ANN SERANNE'S
Good Food &
How to Cook It

BY THE SAME AUTHOR...

The Art of Egg Cookery
Your Home Freezer
The Complete Book of Home Preserving
The Complete Book of Home Baking
Delectable Desserts
The Complete Book of Desserts
The Epicure's Companion (with John Tebbel)
The Complete Book of Home Freezing
America Cooks (Ed.)
The Pots and Pans Cookbook (with Joan Wilson)
The Best of American Cooking

With Eileen Gaden (photographer) . . .

The Blender Cookbook
The Best of Near Eastern Cookery
The Church and Club Woman's Companion
The Sandwich Book

ANN SERANNE'S
Good Food &
How to Cook It

by Ann Seranne

William Morrow & Company, Inc.   New York   1972

Smith, Margaret Ruth
 Ann Seranne's good food & how to cook it.

  1. Cookery. I. Title. II. Title: Good food and how to cook it.
TX715.S66313   641.5   70-188185
ISBN 0-688-00004-5

Dedicated to Wendell Sammet, whose cold lemon soufflé would not rise in his refrigerator, and to the Dullinger boys, two roughnecks aged ten and twelve respectively, who work off their excess energy on rainy days when Mom is out by making butterscotch pies.

Contents

Introduction

I love to cook for men, and this book was originally intended to be especially for them. I have cooked for men for many years and have found in them an appreciative and inquiring audience. I am constantly answering their questions about cooking. So I began to put together a book of really good dishes with man-appeal—a book from which men could easily *learn* to cook, and a useful book for daily meals as well as for cooking for guests.

It was not long, however, before I realized that the book I was writing was not just for men but for everyone who cares about cooking, for men and for women who want to please family and friends.

It is NOT a book for anyone who likes to open a bunch of cans, combine them in a casserole, add a pinch of this, a dash of that (usually too much), and thinks he has created a "gourmet" dish. It is NOT for the man who likes to don a silly apron and hat and burn good steaks on the barbecue. Nor is it a book for the woman who feels she is saving her husband's money by substituting margarine for butter in a delicate dish that calls for a stick of butter, then turns around and buys a gooey, flavorless cake at a commercial bakery for an astronomical sum instead of completing her meal with a simple and inexpensive dessert of fresh or poached fruit or with a hunk of good cheese.

It is a cookbook for everyone who appreciates good food, enjoys cooking, and likes to entertain simply but well. The majority of the recipes are for main dishes, so it is not a general cookbook, nor is it supposed to take the place of one in your kitchen. Rather it is a selection of my favorite recipes, ranging from the simple to the exquisite, that are all relatively easy to make.

The recipes are organized, chapter by chapter, into categories in which the cook is called upon to use similar procedures. This is to make clear fundamentals and techniques which—once you have seen how they repeatedly work the same way despite surface variations—make the difference between a stumbling and a knowledgeable cook. Then you can improvise, change ingredients when necessary, correct a sauce that isn't quite right, and literally graduate from dependence on cookbooks.

This book is not filled with exotic recipes or time-consuming extravagances—no *galantines* or *ballotines,* pheasant *en plumage* or truffled beef—but with good honest dishes that have proved most popular in my own home, dishes ranging from a robust stew or ragout, to poached chicken in a delicate wine sauce, to Wendell Sammet's Cold Lemon Soufflé that failed to rise! Dishes that I call GOOD FOOD.

So let's begin with my idea of what is good food, so that we understand each other right from the beginning. To me the best food in the world is a dish carefully prepared from good, wholesome ingredients. It may be just a baked potato, but the potato itself is the right kind for baking; the skin is crisp and it is split while steaming hot and a big chunk of sweet butter is plopped into the center of its mealy flesh. It may be a casserole of macaroni and cheese, prepared in the morning and baked that evening. But the macaroni is cooked just right, not tough or mushy, the cheese sauce is creamy and golden, made with the best aged American cheddar. It is served hot on hot plates. That's good food! That's good eating!

CARE went into that baked potato and into that casserole of macaroni and cheese, and care is a most essential ingredient in any good dish.

CARE must be taken in seasoning a dish, in dressing a salad, in adding wine to a sauce or spirits to a dessert, for moderation is an important aspect of good cooking. "Season to taste" is an excellent rule, adding pinch by pinch, dash by dash, until the taste is just right. Spices, herbs, and condiments should be used to enhance the flavor of a dish, not to smother it. Garlic and onions, except in a few notable peasant dishes, should also be used judiciously.

Perhaps the greatest crime perpetrated in the home kitchen is overcooking. Overcooking can ruin a fresh egg, a delicate fish, make a tasteless mush of garden-fresh vegetables, and toughen the best roast. CARE to have the dish cooked just long enough often makes the difference between a good and a poor dish.

CARE must also be taken in shopping for the best ingredients, either fresh, in a package, or in a can. Often what appears to be a bargain in the market turns out to be wasteful and so really more expensive than a better-quality product would have been in the first place. Choose vegetables in season that are crisp and bright in color; buy steaks and chops from prime meat; fish impeccably fresh; and the best-quality eggs, butter, cheese, and cream. Margarine may have its place in the kitchen along with other solid shortenings, but it can never take the place of butter in cooking and will never give the flavor and texture to a sauce that creamery butter does. So butter only, please, when you cook these dishes, and honest heavy dairy cream, too.

Afraid of your waistline? Nonsense! Most of those pounds are put on by HOW MUCH you eat rather than by WHAT you eat. Good food never made anyone fat. It's quantity not quality that puts on the pounds.

Afraid of high cholesterol? Then avoid the solid fats on meat (lamb and pork are the worst offenders), but don't give up eggs, cream, butter, and pure olive oil in modest quantities. You need some easily digested fat as much as you need some sugar to help burn off the fats in your body. Doctors and food chemists are finding out that most dietary problems can be solved by good balance in eating rather than by restriction.

A food writer once said of me that I never use one stick of butter where two will do! And that's true. I use eggs, cream, butter lavishly and never dress a salad with anything except fresh and fine olive oil, and the only time I had a slightly high cholesterol count was when I went on a so-called health diet with a friend of mine for a couple of weeks. So back to the butter and cream for me! I still weigh the same as I did in college.

So for you who enjoy good food, who like to cook, who CARE to cook, this book is written.

ANN SERANNE

About the Recipes

There are three types of main-course recipes in this book: Ones that can be made entirely in advance and reheated before serving, and those which can be almost finished, set aside temporarily, and completed quickly. These are the two kinds of dishes I like to cook and serve when I have guests, so I can be with them through most of the preprandial fun. The third type of recipe you are more likely to cook for yourself or family than serve to guests, for while most of the preparation can be done in advance, the dish needs your undivided attention at the stove during the short cooking period.

All of them I have cooked, eaten, and enjoyed not once but many times and I have tried to write them in the greatest possible detail without being boring, beginning with what to put on your market list through to how to serve the dish. The steps of preparation are set down in logical sequence so that after each one everything is ready for the next. This approximates for the home kitchen the orderly procedure French chefs call the *mise en place* ("everything in its place"), but there is nothing fancy about it, it is simply the practical way to get things done.

Within the text of the recipes, ingredients and the amounts required are printed in *italics* so that you may see quickly what is needed for each step of preparation as you go along. The preceding lists of ingredients, on the other hand, are not set up in the conventional way, with every teaspoon and cupful specified, but as market lists, with the amounts of the principal ingredients you need to buy and a list of staples to be checked to be sure you have them on hand. The principal piece of cookware needed to cook the dish is also specified at the beginning; there is no sense in planning to cook a big pot of soup if you don't have a big pot in the house!

And, again, the chapters are organized by method rather than by main ingredient. This seemed to me much the easiest way to make basic principles and procedures clear without being repetitious, and it almost automatically demonstrates how much of cooking is a matter of theme and variations—to which you can sooner or later add variations of your own.

This arrangement, and the careful recipe form, I have used so that this will indeed be a "teaching" cookbook for the inexperienced. But it has not often been necessary to make the recipes very long, the teaching aspect of the book will not get in the way of those who are already knowledgeable cooks.

However, for those who really are beginners, perhaps especially for men who don't know where to begin, most of these introductory sections are devoted to quite rudimentary advice, from how to equip your kitchen to how to chop an onion. Certainly not everyone needs to be told these things, but new cooks starting from scratch do. For them, I have tried to explain everything they will need to know.

Still, a little common sense is needed. No foolproof recipe has yet been written, and two people may cook the same dish from the same recipe and each come up with a different result—both good, I hope. For instance, it is impossible to tell you EXACTLY how long to cook a vegetable. Cooking time depends on the amount of moisture in the vegetable, the amount of liquid used in cooking, the type and degree of heat, and the size and freshness of the vegetable. All I can do is give you an approximate time, tell you how to test for doneness, and warn you over and over again NOT TO OVERCOOK THEM.

How hot is hot? How thick is thick? How soft is soft? These are conditions that influence every recipe. If your high heat is too high and a sauce cooks down too much, you must know how to thin it with a little liquid. If, on the other hand, your low heat is too low or your stew pot is taller than mine and the liquid doesn't evaporate the way mine did, it is a simple matter to raise the heat and boil off some of the excess, or thicken the liquid by stirring in a mixture of flour and butter. Nobody cooking here in New Jersey can tell you in Maine or Wisconsin at what rate the moisture in your dish is going to evaporate in your oven or on top of your stove. So, please, use your own good sense.

Also, nobody can tell you exactly how long it is going to take you to prepare a dish, for everyone works in a different way and at a different pace, so I have not attempted to give approximate preparation times. What difference does it really make? If you like to cook, you will not begrudge the time necessary to prepare a meal as long as the end results are good. What I have attempted to do is to organize and explain each recipe so that you will never find yourself or your kitchen in a turmoil when dinnertime arrives.

With the majority of these main-course dishes are suggestions for accompaniments to serve with them. In planning a menu, if you select your main course first, the rest of the meal is fairly easy to plan. The appetizer should be in direct contrast to the main course, hot versus cold, fish versus meat, plain versus fancy, and so on. Dessert can be practically anything you wish, depending on how much time you want to devote to the making of it, but you can never go wrong by serving fruit *au kirsch,* fresh strawberries or sliced fresh peaches in season, or even a good ice cream with a homemade hot chocolate-rum sauce. Just be sure not to serve a rich, creamy, eggy dessert after a main course that has a rich cream and egg sauce.

Finally, note that when certain dishes suggested as accompaniments are printed with Capital Initial Letters, this means the recipe is in this book and you can find it via the Index.

Equipping the Kitchen

While by no means essential to a good cook, a well-equipped kitchen can save a great deal of time and can do a lot to make the preparation of food more fun.

In addition to a *stove,* which should have a dependable thermostat, and a *refrigerator* with an adequate freezing section, my choice of essential equipment would begin with a good solid *chopping block or board.* Next, *a set of plain, rustable, carbon-steel knives.* There are at least a dozen shapes and sizes, but you can do very well with just two. A *paring knife with a 4½-inch blade tapering to a sharp point,* and a *French chef knife with an 8½-inch blade tapering to a point.* Two such knives of the very best quality you can buy will serve you better than a raft of poor-quality knives. They should be kept razor sharp, because a dull knife is actually more dangerous than a sharp one and also makes your work much harder. To keep them sharp, buy a *butcher's steel* from your butcher and ask him to show you how to use it.

I wouldn't be happy without an *electric blender.* If you don't use it for any other purpose than for making bread crumbs, it will have earned a place in your kitchen.

You will need *an adequate supply of the right size pots and pans and skillets* to prepare dishes for the average number of people you serve. Pots, pans, skillets, and casseroles should be heavy-bottomed for good conduction of heat so that food will cook evenly and won't stick or scorch. Heavy enameled cast iron is—in my opinion—tops.

And you will need *several wooden spoons* to stir food without scratching your pans or imparting a metallic flavor to their contents. A *swivel-bladed paring knife* is a great time-saver for peeling fruits and vegetables, and you should have a pair of tongs for turning chops, chickens, and other foods. A *strong two-tined kitchen fork* is another essential, and *two sizes of wire whisks* for beating eggs and sauces can turn an amateur into a professional practically overnight.

You should have *a small and a large flexible steel spatula* for turning pancakes, loosening tart shells, frosting a cake if you are inclined to such frivolity, and *a couple of rubber spatulas,* the narrow bottle-scraper kind, to scrape out bowls and to fold egg whites into batter—although your hand is better at this than any spatula. Your hands are the best tool you can have in the kitchen and don't be afraid to use them. Don't be brain-washed by television home economists who fear they will contaminate a chop (which is going to be cooked at three to four hundred degrees!) by turning it over in the marinade with their fingers.

You need *a couple of large, long-handled stainless-steel spoons,* or a *bulb-type baster,* though I prefer the large spoon for basting roasts and degreasing sauces.

You need a *colander.* If you plan to cook noodles and spaghetti—and who doesn't?—get one with feet, and get *a couple of fine-mesh sieves* for straining sauces. You need a *general grater,* one of the four-sided varieties which let you grate or shred, and a *small Mouli cheese grater* is a nifty little gadget for grating Parmesan cheese, which I hope you will buy in a large chunk and grate as needed. It freezes well and is far superior, even after being frozen, to the packaged grated cheeses, most often rancid and always stale. And if you are the do-it-yourself type, you might decide you need *a pair of strong poultry shears* for disjointing poultry.

No good cook can get along without a *peppermill* for freshly ground pepper. If you are a purist you may want several—one for white pepper-corns, one for black peppercorns, and one for whole coriander seeds, a great last-minute addition to many vegetables and stews.

You must have a *sturdy metal corkscrew,* and if you don't have an electric blender you will need a *Foley food mill* for puréeing soft fruits and cooked vegetables.

Another must is *a package of cheesecloth* for straining stocks, for wrapping whole fish to be poached, and for many other purposes that you will learn as you work your way through this book. Nice to have, but not vital, is a *wire salad basket* for shaking excess moisture from salad greens.

Essential, of course, to every cook, whether amateur or professional, is *a set of measuring cups,* for dry ingredients and shortening, that come in 1, ½, ⅓, and ¼ cup sizes; also *a set of measuring spoons* in sizes graduating from ¼ teaspoon to 1 tablespoon. For measuring liquids, you need *glass measuring cups* with graduated markings: a 1 cup is a must, but 1 pint and 1 quart will also come in very handy.

In time you will not need to use measuring cups and spoons for most dishes which you make, because experience and good judgment will take their place, but when you first try the recipes in this book, it is the wiser way to success to use them and to use them accurately.

HOW TO MEASURE

To measure flour: Flour does not have to be sifted before it is measured in most of these recipes; any exceptions are stated. Spoon it lightly into dry measuring cup and level off with a straight-edged knife.

To measure sugars: WHITE. Fill dry measuring cup or spoon and level off with a straight-edged knife. BROWN. Pack firmly into measuring cup, pressing down with back of a spoon, and level off.

To measure shortening or tub butter: Pack firmly into measuring cup, taking care to press out air holes, and level off.

To measure stick butter: You just need to know that . . .

      1 stick equals ½ cup or 8 tablespoons
      ½ stick equals ¼ cup or 4 tablespoons
      ¼ stick equals ⅛ cup or 2 tablespoons

WEIGHTS AND MEASURES—EQUIVALENTS:

3 teaspoons	1 tablespoon
4 tablespoons	¼ cup
5 tablespoons plus 1 teaspoon	⅓ cup
12 tablespoons	¾ cup
16 tablespoons	1 cup
2 cups liquid	1 pint
2 pints liquid	1 quart
4 quarts liquid	1 gallon
16 ounces	1 pound
1 fluid ounce	2 tablespoons
16 fluid ounces	1 pint (2 cups)

SIZES OF CANS—EQUIVALENTS:

7¾ to 8½ oz (#½)	Approximately	1 cup
13½ fl. oz. (#300)	"	1¾ cups
1 lb. (#1)	"	2 cups
1 lb. or 15 fl. oz. (#303)	"	2 cups
1 lb. 4 oz. (#2)	"	2½ cups
1 lb. 13 oz. (#2½)	"	3½ cups

BASIC KITCHEN SUPPLIES

If you are a cook, there are certain staples and ingredients that you are always going to have on hand in more or less adequate quantities. For this reason, I have tried throughout this book to make your shopping easier by dividing the ingredients that you need for a recipe into two categories: those you will probably have on hand, but should check to be sure, and those that you will probably have to buy. The following items should be in every well-stocked kitchen at all times:

DAIRY PRODUCTS

Milk
Butter
Eggs
Parmesan cheese
Swiss, Gruyère, Cheddar (one or
  more types) or your favorite
  cheese

PERISHABLES

Lemons
Parsley (or a good dried brand)
Bread
Carrots
Onions
Potatoes
Salad greens
Tomatoes (in season)
Garlic
Shallots (a small basket will last for
  months) or scallions

CANNED GOODS

Whole tomatoes
Stewed tomatoes
Tomato paste
Tomato purée or sauce
Beef consommé
Chicken broth
Canned shortening

Petits pois
Water chestnuts

BOTTLED ITEMS

Olive oil
Cooking oil
Cider vinegar
White wine vinegar
Red wine vinegar
Mustard (Dijon preferred, or
  Mr. Mustard)
Catsup
Chili sauce
Capers
Tabasco
Worcestershire sauce
Mayonnaise
Olives, pickles, gherkins
Vanilla extract (pure, not artificial)

DRY INGREDIENTS

Flour, all-purpose or unbleached
Baking powder
Baking soda
Cream of tartar
Brown sugar
Granulated sugar
Noodles, macaroni, spaghetti
Rice (converted), not instant

SPICES AND HERBS

Every cook needs a selection of herbs and spices. Rather than stock a great variety—apt to be little used and to become tasteless—choose high-quality herbs and spices that are frequently called for. Although there are many brands on the market, in my estimation only one brand is of infinitely superior quality, hence well worth purchasing, even if by mail order. The brand is Spice Islands.

YOU SHOULD HAVE ON HAND THE FOLLOWING

Bay leaves
Cayenne pepper
Cinnamon, powdered and stick
Cloves, whole
Dill weed (not dill seed)
Marjoram
Mustard
Nutmeg, ground
Oregano

Paprika (Hungarian)
Peppercorns (black and white)
Red pepper flakes or dried hot chili peppers
Rosemary
Sage
Sweet basil
Tarragon
Thyme

YOU MIGHT LIKE TO HAVE ON HAND OR BUY AS NEEDED

Allspice
Caraway seeds
Cardamon, ground and whole seeds
Chili powder
Coriander, powdered and whole
Cumin, ground and seeds

Curry powder
Ginger, ground
Poppy seeds
Saffron (threads)
Sesame seeds
Turmeric

A WORD ABOUT PEPPER

PEPPER is the most widely used spice in the world. Some like just a little of it, freshly ground or coarsely cracked; some like a lot; some like the texture and flavor of black pepper, while still others like the aroma and bite of white pepper.

GRINDING makes a great difference in the flavor of pepper. If the corns are ground too fine, they lose much of their flavor-giving oils. Connoisseurs of pepper will buy only the whole peppercorns to grind themselves in a pepper mill or to crush and crack by means of a mortar and pestle.

BOTH BLACK AND WHITE PEPPERCORNS should be on every cook's spice shelf, plus a jar of coarsely cracked black (Java or Tellicherry) pepper for use when you need a large quantity in a hurry.

WHITE PEPPER is preferred for use in cream sauces since it leaves no black specks in the finished dish. It is excellent used quite lavishly on eggs and as a seasoning for plain buttered vegetables.

BLACK PEPPER is best for roasts, Steak au Poivre, meat loaves, spaghetti sauces, stews, ragouts, and, of course, tossed salads, especially the popular Caesar salad.

WINES AND SPIRITS

You will want to have a few bottles of *good dry white and red wines* on hand, a bottle of *Cognac* or *Armagnac,* and one or two, or a selection, of *after-dinner liqueurs.* A bottle of *dry vermouth, ruby port, dry Madeira, imported dry sherry,* and *dark Jamaica rum* are also fairly basic staples for the good cook's kitchen.

Do not waste money buying so-called cooking wines and sherries. It's far better to use no wine at all in a dish than a poor one, for AGAIN a dish is only as good as the ingredients which go into its making. Red wines for cooking should be full-bodied Bordeaux or Burgundies, and there just isn't any substitute for these. White wines should be dry, such as Chablis, Pouilly Fumé or Fuissé, Montrachet, or a pleasant Rhine wine, but an excellent substitute, believe it or not, for dry white wine in a recipe is dry vermouth. I have used it many times in fish, seafood, and poultry dishes requiring a half cup or so rather than opening a new bottle of white wine and have had excellent results. You'll find it specified in several recipes in this book.

Save the tail ends of red wine for marinades or for making wine vinegar.

One caution about using wine in cooking. Always add it early enough to allow the alcohol to boil out. Wine can give a very raw taste to a dish if it is not allowed to simmer for a few minutes.

What You Should Know
About the Onion Family

LEEKS have a more delicate and subtle flavor than onions and are used primarily for soups and stews. They are also good when braised and served as a hot vegetable with a sprinkling of grated Parmesan cheese or when chilled and served vinaigrette.

The coarse green stalks of leeks are usually discarded. Only the thick white stalks are used for chicken soups, light stocks, and vichyssoise. A small portion of the green tops may be left on for meaty soups, ragouts, and pea and bean soups.

Leeks must be carefully cleaned, for generally there is sand imbedded between the layers of the stalks. Cut off and discard the roots and strip off the heavy outside leaves, then cut off as much of the dark green tops as desired. Slit each stalk down the middle to within about 1 inch of the root end, and wash well under cold running water, spreading apart the layers to flush out any sand which might lie there.

Leeks cook quickly in boiling salted water (15 to 20 minutes), and may be served hot or cold.

ONIONS. For a delicate onion flavor, onions should be sautéed in butter or oil just until soft and transparent. For brown or tomato sauces and for other foods requiring a more robust flavor, onions should be cooked until golden. For dark brown beef stews and ragouts they should be browned in a very little fat to add good color and flavor to the sauce.

Small onions measure 1½ to 1¾ inches in diameter and weigh 2 to 3 ounces each (6 or 8 per pound).

Medium onions measure 2 to 2½ inches in diameter and weigh 5 to 6 ounces each (about 3 medium per pound).

Large onions measure 3 to 3½ inches in diameter and weigh 10 to 12 ounces each.

Silver skin onions may be bought in a variety of sizes from the very small, generally used for pickling, to those that are 1 to 1½ inches in diameter (12 to 16 per pound).

SHALLOTS are the glamorous member of the onion family. A few years ago they were rarely found in food markets, but today they are quite common if you know what you are looking for, and there are several mail order houses happy to ship them to you. A pint of shallots goes a long way and will last throughout most of the winter without drying out if kept in a cool dark place. They should not be stored in the refrigerator. Their flavor is less sweet than an onion's, more delicate, and yet more distinct—having a faint suggestion of garlic. Only small quantities are used and they should NEVER be allowed to overbrown lest they give off a bitter flavor.

1 medium shallot weighs about ½ ounce and makes 1 tablespoon when minced.

GARLIC is garlic! Pungent and wonderfully good if you like it. Like shallots, garlic should never be allowed to overbrown or it develops a disagreeable bitter flavor; it should be sautéed in butter or oil over low heat until just pale gold, or be added to a braised dish or stew after the liquid has been added.

If you're a garlic lover you will never press garlic through a garlic press. In some strange way the garlic press squeezes out the essential oils and releases a flavor akin to terpene, a substance found in turpentine.

There is no need to peel garlic cloves that are used in a soup or sauce that is going to be strained or put through a food mill. Just wash and cut each clove in half so the flavor can be released.

To PEEL GARLIC. Place the unpeeled clove on your chopping block or board and give it a whack, with the flat side of a heavy chopping knife or cleaver, just hard enough to crush the garlic so that the papery outer skin can be lifted away. Give the clove another whack, harder this time, and no further chopping is needed. Scoop the smashed garlic up on the side of your knife and transfer it to your skillet or casserole.

There are some dishes, however, in which garlic is best when neatly minced and the recipes so state.

If you object to a garlic odor on your fingers, simply rub your hands with salt and wash with soap and water.

What You Should Know
About Mushrooms

Cultivated mushrooms are available throughout most of the year in three different sizes: small, medium, and large.

Both the small and medium mushrooms are usually picked before the cap has opened and the gills are still covered, while large mushrooms are more mature and are usually opened out into an umbrella shape, exposing the gills.

Small mushrooms weigh about ½ ounce each; there are 30 to 32 per pound.

Medium mushrooms weigh about 1 ounce each; there are 16 to 18 per pound.

Large mushrooms weigh about 1½ ounces each; there are 10 to 12 per pound.

Select firm white mushrooms with smooth unblemished caps. Mushrooms that are brown or discolored are old and are beginning to dry out. They lack both flavor and moisture.

Mushrooms require little preparation except a gentle rinsing in cold water. They should not be peeled. Empty them into a bowl of cold water and rub them lightly between the palms of your hands. If the gills are exposed, turn the mushrooms upside down under cold running water to flush out any sand which might be lurking in the gills.

Trim the base of the stems, cutting off as little as possible, but discarding any part of the stem that is spongy. If the entire stem is spongy, break it away from the cap and discard it.

Place mushrooms on paper towels, cover with more paper towels and pat dry. Then halve, quarter, slice, dice, or mince according to recipe.

Overcooking toughens mushrooms. Sautéed mushrooms should be cooked rapidly over quite high heat in a little butter or oil for just 4 to 5 minutes.

To keep mushrooms pale in color, add lemon juice to the poaching water; or sprinkle a little lemon juice on one side while sautéeing them, and again on the other side when you turn them.

To store, seal in a plastic bag, unwashed, and place in vegetable section of the refrigerator where they will keep fresh for several days.

Slicing, Dicing, Mincing

A COOK'S BEST FRIEND in the kitchen can be his CHOPPING KNIFE, but it can be a dangerous tool if not used correctly. It should be made of heavy carbon steel, which takes a razor sharp edge. The one known as the French chef, or cook's, knife is the perfect shape, the best size for general use, and has an 8- or 8½-inch blade which extends right up through the handle. It should be kept sharp, therefore you need a butcher's steel, which you can usually buy through your butcher, and if you don't know how to use it he will be happy to show you. The second most useful knife in the kitchen for general paring and slicing has exactly the same shape as the French chef's but in miniature. It has a 4- or 4½-inch blade.

These carbon steel knives rust quickly, so they should never be dropped into a sink of water or allowed to soak. If you buy them yourself, you'll take care of them, for they are expensive! They should be wiped off with a cloth immediately after use and placed in a knife rack for safety.

THE COOK'S SECOND BEST FRIEND is his CHOPPING BLOCK. The ideal is a butcher's block on legs, with a rack either across the back or along the sides for holding the knives. If you don't have room for such a unit either beside or in front of your stove, buy a substantial chopping board (for you can't be a good technician in the kitchen if you are afraid of marring your vinyl) and set it on top of a work table, or build it into a work area. Some automatic dishwashers are now being made with butcher board tops.

HOLDING THE KNIFE. Let's begin by holding the knife. Grasp the knife by the handle as if you were going to slice a steak. Look at your hand. Is your index finger stretched out along the blade of the knife? You'll never learn to chop that way! Place your thumb on one side of the blade, as close to the handle as possible. Now wrap your fingers around the handle, letting the knuckle of your index finger rest on the side of the blade opposite your thumb. You are now gripping the top of the blade between your thumb and index finger, while wrapping your other fingers lightly and comfortably around the handle.

SLICING VEGETABLES—*such as carrots and potatoes.* Cut the vegetable in half lengthwise to give you two flat surfaces. Or, if you want the slices to be whole or almost whole, slice a thin strip off one side so the vegetable can lie flat on the board and not slip. Place the vegetable on the board cut-side down. Hold the vegetable firmly with the fingers of your left hand (assuming you are right-handed) and place your thumb at the back end of the vegetable so you can use it as a pusher to move the vegetable into the blade of the knife as you slice. Now, MOST IMPORTANT, point your fingernails back under toward your thumb so that, as you slice, you will be slicing down against your nails. If you will keep them always in this position for slicing, dicing, and mincing, you will never cut your finger or chip a nail. Slice straight down at right angles to the board, making the slices as thick or thin as you wish and pushing them away from the rest of the vegetable with your knife as the blade hits the board.

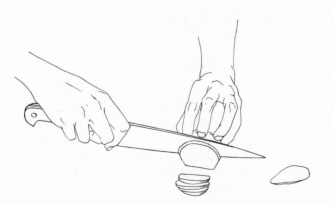

DICING. Slice your vegetable; cut the slices into strips; then, holding a handful of strips together, cut across them at intervals to make dice.

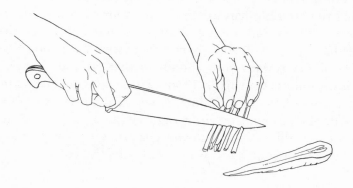

JULIENNE STRIPS. Slice your vegetable lengthwise ⅛ inch thick, then pile two or three slices on top of each other and cut into strips ⅛ inch wide. Cut across the strips to make them whatever length you wish.

DICING OR MINCING *onion, shallots, or garlic.* Peel your onion, shallots, or garlic, but leave on the root end which holds the layers of the vegetable together. Cut the vegetable in half lengthwise, through the root. Place half the vegetable on the board, the cut side facing down and the root end on your left. Slice lengthwise from one side to the other, stopping just short of the root end, thus leaving the slices attached to the root. Then make slices, horizontal to the board, from bottom to top of the vegetable, still leaving them attached at the root. Lastly slice downward from right end of vegetable back leftward to the root—your onion, shallot, or garlic is now diced or minced, depending on how thick or thin you made your slices.

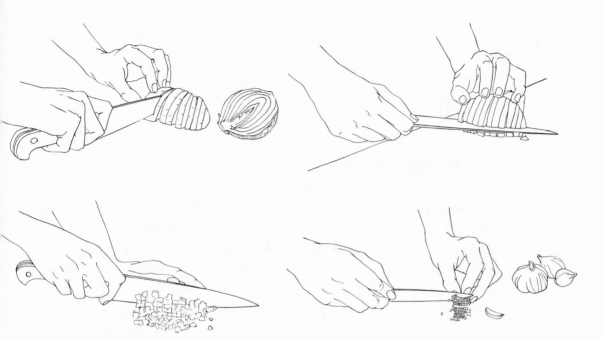

CHOPPING PARSLEY. Pull the parsley clusters from their stems and pile them together on the chopping board. Use a big knife, hold it as usual in your right hand, and hold the back of the blade near the tip with your left hand. Hold the tip of the blade down lightly in one place at the left, and chop up and down rapidly with the right hand in a fan pattern. When the knife has completed about a quarter circle, gather the parsley together into a pile again with the blade, and chop a quarter circle again, repeating until all is finely chopped.

Cooking Terms

Most of the cooking terms used throughout this book are explained in the recipes, but you may wish to use these definitions for easy reference.

ASPIC
: A well-seasoned jelly made with gelatin and stock, or sometimes tomato juice, and usually containing wine or sherry.

AU GRATIN
: Food in a sauce, baked or broiled until the top is brown. Often the surface is sprinkled with buttered bread crumbs or grated cheese.

BAKE
: To cook in the dry heat of an oven. Applies to all oven-cooked foods except meats, which are roasted.

BALLOTINE
: A piece of boneless meat, poultry or fish, stuffed and rolled, usually served hot. When served cold it is called a *galantine*.

BARBECUE
: To roast meats over coals or on a spit. Also applies to broiled meats served with a barbecue sauce.

BASTE
: To spoon liquids over food while it is cooking, such as melted fat and pan juices over meat or syrup over baking apples.

BEAT
: To blend food or liquid thoroughly by rapidly lifting mixture up and over with fork, spoon, wire whisk, rotary or electric beater.

BEURRE MANIÉ
: Butter and flour worked together to a smooth paste; used for thickening sauces.

BLANCH
: To cook food in boiling water until it is

softened or wilted, or to remove strong taste from cabbage, onions, bacon and lemon rind. Also to loosen skin from almonds, tomatoes, peaches, onions.

BLANQUETTE

A savory stew in a white sauce thickened with egg yolks and cream.

BLEND

To combine two or more ingredients thoroughly but less vigorously than by beating.

BOIL

To cook in a liquid which bubbles actively during the cooking period.

BOUQUET GARNI

A small bundle of vegetables and herbs, tied together in cheesecloth for easy removal; used to flavor soups, stews, and sauces. Always contains parsley and bay leaf and leaf of thyme. A pinch of dried thyme takes the place of a fresh thyme leaf.

BRAISE

To brown foods in fat, then cook in tightly covered casserole or skillet in small amount of liquid.

BREAD

To dip food into an egg-milk mixture, then into crumbs.

BROIL

To cook under or over direct heat.

BROTH

Liquid in which meat and/or vegetables have been simmered.

CARAMELIZE

To heat sugar until melted and light brown in color and caramel in flavor.

COMBINE

To mix food together thoroughly as in BLEND.

COURT BOUILLON

A highly seasoned broth for poaching fish or seafood, usually containing white wine.

CREAM

To mix together soft butter and sugar until thoroughly blended and creamy.

CROUTONS

Cubes of bread, toasted or sautéed in butter until crisp and golden; used to garnish soups and salads.

DEGLAZE	To pour liquid into a pan in which meat has been sautéed or roasted and then to cook and stir in all the bits of coagulated meat juices or glaze from bottom and sides of pan.
DEGREASE	To remove fat from surface of a sauce, soup, or broth, or from a pan in which meat is roasting.
DICE	To cut into cube-shaped pieces; page 26.
DOT	To scatter bits of butter or shortening over surface of a dish to be cooked.
DRIPPINGS	Meat juices left in the roasting pan after the fat has been removed.
FILLET	A boneless piece of fish or lean meat.
FINES HERBES	A combination of finely chopped herbs, usually parsley, chives, tarragon, and chervil.
FLAMBÉ	To pour warm brandy or liquor over food, then to ignite it and let flame burn out.
FLAKE	To separate into small thin pieces.
FOLD	To combine delicate ingredients gently with an up and over folding motion; especially refers to incorporating beaten egg whites into a cake batter or soufflé mixture.
FRICASSEE	To cook meat or chicken in butter until it is stiffened, before simmering or braising it in liquid. In a white fricassee the meat is not allowed to brown. In a brown fricassee the meat is sautéed in butter to a golden brown color.
FRY	To cook in hot fat. When the food is only partially covered with fat it is called shallow fried; when immersed in deep fat it is called deep fried.
GLAZE	To coat food with a glossy substance such as jelly, mayonnaise, fruit or meat juices.
GOULASH	A rich stew of meat or poultry.

GRATE	To rub a food over the teeth of a grater until divided into small particles.
GRATINÉ	To brown the top of a sauced dish under a hot broiler. This may be done in a hot oven, but a rich sauce containing egg yolks is apt to curdle unless the dish is set into a shallow pan containing a little water.
GRILL	To broil.
GRIND	To put through food chopper.
JULIENNE	To cut into narrow, lengthwise strips; page 26.
KNEAD	To press and fold dough with palms of hands.
LARD	To cover meat with strips of fat, or to thread strips of fat pork through lean meat with a larding needle.
MACÉDOINE	A mixture of cut-up fruits or vegetables.
MARINATE	Also known as MACERATE. To let foods soak in a flavorful liquid to absorb the flavor or to make them more tender. Macerate is usually applied to fruit soaked in sugar and liquor; marinate is used both for meats soaked in wine with herbs and for pickles put into brine. The soaking mixture is known as the MARINADE.
MINCE	To chop foods very finely; page 26.
PAN BROIL	To cook in a greased skillet over high heat.
PAN FRY	To cook in a skillet in a small amount of fat.
PARBOIL	To partially cook in boiling water.
POACH	To cook in liquid which is barely simmering or is below the boiling point.
PURÉE	To reduce foods to a thick, smooth pulp, free of skins, seeds, and filaments, by pressing them through a sieve or food mill, or by blending in an electric blender.

RAGOUT	A savory stew or goulash.
REDUCE	To lessen the amount of liquid by boiling off part of it in steam, thus concentrating the flavor.
ROUX	A smooth blend of fat and flour cooked together and used to thicken a liquid.
SAUTÉ	To heat and brown food in a small quantity of hot fat until partially or completely cooked.
SCORE	To make shallow slits across the surface with a sharp knife.
SHRED	To cut or tear into thin strips or to put through a shredder.
SIMMER	To cook in liquid which is just at or slightly below the boiling point so that the liquid barely moves.
SLIVER	To cut into very thin strips.
STEAM	To cook food either over steam or surrounded by it in a tightly covered container.
STEW	To cook in liquid below the boiling point.
STOCK	Liquid in which meat, fish and/or vegetables have been cooked. Used to make soups, sauces, and gravies.
TOSS	To mix lightly by lifting with fork or spoon or to flip over.
VINAIGRETTE	Sauce made with a base of oil and vinegar.
WHIP	To beat or whisk rapidly in order to incorporate air.

HEARTY SOUPS
& CHOWDERS

Hearty Soups & Chowders

Most cookbooks begin with a chapter on soups, a lengthy discourse on the merits of the stock pot, and how to make chicken and beef stocks. I'm not going to do this, for the stock pot is now part of our culinary past. There are very acceptable canned beef and chicken broths and consommés on the market, and they are relatively inexpensive. They may be reduced to intensify their flavor; herbs may be added; and simmering removes any trace of the canned flavor. Finally, they are readily available when you need them—and in any quantity. Throughout this book you will not find me recommending many convenience foods, but canned stocks are truly good and are accepted by the best cooks in the country.

This chapter includes only those hearty soups and chowders that make meals in themselves when accompanied by a loaf of hot French or Italian bread—or with sliced, buttered, and toasted crusty bread dropped into the soup and liberally sprinkled with grated Parmesan cheese. Serve them with a glass of wine or a tankard of beer. A scrumptious dessert and good strong coffee will conclude a meal that you can serve to anyone without apology.

Anyone can make a good soup by following four basic rules:

1. Use plenty of good ingredients in a wide variety of compatible flavors.

2. Simmer the soup slowly and take time to remove all the scum that rises to the surface of the liquid and that would cloud the broth if allowed to remain.

3. Season carefully and to taste.

4. Remove every trace of fat from the surface before serving.

PETITE MARMITE HENRI IV

Serves 6. The basis of all good hearty soups is the classic *petite marmite,* of which there are many versions. This one is sufficiently reduced in quantity to be practical for any cook in any kitchen equipped with a heavy 5- or 6-quart kettle or saucepan.

BUY

3 chicken legs and thighs
1 oxtail, cut into pieces; *or* 2
  pounds meaty beef soup bones
1 pound lean brisket of beef, cubed
4 cans beef consommé (10½ ounces
  each)
Carrots
Bunch of leeks
Bunch of celery
2 white turnips *or* 1 large rutabaga
  turnip
2 parsnips
6 small onions
Parsley
Chunk of Parmesan cheese
French bread

HAVE ON HAND

Medium onion
Garlic
Butter
Sugar
Coarsely cracked pepper
Salt
Thyme
Bay leaves

COOKWARE

5- to 6-quart kettle
Small skillet

1. Cut apart *chicken legs* into upper and lower joints, and put into kettle with the *oxtail pieces or soup bones* and the *brisket.* Cover meat

with *cold water,* bring water to a boil, and then simmer for 10 minutes. Drain, and rinse meat with cold water.

2. Return meat to kettle, and add the *4 cans of consommé* and *3 cups water.* Place over heat and bring liquid to a boil.

3. Peel and chop *1 medium onion.* Add to kettle, and simmer the meat and onion over low heat for 2 hours. To make a lovely clear stock, occasionally skim off the scum which rises to the surface.

4. While soup is simmering, wash and dice the following vegetables: *2 carrots, 2 leeks (white part only), 2 stalks celery,* the *white turnips or rutabaga,* and the *parsnips.* Mince *2 cloves garlic.* Set vegetables aside.

5. Peel the *6 small white onions,* and brown them in a small skillet in *1 tablespoon butter* with a sprinkling of *½ teaspoon sugar* to give them a nice caramel color.

6. When soup has simmered for 2 hours, remove the chicken and oxtail, or the soup bones if these were used, to a chopping board. Add all the diced vegetables and the caramelized onions to the broth. Add *¼ teaspoon coarsely cracked pepper, salt to taste, a handful of parsley clusters, ¼ teaspoon thyme,* and *half a bay leaf.* Continue to simmer the soup for 30 minutes.

7. Remove the meat from the chicken bones and meat bones, and cut it all into fine strips. Add the chicken and meat to the broth and simmer for 30 minutes longer.

8. During the last 30 minutes of cooking, grate a big bowl of *Parmesan cheese* and set it aside. Slice, butter, and toast your *French bread,* and keep it warm.

9. When ready to serve, turn the heat off under the kettle so the soup will stop simmering. Tilt the kettle so that any fat on the surface will accumulate on one side. Skim off and discard this fat with your kitchen spoon.

10. Ladle into large soup plates, and serve with the buttered toast. Pass the grated Parmesan separately.

FULL-OF-VEGETABLES SOUP

Serves 6. Serve with hot, crusty French or Italian bread.

BUY

1 oxtail, cut into pieces; *or* 2 pounds meaty beef soup bones
Leeks (if possible)
2 cans beef consommé (10½ ounces each)
1-pound 12-ounce can whole tomatoes
A variety of long-cooking vegetables, such as: white or yellow turnips, parsnips, celery root, Jerusalem artichokes, winter squash *or* pumpkin, carrots
A variety of tender, quick-cooking vegetables such as: cabbage, zucchini, summer squash, fresh peas *or* canned *petits pois,* frozen Frenched green beans *or* frozen artichoke hearts
Parsley

HAVE ON HAND	*COOKWARE*
Butter	5- to 6-quart kettle
Olive oil	
2 medium onions	
Celery	
Garlic	
Salt	
Coarsely cracked pepper	
Oregano, marjoram, *or* tarragon	
Bay leaves	
Cayenne pepper	
Raw rice, macaroni, *or* potatoes (optional)	

1. Wash *oxtail* or *meaty bones* and dry on absorbent paper.

2. Heat *2 tablespoons butter* and *2 tablespoons olive oil* in heavy kettle, and in these brown the soup bones on all sides. For a richly colored broth brown them well, but without burning.

3. While meat is browning, peel and coarsely chop *2 medium onions.* Wash and chop *3 outer stalks celery with leaves* and *2 leeks,* and mince *1 clove garlic.*

4. When meat is brown, add the *2 cans of beef consommé, 1 quart water,* and the prepared vegetables. Add the *can of tomatoes including its liquid, 2 teaspoons salt, ½ teaspoon ground pepper, ½ teaspoon oregano, marjoram, or tarragon* and *1 bay leaf.* Bring liquid to a boil, lower heat, and simmer for 2 hours.

5. While meat is simmering, prepare the long-cooking vegetables: Peel the *turnips, parsnips, celery root, Jerusalem artichokes,* and *squash* or *pumpkin;* scrape the *carrots.* Cut all into dice or thin strips. You should use about 1 quart of diced vegetables in all. Fewer will make a richly brothed soup; more will make a soup as thick as a stew. Do as you prefer.

6. At the end of 2 hours simmering, add the prepared vegetables and simmer for 1 hour longer.

7. Set soup aside to cool a little, then carefully remove any fat which has risen to the surface, and correct the seasoning with salt and pepper, plus a *little cayenne* if you like a zippy soup.

8. Twenty minutes before serving, reheat soup to a simmer. Now is the time to add any of those quick-cooking or canned or frozen vegetables: *shredded cabbage, sliced zucchini or summer squash* (no need to peel these vegetables, just wash and trim), *fresh or canned peas, frozen Frenched green beans or artichoke hearts.* If you wish, you may also add a handful of *raw rice, macaroni,* or *diced raw potatoes.* Simmer for 15 minutes. Chop *some parsley.*

9. Ladle the soup and vegetables into large soup plates or bowls, and sprinkle with chopped parsley.

SANCHOCHO

Serves 8. For the harvest season, here's a wonderful thick soup from Puerto Rico. Although native tropical vegetables are used there, a variety of hard-shelled squash such as butternut, acorn, or Hubbard may be substituted.

BUY

2½ pounds lean beef *or* pork
½ pound pork with bone, such as shoulder or neck

2 large fresh tomatoes *or* a 1-pound can whole tomatoes
1 green pepper
1 sweet red pepper
1 pound summer squash
1 pound zucchini
1 small butternut squash
1 small acorn squash *or* 1-pound piece of pumpkin
1 medium yam
1 medium sweet potato
2 medium white potatoes
2 fresh ears corn *or* 1 can corn kernels
1 hot Spanish sausage (*chorizo*) or 3 hot Italian sausages
2 large, partially green bananas
8-ounce can tomato sauce

HAVE ON HAND

1 large onion
Ground coriander
Salt
Black peppercorns
Dry chili pepper, whole
Saffron threads

COOKWARE

Large heavy kettle

1. Cut the *beef or pork* into bite-size pieces, and put them into the kettle with the *½ pound pork with bone, 4 quarts water, 1 large onion,* peeled and chopped, the *tomatoes,* peeled, the *green and red peppers,* seeded and chopped, *½ teaspoon ground coriander, 3 teaspoons salt, ½ teaspoon ground black pepper,* and *1 hot chili pepper.* Bring liquid to a boil, reduce heat, and simmer for 2 hours.

2. Meanwhile prepare remaining vegetables: Wash, trim, and slice the *summer squash and zucchini.* Peel the *squashes and potatoes,* seed them if necessary, and cut into bite-size chunks. Cut kernels from *corn ears* if using the fresh, or drain *1 cup canned corn.* Slice the *sausage,* or sausages, thickly.

3. When soup has simmered for 2 hours, add the prepared vegetables and sausage. Add the *2 bananas,* peeled and sliced, *½ teaspoon saffron,* and the *can of tomato sauce.* Correct seasoning with *salt and pepper,* and simmer for 45 minutes longer. The vegetables should NOT be overcooked.

4. Serve piping hot in large soup bowls.

LAMB STEW SOUP

Serves 6. Serve with hot, crusty French or Italian bread.

BUY

2½ pounds lamb stew meat, cubed
2 cans chicken broth (13¾ ounces each)
2 cans stewed tomatoes (1 pound each)
Bunch of carrots
Bunch of leeks (if available)
1 summer squash *or* large zucchini

HAVE ON HAND	*COOKWARE*
Cooking oil	Large heavy kettle with lid
Butter	
2 medium onions	
Garlic	
3 stalks celery with tops	
Tarragon	
Coarsely cracked black pepper	
Salt	

1. Heat *2 tablespoons oil* and *2 tablespoons butter* in heavy kettle, and in it brown the *stew meat* well on all sides.

2. While the meat is browning peel and chop *2 medium onions* and *2 large cloves garlic;* chop *3 stalks celery with tops*.

3. When meat is brown, turn heat very low, sprinkle the chopped vegetables over the meat, cover the kettle tightly and let the vegetables braise in their own liquid for 10 minutes.

4. Add the *2 cans chicken broth* and *3 cups water*, the *2 cans stewed tomatoes, ½ teaspoon dried tarragon, ½ teaspoon cracked pepper,* and *1 teaspoon salt*. Bring liquid to a boil, reduce heat, and simmer for 3 hours.

5. While soup is simmering scrape *5 or 6 carrots* and cut into julienne strips. Wash thoroughly and slice the white part of *4 or 5 leeks*.

6. Set soup aside to cool a little, then remove any fat which has accumulated on the surface. Correct the seasoning with salt and pepper.

7. One hour before serving reheat soup to a simmer. Add prepared carrots and leeks and simmer for 30 minutes.

8. Wash and dice the *summer squash or zucchini.* At the end of the 30-minute simmering, add the squash or zucchini, and simmer for 20 minutes longer.

9. Ladle into soup plates.

ONION SOUP

Serves 6. A fabulous late-supper soup with great restorative powers!

BUY

6 large Spanish onions
3 cans beef consommé (10½ ounces each)
Swiss, Gruyère, *or* Parmesan cheese
French bread

HAVE ON HAND	*COOKWARE*
Garlic	Large heavy saucepan with lid
Butter	1 large earthenware casserole or
Salt	6 individual ones
Black peppercorns	
Port wine	

1. Peel and slice *onions* thinly. Put on sunglasses and you won't cry —as much. Peel and mince *1 clove garlic.*

2. Melt *1 stick butter (½ cup)* in heavy saucepan. Add onions and garlic and cook over low heat for about 20 minutes, or until onions are wilted and transparent, but not brown.

3. Add the *3 cans beef consommé* and *3 cups water,* and season to taste with *salt* and *plenty of freshly ground black pepper.* Easy on the salt for the consommé contains salt. Bring liquid to a boil and simmer for 30 minutes.

4. Set soup aside to cool, partially covered with lid to saucepan.

5. Grate about *1 cup of your cheese*. Slice the *French bread* sort of slantwise. Then toast it—the best way to do this is to place the slices on a baking sheet and place it under the broiler, about 4 inches away from the source of heat. Watch carefully until just golden, then turn and toast the other side. You can, if you wish, butter one side first either with plain or with garlic butter.

6. Before serving, reheat the soup to simmering and stir in *½ cup Port wine*. Ladle into one large earthenware casserole or 6 individual ones. Float slices of French toast on top, and sprinkle the toast generously with the grated cheese.

7. Bake in a preheated 375° F. oven, or place under broiler heat until cheese melts and soup is boiling around the edges.

8. Serve bubbling hot with the remaining toast.

MINESTRONE AND BORSCHT

Everyone should know how to make minestrone and borscht—good as meals in themselves or as first courses if served in smaller quantities.

Minestrone is the vegetable soup of Italy and there are as many variations as there are regions of Italy. The following recipe has the flavor of Milan; to change it to a Genovese version you must stir *pesto* into it just before serving. *Pesto* is a marvelous combination of garlic, fresh sweet basil, pine nuts, and Parmesan cheese, all ground and mashed to a paste with olive oil. It is a favorite spaghetti sauce in Northern Italy. Unfortunately the pleasure of enjoying *spaghetti al pesto* is only for those of you who are able to beg, borrow, or steal a big bunch of fresh sweet basil; *pesto* cannot be made from the dried.

MINESTRONE IN THE MANNER OF MILAN

A meal for 6

BUY

2 ounces salt pork
2 leeks (if possible)
1-pound 12-ounce can Italian-style whole tomatoes with basil
Small cabbage
1 medium *or* 2 small zucchini
1-pound can chick peas (garbanzos)
Parsley

HAVE ON HAND

1 medium onion
Garlic
Olive oil
1 carrot
Celery
Salt
Coarsely cracked peppercorns
Oregano *or* sweet basil
Elbow macaroni *or* rice
Parmesan cheese, grated

COOKWARE

Large heavy saucepan *or* kettle

1. Dice the *salt pork*. Clean and chop the *leeks*. Peel and slice *1 medium onion*. Peel and mince *1 clove garlic*.

2. Put the salt pork in the heavy saucepan with *1 tablespoon olive oil*, the leeks, onion, and garlic. Cook over low heat for about 10 minutes, or until onion is transparent but not brown.

3. While the onion is cooking, scrape and dice *1 carrot*. Chop *enough celery to measure 1 cup*. Add the carrot and celery to the onions, and cover and cook over low heat for 2 to 3 minutes.

4. Add the *tomatoes with their liquid, 1 teaspoon salt, ½ teaspoon pepper, ½ teaspoon oregano or sweet basil,* and *6 cups water*. Bring liquid to a boil and simmer for 1 hour.

5. Meanwhile remove coarse outer leaves from *cabbage*. Cut in half and reserve one half for some other use. Cut away and discard the core from the remaining half, and shred the leaves thinly. Add cabbage to soup and continue to simmer for 30 minutes.

6. Set soup aside to cool a little, and remove any fat from surface.

7. Wash, trim, and slice the *zucchini*.

8. Half an hour before serving, reheat soup to simmering. Add the zucchini and *½ cup elbow macaroni or raw rice*. Drain the *can of chick peas* and add. Simmer for 20 minutes.

9. Just before serving, stir in *½ cup grated Parmesan cheese*. Ladle into serving plates or bowls and serve *more grated cheese* separately.

NOTE: When you add the zucchini, you may if you wish add other vegetables, such as strips of eggplant, sliced mushrooms, leaves of spinach, sliced green beans, peas, corn kernels.

PESTO

18 large fresh sweet-basil leaves
½ cup olive oil
½ cup freshly grated Parmesan cheese
½ teaspoon salt
⅓ cup pine nuts
5 gloves garlic, peeled

Put all ingredients into container of an electric blender. Blend at high speed for 30 seconds, or to a thick smooth sauce, stirring down if necessary with a rubber spatula. For Minestrone in the Manner of Genoa, add 2 tablespoons of pesto to the soup just before serving.

SPAGHETTI AL PESTO

Serves 2

1. Cook ½ pound thin spaghetti in rapidly boiling salted water for 10 minutes, or until just tender.

2. Fork spaghetti into large mixing bowl, and add a chunk of butter, the Pesto sauce, and 3 tablespoons hot spaghetti water. Toss until butter is melted. Serve with additional grated Parmesan.

BORSCHT

A meal for 6

BUY

2 pounds brisket of beef
4 cans beef consommé (10½ ounces each)
8 medium beets
Small cabagge
Sour cream

HAVE ON HAND

Peppercorns
Garlic
1 large onion
Bay leaves
Salt and pepper
Dill weed
Lemon

COOKWARE

Heavy kettle with lid
Large saucepan

1. Put the *brisket* into the heavy kettle with *3 quarts water,* the *4 cans of beef consommé,* ½ *teaspoon peppercorns, 1 large clove garlic,* halved, *1 large onion,* quartered, *1 large bay leaf* and *1½ teaspoons salt.* Bring liquid to a boil, skimming the scum from surface several times until liquid is clear. Partially cover, and simmer for 3 hours.

2. Meanwhile peel the *beets*. Remove outer coarse and wilted leaves from the *cabbage,* cut out and discard the core, and shred the leaves finely. Set vegetables aside.

3. Add beets to kettle, and simmer for 1 hour longer.

4. Remove beets and brisket—the meat should be saved for another use. Now strain the soup broth into the large saucepan. Add the shredded cabbage to the strained broth. Grate the beets, or cut them into thin strips, and add. Bring broth again to a simmer, and cook over low heat for 30 minutes. Set aside until needed.

5. When ready to serve, reheat soup to a simmer, and stir in *½ tea-spoon dill weed* and *2 to 3 tablespoons lemon juice* to taste. Correct seasoning with *salt and pepper.*

6. Serve with a dollop of *sour cream* on top.

NOTE: Save the brisket for lunch the next day. Slice it across the grain, and serve it with horseradish and slices of buttered pumpernickel bread.

KIDNEY-BEAN AND LENTIL SOUP

Serves 8. Bean, split-pea, and lentil soups all make hearty meals. They are better (to me at least) served with buttered dark or pumpernickel bread than with French or Italian bread.

BUY

1 pound kidney beans
½ pound lentils
3 cans chicken broth (13¾ ounces each)
Parsley

HAVE ON HAND

Celery
1 carrot
Garlic
2 medium onions
Bay leaves
Salt

Peppercorns
Salad oil
Butter
Red wine vinegar

COOKWARE

Large heavy kettle with lid
Heavy saucepan

1. Soak *beans and lentils* overnight in *plenty of cold water to cover.*

2. Next day drain the water off. Put beans and lentils in large kettle, and add *2 stalks celery with leaves,* chopped, *1 carrot,* chopped, *2 cloves garlic,* chopped, *2 medium onions,* chopped, *6 sprigs parsley, 1 large bay leaf, 1 teaspoon salt, ½ teaspoon peppercorns,* the *3 cans chicken broth, 6 cups water,* and *1 tablespoon salad oil.*

3. Bring liquid to a boil, and remove any scum that appears on the surface. Partially cover, and cook over low heat for 1½ to 2 hours, or until beans and lentils are very tender.

4. Remove from heat and let cool a little; then strain beans and liquid through a sieve into a large saucepan, pressing through as much as possible of the beans and vegetables. Or blend 2 cups at a time in an electric blender, being sure to cover container each time before blending. Set aside until needed, or cool and refrigerate. Chop *2 tablespoons parsley,* and set aside.

5. Before serving, return strained soup to heat and bring to a simmer. Correct seasoning with salt. Add *2 tablespoons butter, 3 tablespoons red wine vinegar,* and the parsley. Stir just until butter is melted.

6. Serve each portion with a sprinkling of *freshly ground black pepper.*

BLACK-BEAN SOUP

Serves 8. Always pick over and wash the beans well. Occasionally small pebbles get mixed in, so discard anything that doesn't look one hundred per cent beanish.

BUY

1 pound black beans
Leeks
Sour cream (optional)

HAVE ON HAND	*COOKWARE*
Salt	Large heavy kettle
Black Pepper	Large 3-quart saucepan
Celery	Skillet
1 large onion	
Garlic	
Salad oil	
Ham bone (optional)	
Bay leaves	
Lemon	
Madeira *or* sherry wine	

1. Wash *beans,* and soak them overnight in a large kettle in *3 quarts water.*

2. Next day, do not drain. Add to beans and liquid *3 teaspoons salt* and *½ teaspoon pepper;* bring to a boil.

3. While beans and liquid are coming to a boil, chop *1 stalk celery with leaves, 1 large onion, 2 cloves garlic,* and the *white part of 2 leeks.* In skillet, heat *¼ cup oil.* To it add the prepared vegetables, and cook for about 10 minutes, or just until the onion starts to turn pale gold. Add oil and vegetables to the beans. Add a *ham bone* if you happen to have one, and *1 large bay leaf.* Simmer for 2 hours, or until beans are very tender, adding a little more water from time to time if needed.

4. Remove soup from heat, and let cool a little. Discard ham bone; then strain beans and liquid through a sieve, pressing as much of them as possible into a large saucepan. Or blend 2 cups at a time in an electric blender. Do be careful, for the bean purée can be very hot. And be sure to cover blender container each time before blending. Set soup aside until needed, or cool and refrigerate.

5. Before serving, return strained soup to heat and bring to a simmer. Correct the seasoning with salt. If the purée is too thick for your taste, thin it with a *little water.*

6. Slice a *lemon* very thinly. Stir *½ cup Madeira or sherry* into the soup, and ladle into big soup plates or bowls. Float a couple of the lemon slices on each serving, and serve *sour cream* separately.

OYSTER STEW

A meal for 2. Serve with toasted pilot crackers and sweet butter.

BUY

1 pint milk
1 pint heavy cream
24 freshly shucked oysters with their liquid (together, 1 pint)

HAVE ON HAND	*COOKWARE*
Butter	Heavy saucepan
Salt	
Pepper	
Paprika	

1. Heat *2 cups milk* and the *cream* in the heavy saucepan just to a simmer.

2. Add the *oysters and their liquor, 2 tablespoons butter,* a *little salt,* and *freshly ground black pepper* to taste. Let the oysters steep in the hot milk-cream mixture over very low heat until their edges begin to curl, which they should do almost immediately.

3. Remove stew from the heat, and pour into large soup bowls. Sprinkle with *paprika,* and float a small chunk of butter on top of each serving.

JANE'S LOBSTER STEW

A meal for 2. Jane Nickerson, former food editor of the *New York Times,* gave me this recipe for lobster stew—nothing but fresh lobster, sweet butter, milk, and cream. Not even salt or pepper is needed. It's best, Jane said, if made a day before you plan to serve it. She was right; the flavor does seem to develop and mellow in the refrigerator overnight. Serve with melba toast or hot corn muffins and a glass of dry sherry.

BUY

A 1½-pound very lively lobster
1 stick sweet butter (and don't you DARE buy margarine)
1 pint heavy cream

HAVE ON HAND	*COOKWARE*
Salt	Large kettle with lid
1 pint milk	Heavy saucepan with lid

1. In large kettle bring to a boil *4 quarts water* into which you have put *4 tablespoons salt*. When rapidly boiling, plunge the *live lobster,* head first, into the pot; cover pot, and bring water back to just a simmer. Simmer the lobster for 7 minutes, then turn off heat, and let the lobster remain in the salted water until cool enough to handle.

2. Split lobster and extract every little bit of the meat, discarding ONLY the intestinal vein that runs down the back and the sac that lies in the head. Reserve the green liver (tomalley) and the pink coral. Cut the meat into good-size chunks.

3. In heavy saucepan heat *6 tablespoons sweet butter,* and in it simmer the liver and coral for 7 minutes. Then add the lobster meat, and cook over very low heat for 5 minutes longer, stirring and tossing the lobster occasionally in the mixture. Remove saucepan from heat.

4. Very gradually pour in first the *milk* and then the *cream,* just a trickle at a time, stirring constantly; continue to stir until the rich milk turns to a delicate pink color. Cover saucepan and refrigerate for a least 6 hours, or overnight.

5. To serve, reheat to steaming hot, but do not let it boil.

MEDITERRANEAN CLAM OR MUSSEL SOUP

Serves 4. Serve with hot garlic bread.

BUY

48 Littleneck hard-shelled clams *or* mussels
Bunch of leeks
Parsley
1-pound can whole tomatoes
Saffron (filaments, not powder)

HAVE ON HAND

Onion (if you can't buy leeks)
Garlic
Olive oil
Bay leaves
Thyme
Dry white wine *or* dry vermouth
Salt
Peppercorns

COOKWARE

Large heavy kettle with lid

1. Soak the *clams or mussels* in *salted water* for half an hour, then scrub each one with a stiff brush and rinse well to remove any sand from the shells. If you are using mussels you will have to scrape off any seaweed, barnacles, or beard sticking to the shells. Set shellfish aside.

2. Trim, clean, and chop enough *white part of the leeks to measure 1½ cups* (or use *½ cup finely chopped onion*). Chop *3 large cloves garlic.* Mince enough *parsley clusters to measure 3 tablespoons.* Open *can of tomatoes,* drain well, and chop the tomatoes.

3. Measure *½ cup olive oil* into the kettle and heat it gently. Add the leeks or onions, and let them stew in the hot oil over low heat for about 10 minutes, or until soft but not brown.

4. Add garlic and drained, chopped tomatoes, mix well with the leeks, and simmer for 10 minutes longer.

5. Add the minced parsley, *1 bay leaf, ½ teaspoon dried thyme, 1 cup*

dry white wine or dry vermouth, 2 cups water, and *1 teaspoon saffron.* Bring to a boil, then simmer for 10 minutes.

6. Add the clams or mussels, cover tightly, and cook for 10 to 15 minutes, or until shells are open, stirring occasionally with a wooden spoon. Add a *little salt* to taste and about ½ *teaspoon freshly ground black pepper.*

7. Remove from heat, and ladle into large soup bowls.

CLAMS OR MUSSELS À LA NORMANDE

Serves 4. Serve with hot French bread.

BUY

4 pounds mussels *or* littleneck clams
Parsley
8-ounce container heavy cream

HAVE ON HAND	COOKWARE
Dry white wine	Large heavy kettle with lid
Shallots *or* onion	
Butter	
Pepper	

1. Soak and clean the *clams or mussels* as in preceding recipe.

2. Into a heavy kettle put *1 cup dry white wine, 2 tablespoons minced shallots or onion, 1 tablespoon minced parsley, 2 tablespoons butter,* and about ½ *teaspoon freshly ground black pepper.*

3. Add the mussels or clams and place the kettle over high heat. Cover tightly and cook for 10 to 15 minutes, or until shells have opened, stirring occasionally with a wooden spoon.

4. Remove cover, turn heat to low, and gradually stir the *cream* into the liquid in the kettle. Correct the seasoning of the broth with salt if necessary.

5. Ladle into large soup bowls, and sprinkle each serving with a *little more chopped parsley.*

BOUILLABAISSE

According to connoisseurs, no true bouillabaisse can be made without the unusual varieties of fish which swim in the Mediterranean—the *rascasse* or hog fish, the *baudroie* or devil fish, the *rouget* or rooster of the sea, the *loup de mer* or sea wolf, and others. No apology, however, really need be made to any Marseille gourmet for recipes that make use of the best fresh fish available in our own American markets.

At least four varieties of fish are needed. These should include thick slices of heavy fish such as red snapper or striped bass; cod steaks; tender fillets of sole or flounder, or other boned fish; and sections of fresh eel. Then you need lobsters and mussels, if you can find good ones. If not, you can substitute cherrystone clams. You will also need a few heads and bones to make a basic fish stock.

The following recipe is a most delicious and time-honored version of bouillabaisse which came originally from Provence. There is a considerable amount of work connected with its preparation, but the fish stock and the bouillabaisse broth may be made the day before and the entire production assembled early the day you are going to serve it, leaving only the final cooking to be done before serving.

BOUILLABAISSE IN THE MANNER OF PROVENCE

Serves 4. Serve with toasted garlic bread.

BUY

2 pounds fish bones, heads, and trimmings
Bunch of leeks (if available)
2 large ripe tomatoes *or* a 1-pound can whole tomatoes
Parsley
1 bottle dry white wine (3 cups)
Saffron threads, if you don't have
4 slices heavy fish with bones, cut about 2 inches thick, such as red snapper or striped bass

2 thick cod steaks
8 pieces of eel, each about 3 inches long
4 boneless fillets of gray or lemon sole *or* flounder
2 small lobsters (about 1 pound each)
1 dozen mussels *or* cherrystone clams
French bread

HAVE ON HAND	*COOKWARE*
Bay leaves	2½-quart saucepan
Thyme	6- to 7-quart heatproof casserole with
Salt	cover
Peppercorns	
Onions (if leeks are not available)	
Garlic	
Olive oil	
Butter	

MAKE FISH STOCK A DAY IN ADVANCE:

1. Wash *fish bones, heads, and trimmings,* and put them into the saucepan with *6 cups water, 1 bay leaf, a pinch of thyme, 1 teaspoon salt,* and *½ teaspoon peppercorns.*

2. Bring liquid to a boil, then reduce heat and simmer for 20 minutes. Do not overcook; this length of time is sufficient to extract all the good flavor and juices from the fish and bones.

3. Strain stock into a large bowl and set aside. Discard fish trimmings. Wash saucepan.

MAKE COURT BOUILLON A DAY IN ADVANCE:

1. Trim, wash well, and chop enough *white part of leeks to measure 1½ cups* (or use ½ cup chopped onion). Mince *3 cloves garlic.* Peel and chop the *fresh tomatoes* (or drain and chop the *canned tomatoes*). Squeeze out excess juice and seeds. Chop enough *parsley clusters to measure 2 tablespoons.* Set vegetables aside.

2. In the saucepan gently heat *½ cup olive oil.* Add the leeks or onion and cook over low heat for 10 minutes, or until vegetable is tender, but not brown.

3. Add the garlic and tomatoes, mix well with the leeks or onion, and simmer for 10 minutes longer.

4. Add the parsley, *1 quart of your fish stock, 1 bay leaf, ½ teaspoon dried thyme,* and *1 bottle dry white wine (3 cups).* Bring slowly to a boil, then sprinkle with *1 teaspoon saffron* and simmer for 20 minutes. Season to taste with *salt* and *freshly ground pepper.* Remove from heat and cool, then chill in refrigerator until the next day.

NEXT MORNING, MAKE THE BOUILLABAISSE:

1. Oil the bottom of your heavy casserole with *olive oil.* Arrange the *heavy fish, cod steaks,* and *eel* in the casserole. Place the tender fillets on top.

2. Pour the cold court-bouillon over the fish. Now cover the casserole, and place it in the refrigerator until time to cook.

3. Meanwhile split *lobsters* if you did not have this done at the fish market (see Index under live lobsters), and remove intestinal vein and sac in back of head. Split lobster shells and meat into pieces. Remove and crack the claws. Store in refrigerator.

4. Wash and scrub the *mussels or cherrystone clams* thoroughly, and keep cold.

5. Half an hour before you are ready to serve the bouillabaisse, place the casserole over direct heat and remove the cover. Watch carefully until the broth begins to simmer.

6. As soon as the broth begins to simmer, add the lobster pieces, cover casserole tightly, and cook over low heat for 15 minutes.

7. While the bouillabaisse cooks, slice the *French bread.* Spread each slice with *butter* and rub with a *cut clove of garlic.* Arrange slice on a baking sheet.

8. Add mussels or cherrystones to casserole, cover it again, and cook for 5 to 10 minutes longer, or until shells have opened.

9. Place baking sheet under broiler heat for 2 to 3 minutes, or until bread is toasted.

10. Bring the casserole to the table and serve the bouillabaisse in large soup plates with the garlic toast. Serve a piece of each kind of the fish to each person, along with plenty of the aromatic broth.

STEWS & GOULASHES

Stews & Goulashes

Where does a hearty soup leave off and a stew begin? I don't honestly know. In both, the meat and vegetables are usually cut into manageable pieces and are simmered in liquid from the start. I guess if someone pinned me down, I would say that a stew is thick enough to be served on a plate rather than in a soup bowl. Then where does poaching come in? Poaching is akin to stewing, stewing is kissin' cousin to braising; fricassees are related to both stews and sautés, and the difference between a sauté and a fricassee is trivial.

Often I feel about food the way Abbott and Costello felt about baseball in their wonderfully funny routine: "WHO's on first? No, WHO's on second? . . ." When I read Julia Child's great book, *Mastering the Art of French Cooking,* then reread Louis Diat's articles, "Tricks of My Trade," published in *Gourmet Magazine* when I was executive editor, I still get confused and have to start all over again, sorting out methods and techniques. So don't be critical if I put *blanquette de veau* under stews and Julia puts it some place else. I have organized the recipes in this book according to categories in which the cook is called upon to use similar procedures, so that you will learn the basic techniques of each category and will then be able, without bothering with a cookbook, to improvise dishes of your own from ingredients that you have on hand.

Some of the greatest dishes in the world are stews. Most of them are robust dishes that men enjoy eating and like to prepare. They are relatively inexpensive and, although they take a long time to cook, they don't take long to prepare. Moreover, they are always better if cooked a day in advance and reheated when needed.

Like hearty soups, or chowders, stews, goulashes, and braised dishes need little else to make a delicious and satisfying meal. A good tossed salad and some hot French bread to mop up the rich gravy are quite sufficient with them, although they are often served with rice, buttered noodles, dumplings, or mashed or boiled potatoes. Some accompaniments are traditional, such as noodles with Hungarian goulash or *risotto* with *osso buco,* but it doesn't really matter as long as you have something good with which to sop up the sauce.

There are two types of stews: rich, dark-colored stews, often flavored with red wine, and more delicate ones with a fragrant, light-colored sauce, sometimes containing white wine.

The first essential in making a dark stew is the correct browning of the meat. If you don't learn this, you will never make a stew with a really good, rich, dark sauce. Some short cuts have NO place in fine cooking, and one of these is the addition of bottled caramelized products to give a rich color to a sauce. Your stew will look just great, but it will taste lousy!

The meat must be really browned and not allowed to steam in its own juices. So begin at the butcher's. Don't let him cut your meat into chunks, let alone buy it already cut and packaged as stew meat. Rather, ask your butcher to give you thick slabs of lean meat, as many slabs as needed to amount to the weight of the meat specified in the recipe. With a heavy-duty chef's knife, and a wooden chopping block or board, it's very easy to cut the slabs into cubes yourself.

When meat is cut ahead of cooking time, all cut surfaces "bleed" and flavor is lost that should have gone into your stew. If you *do* buy your meat pre-cut, you must dry all surfaces of the meat with paper towels before putting it in the hot fat, for wet surfaces will not brown.

The meat is put into very hot fat. Use bacon drippings, any of the canned shortenings, or olive oil (the best), but NOT BUTTER. Butter burns at the high temperature needed to brown the meat. And no flour, please. If you flour the meat and then brown it in hot fat, all you're doing is burning the fat and flour!

Use a heavy-bottomed frying pan or skillet, and a large one. When the oil or fat is very hot, brown only as many cubes of meat at one time as can fit comfortably into the pan without one piece touching another. Meat needs plenty of room to brown well. Crowding the pan reduces the temperature of the fat, and the meat simmers instead of browning. Don't worry if some of the edges on the cubes get black. This won't hurt your stew any more than the crisp black edges on a broiled steak or double lamb chop spoil their flavor.

TO MAKE A GOOD DARK STEW:

1. Cut your meat into cubes yourself, but if you *have* bought pre-cut meat, wipe all surfaces well with absorbent paper.

2. Don't flour your meat.

3. Use a large, heavy skillet.

4. Use oil or shortening instead of butter, and have it smoking hot.

5. Don't brown too many chunks of meat at a time.

As the meat browns, transfer the cubes to a heavy casserole or Dutch oven. Then pour off all but a couple of tablespoons of fat, and in it brown some chopped onions and carrots, stirring them around so they pick up all the little brown pieces of meat glaze from the bottom and sides of the skillet. These chopped vegetables are known as the flavor-vegetables, and a chef's trick in browning them for a dark stew is to sprinkle them with a tiny bit of sugar—about 1 teaspoon. The sugar caramelizes, adding a rich color to the gravy without making the sauce sweet.

After the meat and vegetables are browned, enough liquid must be added to just cover the meat. This liquid may be stock, wine, or tomato juice—almost any liquid is better than plain water.

STEWS SHOULD NEVER BE ALLOWED TO BOIL. After the liquid reaches the simmering point, a good precaution is to place an asbestos pad between the casserole and the direct heat, unless you are sure you can control the heat sufficiently to keep the stew at no more than the simmering point.

Whole vegetables that are to be served with the meat are added during the last part of cooking, so they will not be overcooked.

Use a wooden spoon to stir the stew from time to time, and stir gently, moving the meat and whole vegetables around carefully to prevent mashing them.

In *haute cuisine* the sauce is usually strained to make it velvet smooth, but in *cuisine bourgeoise* (home-style) the tiny bits of flavor-vegetables are left in the sauce, giving it a coarser texture. Either way, the sauce should have good body, but it should never be too thick. It may be thickened with flour, cornstarch, or arrowroot mixed with cold water, or with a flour and butter paste known as *beurre manié*. Whichever method is used, add the thickening agent gradually, for nobody can tell you exactly how much is needed. The amount depends on how fast the stew was simmered and how long it was cooked. So use your common sense.

Now you're cooking!

BOEUF BOURGUIGNONNE

A perfect party dish for 10 or 12. Serve with boiled or mashed potatoes or garlic bread. Try Cheesecake for dessert.

BUY

5 pounds top round, in slabs cut 1½ inches thick
½ pound bacon
Carrots
Leeks
Parsley
4 medium onions
1 bottle good Burgundy wine
2 pounds small white onions
1 pound medium mushrooms

HAVE ON HAND

Olive oil *or* shortening
Garlic
Salt
Coarsely cracked pepper
Cognac
Thyme
Bay leaves
Flour
Butter
Sugar
1 lemon

COOKWARE

Large heavy skillet
5-quart heavy casserole, *or*
    Dutch oven, with cover
2 8-inch skillets, one with lid

ADVANCE PREPARATION:

1. Cut *beef* into 1½-inch cubes.

2. In heavy skillet heat *4 tablespoons olive oil or shortening* until smoking hot. Place as many cubes of beef in the skillet as will fit com-

fortably without touching one another, and brown on all sides in the hot oil or shortening. As cubes brown, transfer them to the heavy casserole or Dutch oven and keep warm. Add more oil or shortening as needed.

3. While meat is browning, shred the *bacon.* Scrape and coarsely chop *2 carrots.* Remove most of the green stalks from *3 leeks,* split and wash well to remove any trace of sand, then slice. Chop *½ cup parsley.* Peel and coarsely chop *4 medium onions.* Peel and mince *4 cloves garlic.*

4. When all meat is brown and in the casserole, sprinkle with *2 teaspoons salt* and *½ teaspoon coarsely cracked pepper.* Pour *½ cup cognac* over the meat and set aflame. Let the flame die out.

5. Put bacon in fat remaining in skillet, and cook over moderate heat for 2 to 3 minutes, or until fat starts to be rendered out. Add carrots, leeks, 3 tablespoons of the chopped parsley, and the chopped onion, and continue to cook, stirring occasionally, until vegetables and bacon are a nice brown. Add contents of skillet to the casserole.

6. Add to casserole *½ teaspoon thyme, 2 bay leaves,* the minced garlic, *the bottle of Burgundy,* and *enough water to just cover* the meat and vegetables. Bring to a simmer on top of the stove, then transfer to the oven, preheated to 325° F.; cover casserole and cook for 2 hours.

7. In a small bowl mix *2 tablespoons each of flour and butter* to a smooth paste. Remove casserole from oven. Blend the flour-butter paste with a little of the hot liquid, then stir this slowly into liquid in casserole. Cover casserole and return to the oven. Cook for 2 to 3 hours longer.

8. Finish boeuf bourguignonne so that it will be ready to serve, or having let it cool, refrigerate it, and then complete it next day. Before reheating, remove any fat from surface.

TO FINISH:

9. The casserole is still in the oven, or has been placed there for reheating. Now peel the *small white onions.* Wash *mushrooms* and trim stems. In a small skillet melt *2 tablespoons butter.* Add onions and sprinkle with *1 teaspoon sugar.* Cook over brisk heat, shaking pan frequently to toss the onions in the butter and sugar until golden brown. Add *2 tablespoons water,* cover skillet, and cook over low heat for 10 minutes.

10. In another small skillet heat *2 tablespoons butter,* and in it sauté mushrooms, cap side down, until lightly browned. Turn mushrooms, sprinkle with *juice of ½ lemon,* and cook for 2 minutes longer.

11. Remove casserole from oven to top of stove. Carefully tip casserole and skim off any excess fat from surface of sauce. Correct seasoning of sauce with *salt* and *pepper,* and add *juice of remaining ½ lemon.* Fold in onions and arrange mushrooms on top. Sprinkle with *remaining chopped parsley,* and serve directly from the casserole.

HUNGARIAN GOULASH

Serves 6. Serve with hot buttered noodles. If desired, sauté some fresh bread crumbs (use your blender for these) in butter with 1 clove garlic, minced. When crumbs are golden, sprinkle on top of the buttered noodles. Good!

BUY

3 pounds top round, in slabs cut 1½ inches thick
2 pounds onions
6-ounce can tomato paste

HAVE ON HAND

Cooking oil *or* bacon drippings
Bay leaves
2 cans ale *or* beer (12 ounces each)
Salt and pepper
Paprika

COOKWARE

Large heavy skillet
4-quart heavy casserole with cover

ADVANCE PREPARATION:

1. Cut *meat* into 1½-inch cubes.

2. In skillet heat ¼ *cup oil or bacon drippings* until smoking. Place as many cubes of beef in the skillet as will fit comfortably without touching one another, and brown well on all sides in the hot oil or drippings. Transfer meat to a heavy casserole when brown. Add more oil or drippings if needed.

3. While meat is browning, peel and slice the *onions.*

4. When all meat is browned and in casserole, add the onions and *1 large bay leaf.* Cover casserole, and cook over low heat for 10 minutes, to wilt and soften the onions.

5. Add the *2 cans ale or beer;* add the *can of tomato paste;* and bring liquid to a boil. Cover casserole, and cook over very low heat for 2½ hours, or until meat is tender.

6. Finish and serve, or cool and then refrigerate. Reheat next day, but first remove any fat accumulated on surface.

TO FINISH:

Correct seasoning of the hot goulash with *salt and pepper.* Stir in *1 table-spoon paprika.* Keep over low heat until ready to serve.

SZEKELY GOULASH

Serves 4. Serve with small boiled potatoes.

BUY

3 pounds pork tenderloin
3 pounds fresh *or* canned sauerkraut
1-pound can solid-pack tomatoes
13½-ounce can chicken broth
8-ounce container dairy sour cream

HAVE ON HAND

2 large onions
Garlic
Bacon drippings
Caraway seeds
Coarsely cracked pepper
Salt
Hungarian paprika *or* American
  paprika and red pepper
Flour
Fresh dill *or* dried dill weed

COOKWARE

Large heavy kettle with lid

1. Cut the *pork tenderloin* into 1-inch cubes. Peel and chop *2 large onions;* peel and mince *4 large cloves garlic.* Rinse the *sauerkraut* in two changes of cold water. Drain well.

2. Heat *⅓ cup bacon drippings* in a large heavy kettle, and in it

brown the pork cubes lightly on all sides. Add the chopped onions, minced garlic, the sauerkraut, *1 tablespoon caraway seeds,* the *tomatoes with liquid,* and ¼ *teaspoon coarsely cracked pepper.* Toss all together gently, cover, and simmer over low heat for 1½ hours, or until pork is tender.

3. Sprinkle the stew with *3 tablespoons Hungarian paprika; or 2 tablespoons American paprika plus ¼ teaspoon red pepper.* Add ½ *cup chicken broth,* and stir well. Cover, and simmer for 15 minutes.

4. Taste goulash, and add *a little salt* if needed. Combine ½ *cup of remaining chicken stock* with *2 tablespoons flour* and *1 cup sour cream.* Stir gently into the meat-and-sauerkraut mixture, and cook until the goulash is hot and the liquid is thickened.

5. Serve sprinkled with *chopped fresh dill or dried dill weed.*

CARBONNADE FLAMANDE

Serves 6. This Flemish beef-and-beer stew is traditionally served with boiled potatoes. A tossed green salad goes well with it, of course, and beer is the best beverage. Apple Crunch is an easy and suitable dessert.

BUY

2 pounds onions
3 pounds chuck steak, cut in a slab about 1 inch thick

HAVE ON HAND	*COOKWARE*
Cooking oil *or* beef fat	Large heavy skillet
Parsley	4-quart casserole with cover
Salt and pepper	
Thyme	
Garlic	
1½ quarts beer	
Flour	
Butter	

1. Peel and thinly slice the *onions.*

2. In heavy skillet heat ¼ *cup cooking oil or beef fat* until quite hot, but not smoking. Add onions and sauté over moderate heat for about

10 minutes, stirring frequently, until onions are lightly browned. Transfer onions with slotted spoon to the casserole.

3. While onions are browning, cut *meat* into 1-inch cubes. Chop some *parsley* and set aside.

4. When onions are in the casserole, increase heat under skillet until the fat remaining in it is smoking hot; now brown the meat cubes well on all sides, a few at a time. As the cubes are browned place them on the bed of onions in the casserole.

5. Sprinkle the meat with *1 teaspoon salt, ¼ teaspoon pepper, ½ teaspoon thyme, 4 cloves garlic, minced.* Add the *quart of beer.* Cover and cook over low heat for 2½ hours. The liquid should not boil, instead it should barely bubble or simmer. Remove cover, and if there is too much liquid, cook for 20 minutes with cover off to let the liquid reduce a little. There should be about 3 cups liquid.

6. Carefully skim off any excess fat from surface of liquid. In small bowl or cup combine *2 tablespoons each flour and butter* to a smooth paste. Stir in a little of the hot liquid, then stir mixture slowly into the ingredients in casserole. Cook, stirring, until sauce is slightly thickened.

7. Sprinkle with parsley and serve. Or cook, partially cool, and then refrigerate. When ready to serve, cover casserole and return to a simmer. Simmer for 4 or 5 minutes, or until meat is thoroughly hot.

TEXAS CHILI

Serves 6. This is one of the easiest and best chilis I have ever eaten. Serve it with cooked rice and with canned kidney beans, simply heated in their own liquid and drained before serving, or with Sopa de Arroz, a combination of rice and *garbanzos* (chick peas). Serve bowls of shredded lettuce and finely chopped onion on the side to be sprinkled over the chili. Canned tamales make a suitable first course, or guacamole with fritos. Try an easy Caramel Flan for dessert.

BUY

3 pounds round steak, cut in slabs ½ inch thick
2 cans beef broth (13¾ ounces each)

HAVE ON HAND	*COOKWARE*
Cooking oil	12-inch heavy, deep skillet,
Chili powder	*or* chicken fryer, with cover
Flour	
Cumin seeds	
Oregano	
Salt	
Garlic	

1. Cut *steak* into ½-inch cubes.

2. In skillet heat *6 tablespoons cooking oil* until smoking hot. Add meat and cook, stirring and tossing the meat in the hot oil, until it loses all red color. It won't brown since the cubes are too small and there are so many in the pan.

3. Stir in *6 tablespoons chili powder* and *6 tablespoons flour.* Add *1 teaspoon cumin seeds, 1 teaspoon oregano, 1 teaspoon salt,* the *2 cans of beef broth* and *3 cloves garlic,* minced. Bring to a simmer, then almost completely cover, and cook over very low heat for 4 to 6 hours. The longer it cooks (without boiling) the better it is. In Texas the chili is allowed to cook for as long as 24 hours.

4. Serve with the accompaniments suggested above. If to be served in a day or so, cool and refrigerate. When ready to serve, reheat to a simmer and let it sit over low heat until you are good and ready to set it on the table.

CHILI CON POLLO

Serves 4. If you like chilis you will enjoy this for a change. It really is not so much a stew as a braised dish, but it seems to fit logically here.

BUY

4-pound roasting chicken, quartered or cut into serving pieces
13¾-ounce can chicken broth
2 1-pound cans whole tomatoes

<table>
<tr><td>HAVE ON HAND</td><td>COOKWARE</td></tr>
</table>

Salt and pepper	Heavy kettle with lid
Chili powder	
Cumin, ground	
Oregano	
Garlic	
Onions	
Flour	
Lemon	

1. Put *chicken* into a heavy kettle, and add the *chicken broth, 1 tea-spoon salt, ¼ teaspoon pepper,* the *canned whole tomatoes and their juice, 4 tablespoons chili powder, 1 teaspoon ground cumin,* and *1 tea-spoon oregano.* Bring liquid to a boil.

2. While liquid is coming to a boil, peel and chop *2 cloves garlic.* Peel and chop *2 cups onions.* Add garlic and onions to a kettle, partially cover, and simmer over low heat for 1½ hours, or until chicken is very tender.

3. Remove chicken from broth with slotted spoon, discard bones, and cut meat into large pieces.

4. In small bowl combine *4 tablespoons flour, 4 tablespoons water,* and *juice of ½ lemon.* Bring liquid in kettle to a rolling boil. Gradually stir flour mixture into liquid, and cook, continuing to stir, until sauce is thickened.

5. Add chicken to kettle, reduce heat, and cook for 10 minutes.

NOTE: There is an excellent brand of frozen tortillas on the market. Follow the directions on package for making tacos, and use any leftover chicken for the filling. Top with shredded lettuce.

COUSCOUS

Serves 8. This is the national dish of North Africa, and if you've never made it, do try it for it is quite a marvelous meal. In essence, it is a simple lamb-and-vegetable stew served with steamed hard wheat, or semolina, called *couscous,* from which the dish takes its name. The stew is served with two different sauces, one mild and the other extremely hot. There are many different recipes for *couscous;* this one is rather simple, but delicious. A more exotic version includes raisins and almonds.

IN ADVANCE

Order two 1-pound boxes of *couscous.*
Check your spice shelf.

BUY

4 pounds lean leg or shoulder of lamb, cut into 1½-inch cubes
1½ pounds onions
8 tomatoes, *or* a 2-pound 3-ounce can Italian plum tomatoes
1½ pounds zucchini *or* yellow squash
1-pound 4-ounce can chick peas (garbanzos)
8 small carrots
1 pound white turnips
1 large rutabaga turnip *or* 1 pound pumpkin
3 green peppers
Small can tomato paste

HAVE ON HAND

Olive oil
Garlic
Bay leaves
Thyme
Oregano
Rosemary
Pepper
Salt
Dried hot chili peppers
½ cup (1 stick) butter
Paprika
Ground coriander
Cayenne pepper
Cheesecloth

COOKWARE

A large heavy kettle with lid, and a colander with handles that can sit on top of the kettle without falling in; *or,* in place of these two items, a special cooker known as a *couscousière.*
Small saucepan

1. In the heavy kettle heat *4 tablespoons olive oil* and in it brown the *lamb* well on all sides.

2. While lamb is browning, peel and coarsely slice the *onions.* Mince *3 cloves garlic.* Peel and quarter *the tomatoes* and squeeze out excess moisture and seeds. Wash *zucchini,* then split, and cut into 1½-inch lengths.

3. When lamb is brown, reduce heat to moderate, and add onions. Let these brown lightly. Then add garlic, tomatoes, HALF of the zucchini, *1 bay leaf, ½ teaspoon each thyme and oregano,* and *¼ teaspoon each rosemary and pepper.* Drain and add *the chick peas.* Add *2 quarts water,* or enough to just cover meat and vegetables, and season liquid with *salt* to taste. Bring liquid to a boil, reduce heat, partially cover, and simmer without stirring for 1 hour.

4. While the stew is simmering for the first hour, empty the *2 pounds couscous (semolina)* into a large mixing bowl, and pour over it about *1 cup boiling water* to make the grains swell. Stir well with a fork, and let stand for 20 minutes. Repeat this three times. Then line a colander with cheesecloth and empty the couscous into it. Crumble the couscous with your fingers to get rid of any lumps.

5. While you're paying some attention to the couscous, scrape the *carrots,* and peel the *white turnips* and quarter them. Peel and cut the *rutabaga or pumpkin* into chunks. Seed the *green peppers* and cut them into strips.

6. Now add to your stew the rest of the zucchini, the carrots, turnips, rutabaga or pumpkin, green peppers, and *2 hot chili peppers.* Add a little more water if necessary to just cover the ingredients. Set the colander with the couscous in it over the stew. Dot the couscous with *4 tablespoons butter,* and sprinkle it lightly with *salt and pepper.* Cover the colander with the lid of the kettle, and simmer the stew for 1 hour longer.

7. Make the Hot Sauce; Measure *1 cup of the liquid from the stew* into a small serving bowl, and stir in *2 tablespoons tomato paste, ½ teaspoon paprika, ¼ teaspoon ground coriander,* and from *¼ to 1 teaspoon cayenne pepper* to taste. The sauce should be VERY hot.

8. In small saucepan melt 4 tablespoons butter.

9. To serve: Pile the couscous in a cone shape on a platter, and pour the melted butter over it. Ladle meat and vegetables plus a little of the liquid into a big tureen or serving bowl. Serve remaining liquid separately from a sauce boat. Serve the Hot Sauce in a bowl with a tiny spoon.

NOTE: Other vegetables may be added to this lamb stew, such as artichoke hearts, sliced eggplant, winter squash, and so on. One-half cup each of seedless raisins and blanched almonds may also be added about 15 minutes before the stew is ready to be served.

LAMB STEW À LA RITZ

Serves 6

BUY

3 pounds shoulder of lamb, cut into rather large pieces
3 medium size onions
3 pounds small potatoes
Bunch of leeks
Celery
18 small white onions
6 white turnips
6 carrots
Small can tomato paste
Parsley

HAVE ON HAND

Garlic
Salt
Peppercorns
Tarragon

COOKWARE

2 large heavy saucepans
or kettles

1. Put *lamb* into the saucepan, and cover with *cold water*. Bring water to a boil, and boil for 5 minutes. Drain lamb, discarding the water; rinse the meat in fresh cold water.

2. Clean the saucepan, and return the meat to it. Add *2 quarts water,* and bring water slowly to a boil.

3. While stew is heating, peel and chop *3 medium onions;* peel and chop *4 of the potatoes;* discard green stalks from *3 or 4 leeks,* wash thoroughly and chop. Chop *4 stalks celery.* Peel and mince *1 clove garlic.* Add the vegetables to the meat. Add *3 teaspoons salt, ½ teaspoon peppercorns,* and *½ teaspoon tarragon.* Simmer the stew gently for 1 hour.

4. Meanwhile peel the *18 small white onions.* Peel *remaining potatoes* and put into a bowl of cold water. Peel and quarter *the turnips* and add to potatoes. Scrape *carrots* and cut each into 6 pieces. Chop *1 tablespoon parsley.*

5. Transfer the meat to another saucepan or kettle. Carefully skim off any fat from top of the broth. Then strain broth through a sieve, or food mill, pressing and rubbing as much of the cooked vegetables through as possible. Pour the broth over the meat, and stir in *2 tablespoons tomato paste*. Correct seasoning with *salt and pepper*. Place the prepared vegetables on top of the meat, and sprinkle with *parsley*.

6. Bring broth to a boil and simmer for 45 minutes, or until meat and vegetables are tender.

BLANQUETTE DE VEAU

Serves 6. Serve with cooked rice and a colorful vegetable in season. A simple fruit dessert such as Strawberries Romanoff or Peaches Baked in Cointreau is called for here.

BUY

3 pounds boned shoulder of veal, cut into 1½-inch cubes
2 cans chicken broth (13¾ ounces each)
Parsley
18 small white onions
18 small mushroom caps
8-ounce container heavy cream

HAVE ON HAND

Dry white wine *or* dry vermouth
Large onion
Whole cloves
Carrots
Celery
Garlic
Peppercorns
Bay leaf
Thyme
Butter (at room temperature)
Flour

Salt
White pepper
3 eggs
1 lemon

Large heavy kettle with lid
Small saucepan for white onions

1. Put *veal* into a heavy kettle, and cover generously with *salted water*. Bring water to a boil, then simmer for 5 minutes, skimming off foam as it rises to surface. Place the kettle under cold running water to refresh and cool the meat. Drain well, leaving meat in the kettle.

2. Add the *2 cans chicken broth, 2 cups water,* and *1 cup dry white wine or dry Vermouth.* Add *1 large onion stuck with 3 cloves,* and *2 large or 3 small carrots, scraped and cut into strips.*

3. Tie *1 stalk celery with leaves, 3 sprigs parsley, 1 clove garlic, halved, ¼ teaspoon peppercorns, 1 bay leaf,* and *½ teaspoon thyme* in a cheesecloth bag, and add to kettle. Add *½ teaspoon salt* and bring liquid to a boil, skimming off any scum which appears on surface. Partially cover, and simmer over low heat for 1½ hours.

4. Meanwhile peel the *18 small white onions.* Simmer them in salted water to cover until barely fork tender, then set aside. Wash, trim, and dry *mushrooms;* chop some *parsley;* set both aside.

5. When meat is fork tender, discard the spice bag and the large onion.

6. In cup or small bowl combine *4 tablespoons soft butter* and *6 tablespoons flour* with a little of the hot liquid from the kettle; stir this little by little into remaining liquid in kettle. Cook for 5 minutes longer, constantly stirring. Add the mushrooms, and cook for another 5 minutes. Correct seasoning of the sauce to taste with *salt* and *white pepper.* Drain the onions, and add to stew.

7. When ready to serve, combine *3 egg yolks with 2 tablespoons lemon juice* and *1 cup of heavy cream.* Stir this mixture gradually into sauce in kettle. DO NOT LET THE SAUCE BOIL while adding or after adding the egg yolks. If it is necessary to keep the stew hot, set the kettle over a large pan of hot, but not boiling, water.

8. Ladle stew into a large serving dish or soup tureen, and sprinkle with the chopped parsley.

CHICKEN BARBAN

Serves 4. Serve with buttered noodles. This is a rich unctuous dish and should be followed by a simple dessert. A big bowl of fresh strawberries and a side dish of confectioners' sugar to dip them in would be perfection.

BUY
3½-pound frying chicken, cut into serving portions
4 carrots
8 small onions
8 small potatoes
2 cans chicken broth (13¾ ounces each)
8-ounce container heavy cream
Parsley

HAVE ON HAND
Garlic
Dry white wine *or* dry vermouth
Cayenne
Curry powder
Bay leaves
Thyme
Salt and pepper
Flour
Butter (at room temperature)
Lemons
Eggs

COOKWARE
2½- to 3-quart top-of-stove casserole with cover

1. Soak *chicken pieces* in cold water for 30 minutes. Meanwhile scrape the *carrots* and halve them lengthwise. Peel *onions*. Peel *potatoes* and drop into cold water with the chicken. Mince *1 clove garlic*.

2. Dry chicken pieces on absorbent paper, and put them in the casserole. Add *the chicken broth* and ½ *cup dry white wine or dry vermouth*. Add minced garlic, *dash cayenne pepper, ¼ teaspoon curry powder, 1 bay leaf* and ¼ *teaspoon thyme*. Bring liquid to a simmer, cover casserole, and continue to simmer for 15 minutes.

3. Add carrots, onions, potatoes, and a *little salt and pepper to taste*.

Be careful with the salt since the chicken broth contains salt. Cover and simmer for 45 minutes longer. Discard bay leaf.

4. In a small bowl or cup mix *4 tablespoons flour* and *4 tablespoons soft butter* to a smooth paste. Stir a little of the liquid from the casserole into the paste, then stir the mixture gradually into liquid in casserole. Cook over low heat, uncovered, for 10 minutes.

5. Finish and serve, or cool and reheat when needed.

TO FINISH:

Chop a *little parsley* and set aside.

6. When liquid is hot, add the *juice of 1½ lemons*. In a small bowl combine *2 egg yolks* and *½ cup heavy cream*. Stir egg mixture into sauce in casserole, and heat to serving temperature, stirring constantly. DO NOT LET THE SAUCE BOIL or the egg will curdle. Sprinkle with a little chopped parsley and serve.

BRAISED DISHES

Braising

Poultry, lamb, pork, veal, and beef may all be braised (yes, fish, too). Usually this method of cooking is reserved for less tender and less expensive cuts of beef such as chuck, top or bottom round, rump, neck, brisket, oxtails, and short ribs, these frequently being marinated for 6 to 24 hours to tenderize them before they are cooked.

The meat may be cooked in one piece or cut into serving portions. Always less liquid is used in braising than in stews, ragouts, and goulashes. This means that whether the dish is cooked on top of the stove or in the oven, frequent basting is essential in order to cook the top of the meat as well as the bottom.

The meat is first seasoned with salt and rolled in a small amount of flour, then it is browned in fat or oil over moderately high heat. The bottom of the braising kettle is often spread with chopped vegetables, and the browned meat placed on top of them.

The braising liquid may be any combination of wine, stock, and tomato juice or water, and when the dish is finished the liquid should have been reduced to about half the original quantity.

A good trick to remember when braising: Each time you baste, skim off any fat that has risen to the surface of the cooking liquid and you will never have a greasy sauce.

PEGGY'S BRAISED OXTAILS

Serves 8. These are powerful good eating! Yet I know many food lovers who blanch at the thought. Why? The tail of the ox is nothing more nor less than an extension of the backbone, along which are the cuts of steaks, roast beef, and stew meat that we eat without thinking a thing of it! Here you have one of the best recipes for oxtails that I know of. Serve with small boiled potatoes and a buttered mixed julienne of carrots and white turnips. Peach Melba or Coupe aux Marrons for dessert.

BUY

4 oxtails, skinned and cut into sections
Parsley
2 cans beef consommé (10½ ounces each)
1-pound can whole tomatoes

HAVE ON HAND	COOKWARE
Celery	Large heavy skillet
Carrots	Heavy casserole, *or* Dutch oven,
Garlic	with cover
Butter	2-quart saucepan
Olive oil	
Bay leaves	
Flour	
Cognac	
Pepper	
Nutmeg	
Lemon	
Salt	
Madeira *or* Marsala	

1. Soak *oxtails* in *lukewarm water* for 1 hour, changing water every 15 minutes. Drain and dry well.

2. While oxtails are soaking, chop *4 stalks celery, 2 carrots,* and *2 tablespoons parsley.* Mince *1 clove garlic.*

3. In heavy skillet heat *4 tablespoons each butter and olive oil,* and in it brown oxtail pieces over moderate heat, a few at a time.

4. *Butter* bottom of a heavy casserole or Dutch oven, and sprinkle bottom with the chopped celery, half the parsley, and the garlic. As the oxtails brown, place them on this bed of vegetables; when all are brown, add *1 bay leaf.*

5. To fat remaining in skillet add the chopped carrots, and cook until they are lightly browned. Stir in *2 tablespoons flour,* then gradually stir in *1 can of the consommé,* cooking and stirring in all the brown bits from bottom and side of skillet. Add carrots and sauce to casserole.

6. Add to casserole *remaining can of consommé* and *¼ cup cognac.* Drain the *tomatoes,* then chop them and add to casserole. Add *½ teaspoon pepper, ¼ teaspoon nutmeg,* and the *juice of ½ lemon.*

7. Cover casserole tightly; braise on top of the stove, or in a preheated 325° F. oven, for 2½ to 3 hours, checking occasionally to make sure the stew is NOT boiling. If it is boiling, reduce heat to keep liquid at a low simmer.

8. When ready to serve, transfer the pieces of oxtails to a serving dish. Strain the gravy into a saucepan, pressing as much of the cooked vegetables as possible through the sieve.

9. Return gravy to heat, and correct seasoning with *salt.* Stir in *½ cup of Madeira or Marsala,* and heat to simmering. Pour gravy over oxtails, and sprinkle on the *remaining chopped parsley.*

OSSO BUCO

Serves 6 to 9. This is a well-known Italian braised dish. The name means marrow bone. It is made with the meaty forelegs of young veal, which are sawed into 3-inch pieces. Each piece with its surrounding layer of meat forms a sort of individual circular steak with marrow in the center of the bone.

Serve this dish with plain rice or Risotto, small buttered carrots, and hot Italian bread. Antipasto makes a suitable first course. Fresh fruit and cheese, or a fruit compote, or Lemon Sherbet are suggestions for dessert. Espresso coffee, of course.

BUY

3 forelegs of young veal, each cut into three 3-inch portions
Carrots
Celery
10½-ounce can beef consommé

HAVE ON HAND	*COOKWARE*
Butter	Large heavy kettle *or*
Olive oil	top-of-the-stove casserole
Flour	
Garlic	
Onion	
Salt	
Coarsely ground pepper	
Rosemary	
Sage	
Dry white wine	
Tomato paste	
1 lemon	

1. In kettle or casserole over moderate heat, put *2 tablespoons each butter and olive oil*. Roll the *pieces of veal* in *flour*, and sauté them in the hot oil mixture until brown on all sides, turning frequently.

2. While the bones are browning, scrape and chop *2 small carrots*. Peel and chop *1 clove garlic* and *1 medium onion*. Chop enough *celery stalks to measure 1 cup*.

3. When all the bones are brown, set them on their sides to hold the marrow in, and sprinkle with *1 teaspoon salt* and *½ teaspoon coarsely ground pepper*. Add the prepared vegetables and *1 teaspoon rosemary* and *½ teaspoon sage*. Cover kettle or casserole, and let the vegetables steam over moderate heat for 10 minutes.

4. Add *1½ cups white wine*, the *can of beef consommé, 2 tablespoons tomato paste*, and *about 1 consommé can full of water*, or enough to barely cover the bones with liquid. Cover kettle or casserole, and simmer over low heat for 2 hours.

5. While bones are simmering, prepare an Italian seasoning mixture known as the *gremolada:* With a vegetable peeler remove the *thin yellow rind from 1 lemon,* and cut rind into very fine slivers. Peel and mince

2 large cloves garlic; chop *3 tablespoons parsley.* Combine rind, garlic, and parsley, then set aside.

6. Finish dish and serve, or set it aside and reheat when needed. To finish: Bring liquid in kettle or casserole to a simmer, stir in the gremolada, and simmer for 1 to 2 minutes longer.

BRAISED LAMB SHANKS

Serves 4. Serve with boiled potatoes or cooked rice. Prunes in Port Wine for dessert.

BUY

4 lamb shanks
1-pound can Italian plum tomatoes

HAVE ON HAND	*COOKWARE*
Garlic	Large heavy casserole *or*
2 carrots	Dutch oven
1 large onion	Heavy skillet
2 stalks celery with leaves	
Olive oil	
Bay leaves	
Oregano	
Thyme	

1. Soak the *lamb shanks* in *lukewarm water* for 20 minutes. Drain and dry well on paper towels.

2. While the lamb shanks are soaking, peel and mince *3 cloves garlic;* scrape *2 carrots* and cut them into thin julienne strips; peel and thinly slice *1 large onion;* and thinly slice *2 stalks celery with leaves. Oil* the bottom of the casserole or Dutch oven, and lay on it the prepared vegetables.

3. In skillet heat *½ cup olive oil,* and in it brown the lamb shanks well on all sides. As they brown transfer them to the casserole, placing them on top of the bed of vegetables.

4. When all the shanks are in the casserole, add *2 bay leaves,* crum-

bled, *½ teaspoon oregano, ½ teaspoon thyme,* the *can of tomatoes in-cluding its liquid,* and *1 cup water.*

5. Cover casserole or Dutch oven tightly, and braise on top of the stove, or in a 350° F. oven, for 2 to 2½ hours, checking occasionally to make sure the liquid is not cooking too rapidly. It should just simmer. If necessary, reduce the heat.

6. Finish and serve, or set aside, partially covered, and reheat when needed. To finish: Skim off all the fat floating on the surface of the sauce.

OVEN-BRAISED POT ROAST

Serves 8. Small whole carrots and peeled onions and potatoes may be added to the casserole 1 hour before roast is done. Or, potatoes may be cooked separately to serve with the roast. Actually, I prefer mashed po-tatoes.

BUY

4 to 5 pounds boneless pot roast, larded and tied
Parsley
10½-ounce can beef consommé
1 bottle good red wine
1 pound mushrooms

HAVE ON HAND

3 stalks celery with leaves
1 medium onion
1 large carrot
Garlic
Salt and pepper
Thyme
Bay leaf
Cloves, whole
Peppercorns
Red wine vinegar
Cooking oil
Cognac *or* brandy
Cornstarch
Port *or* Madeira

COOKWARE

Heavy casserole, *or* Dutch oven, with cover
2-quart saucepan

ONE DAY IN ADVANCE:

1. Coarsely cut *3 stalks celery with leaves;* peel and coarsely chop *1 medium onion;* slice *1 large carrot;* cut *2 cloves garlic* in half (no need to peel); and chop *¼ cup parsley.* Put half of these vegetables in a large pyrex bowl or porcelain-lined casserole. Rub the *pot roast* with *salt* and *pepper,* and place it on the bed of vegetables. Sprinkle with *½ teaspoon thyme,* and add *1 bay leaf, 3 whole cloves, 1 teaspoon salt,* and *½ teaspoon peppercorns.* Cover the meat with the *rest of the vegetables,* and pour over all *2 cups red wine* and *½ cup red wine vinegar.* Cover container, and refrigerate for 12 to 24 hours, turning the meat occasionally.

WHEN READY TO COOK:

2. Remove meat from casserole, and be sure to save the marinade! Dry the meat well with paper towels, for it must be browned in hot fat to seal in the juices before it is braised, and meat that is wet will not brown nicely and will cause the fat to splatter.

3. Pour the reserved marinade into a saucepan, bring to a boil, and then reduce to a simmer while the meat is browning.

4. Heat *4 tablespoons good cooking oil* in the heavy casserole or Dutch oven over moderately high heat until very hot. Place roast carefully in the hot fat and cook until it is dark brown, but not burnt, turning it with two wooden spoons until brown on all sides. Do not pierce meat by turning it with a fork or the juices will run out and splatter. When meat is browned, pour off excess fat from casserole; return casserole to the stove and turn heat to moderate.

5. Pour *⅓ cup cognac or brandy* over the roast, ignite it and let the flame burn out. This loosens all the brown bits of meat glaze from bottom of the casserole, and gives the gravy a super-duper flavor.

6. Preheat oven to 300° F.

7. Add the *can of consommé* and the *marinade* (liquid and vegetables) to the casserole, and bring the liquid to a boil. Cover tightly and braise in the low oven for 4 hours, checking occasionally to make sure the liquid is not boiling. It should barely simmer. If necessary, reduce oven temperature to 250° F. If adding whole vegetables, add them at the end of 3 hours cooking.

8. Meanwhile wash *mushrooms,* trim ends of stems, and dry well on paper towels.

9. When meat is cooked, place it on a hot platter. Remove the whole vegetables, if used, with a slotted spoon and arrange around the roast. Keep dish warm while you make the gravy. If desired, cover platter with aluminum foil and return to the oven (heat off).

10. Strain liquid in casserole through a sieve into the saucepan, pressing as much of the chopped vegetables as possible through the sieve with a wooden spoon. Skim off all fat from surface of liquid with a metal spoon, reserving 2 tablespoons. Bring the defatted liquid to a boil, then simmer while cooking the mushrooms.

11. Return the emptied casserole to direct heat, and add the *2 tablespoons reserved fat*. In it sauté mushrooms until lightly browned. Add the strained hot liquid, and correct the seasoning with *salt and pepper*.

12. Combine *1 tablespoon cornstarch* and *2 tablespoons Port or Madeira wine,* and stir into the hot liquid. Cook, stirring, for 1 minute. Keep over low heat for 3 minutes, then pour a little gravy over the roast and garnish with mushrooms. Serve the rest of the gravy separately.

CECELIA'S SAUERBRATEN

Serves 8. Mashed potatoes may not be as traditional with sauerbraten as noodles or dumplings, but I still like them best for soaking up the rich gravy. Buttered string beans, broccoli, or Brussels sprouts are good complementary vegetables. And a homespun Brown Betty or Shoo-fly Pie for dessert. Enjoy anything leftover from these for breakfast. Great!

BUY

5- to 6-pound, rolled, top eye *or* bottom round of beef
2 cans beef consommé (10½ ounces each)
Parsley

HAVE ON HAND

Red wine vinegar
Dry red wine
Peppercorns
Salt

Bay leaves
Cloves (whole)
Nutmeg
Garlic
Lemon
Onion
2 stalks celery
2 carrots
Cornstarch *or* arrowroot

COOKWARE

Heavy kettle, or Dutch oven,
  with cover
2-quart saucepan

TWO DAYS IN ADVANCE:

1. Put the beef into a large pyrex or porcelain-lined container, and pour in *1 cup red wine vinegar*, and *½ bottle dry red wine.* Then add *1 teaspoon peppercorns, 1 teaspoon salt, a large bay leaf, 6 cloves, ¼ teaspoon nutmeg, 2 cloves garlic,* split, *2 strips lemon rind, 1 onion,* halved, *2 large stalks celery,* coarsely sliced, *2 carrots,* cut into strips, and *a few sprigs parsley.* Cover the container and let sit in a cool place for 2 days, turning the meat occasionally.

2. Remove meat from the marinade, reserving the marinade, and pat meat dry with paper towels.

3. Set the kettle or Dutch oven over moderate heat; when it is hot, place the meat in it, fat side down. Brown the meat well, turning it until good and brown on all sides. Don't rush this, for you don't want to burn the roast. The browning process should take about half an hour in all.

4. When roast is brown reduce heat to very low, add *1 can of the consommé,* cover kettle tightly, and begin the long slow braising over low heat.

5. Pour the *reserved marinade* into the saucepan, and bring it to a simmer. Let it simmer quietly.

6. Total braising time for the meat is from 3 to 3½ hours. During this time remove the cover occasionally and baste the meat with some of the hot marinade and the *remaining can of consommé* until all of them have been added.

TO FINISH:

7. Remove the meat to a hot platter. Strain the gravy into the saucepan, pressing as much of the cooked vegetables through the sieve as possible, or better still use a food mill.

8. Combine *1 tablespoon cornstarch or arrowroot* with *2 tablespoons water*. Remove excess fat from surface of the gravy, then bring gravy to a boil. Stir in the starch mixture and cook, stirring constantly, for about 1 minute. Pour a little of the gravy over the roast, and serve the rest separately.

SWISS STEAK

Serves 4. The recipe may be doubled. This is an easy braised dish for the junior members of the family to make. It smells like dried-onion soup when it is cooking but, fortunately, does not taste like it! Serve with boiled or mashed potatoes, or with French bread for dunking, and a tossed salad. And the Dullinger boys' Butterscotch Pie for dessert.

BUY

1½ pounds chuck steak, cut 1-inch thick
½ pound mushrooms
2 green peppers
Box onion soup mix
1-pound can stewed tomatoes

HAVE ON HAND

Flour
Cooking oil
Salt and coarsely cracked pepper
Thyme
Worcestershire sauce
Parsley, fresh or dried

COOKWARE

12-inch heavy skillet with
   tight-fitting lid

1. Place *steak* on waxed paper on chopping board or work table and sprinkle with *¼ cup flour.* Pound flour into the steak with a steak pounder, a wooden mallet, or the side of a heavy plate. Turn steak several times, rub with flour, and pound in as much of it as possible. Reserve any remaining flour.

2. In heavy skillet heat *2 tablespoons cooking oil* until smoking hot. Place steak in the hot skillet and brown well on both sides over moderate heat.

3. While steak is browning, wash *mushrooms,* trim stem ends, and dry on paper towels; then slice coarsely. Seed *green peppers* and slice coarsely. Set vegetables aside.

4. When steak is well browned, but not burned, sprinkle it with *reserved flour, 1 envelope onion soup mix,* the sliced mushrooms and green peppers, *¼ teaspoon salt, ¼ teaspoon pepper,* and *¼ teaspoon thyme.* Add *tomatoes, 1 tablespoon Worcestershire sauce,* and *¼ cup water.* Cover skillet, turn heat to very low, and let the steak braise for 2 to 2½ hours, turning steak occasionally and spooning some of the pan sauce over it.

5. To serve, cut steak into 4 equal portions, or slice, and transfer to serving platter. Pour sauce over meat, and sprinkle with *1 tablespoon chopped parsley.*

CHOUCROUTE GARNIE

This is a fancy name for a simple but substantial meal that originated in Alsace-Lorraine. The secret of a really good *choucroute* is in the thorough washing of the sauerkraut before it is cooked. Few people in America are aware of this essential step, which in Europe is just automatic. Then they wonder why their dish of sauerkraut is too tart or too salty and why the kids don't like it. Many independent butcher shops in rural areas in the East make their own sauerkraut, but if this is not available to you, buy it in cans or jars, not in plastic pouches. The pouches contain a quick-processed sauerkraut that tastes so strongly of sulphur that it is practically inedible.

Serves 8. Serve with Dijon mustard, small tart pickles or *cornichons,* and slices of dark bread. Beer is the best beverage accompaniment. You can serve a good rich dessert after this entrée if you wish.

BUY

4 pounds fresh *or* canned sauerkraut
1 bottle dry white Alsatian wine
3-pound smoked boneless pork shoulder butt
4 large carrots
8 medium onions

8 knockwurst *or* frankfurters
8 large potatoes
1 pound sliced Canadian bacon

HAVE ON HAND

Bacon drippings
Garlic
Bay leaves
Coarsely cracked pepper
Juniper berries *or* gin
Cooking oil

COOKWARE

Large heavy casserole, *or*
   kettle, with lid
Saucepan for potatoes

1. Empty *sauerkraut* into a large basin or sink of cold water. Rinse sauerkraut well, pulling apart any lumps. Drain and repeat once or twice more until sauerkraut tastes bland, not sour or salty. Drain well and squeeze out excess moisture.

2. In heavy casserole or kettle heat *2 tablespoons bacon drippings.* Pile the sauerkraut into the casserole and cook for a few minutes, tossing the sauerkraut in the hot drippings. Add *3 cloves garlic,* chopped, *1 large bay leaf, ½ teaspoon coarsely cracked black pepper, 2 tablespoons juniper berries or 4 tablespoons gin* and the *bottle of white wine.* Bury the *pork shoulder* deeply in the center of the sauerkraut. Bring liquid to a simmer, cover kettle and simmer for 3 hours. The liquid should not boil.

3. Meanwhile scrape and quarter *the carrots* and peel *the onions.* When choucroute has braised for 3 hours, add the carrots and onions, then cover and simmer for 1 hour longer.

4. Add *knockwurst or frankfurters;* cover and simmer for 30 minutes longer.

5. Meanwhile peel *potatoes,* and boil in salted water until tender. Drain and keep warm.

6. In skillet sauté the *Canadian bacon* in a *little oil* until edges are frizzled and slices are lightly browned on both sides.

7. To serve: Pile the sauerkraut in the center of a large platter, moisten with the pot liquor, and cover with slices of pork shoulder. Garnish platter with carrots, onions, bacon, knockwurst and potatoes.

SWEDISH MEAT BALLS

Serves 4. These tender meat balls are good for either a small sit-down dinner or served in a chafing dish on a buffet table—in the latter case you would probably want to double the recipe. Serve traditionally, with thinly sliced sour pickles and with lingonberries (canned lingonberries are available at shops carrying gourmet items), or serve with a tart cranberry sauce. Small boiled potatoes, tossed with butter and chopped fresh dill, make a perfect accompaniment. Smoked salmon would be a good appetizer, and baked apples, or Prunes in Port Wine, would be an excellent ending.

BUY

½ pound ground lean chuck
¼ pound ground veal
¼ pound ground lean pork
8-ounce container light cream

HAVE ON HAND

Butter
Onion
Fresh bread
Milk
Egg
Salt and pepper
Flour

COOKWARE

10-inch heavy skillet

1. In skillet melt *1 tablespoon butter,* and in it sauté *3 tablespoons minced onion* until golden brown and tender.

2. While onion is browning remove crusts from *4 slices bread;* crumb the bread in a blender, or by picking it apart with thumb and forefinger. You should have a good cup of soft bread crumbs.

3. Empty bread into mixing bowl and add *1 cup milk.* Stir until bread absorbs most of the milk. Then stir in the cooked onion, the *ground meats, 1 egg, 1 teaspoon salt,* and *¼ teaspoon pepper;* mix thoroughly.

4. Measure *¼ cup flour* onto a piece of waxed paper. Shape meat

mixture into balls about 1 inch in diameter, and roll in the flour to coat them on all sides. Reserve leftover flour.

5. In same skillet melt *3 tablespoons butter,* and in it sauté meat balls until well browned all over, shaking pan frequently to roll and toss them in the hot butter. As they brown, remove with slotted spoon to a plate or pan.

6. When all meat balls are browned, stir *1 tablespoon of the reserved flour* into juices remaining in skillet. Gradually stir in the *cream,* and cook, stirring, until sauce is slightly thickened. Return meat balls to sauce, cover and cook over very low heat for 20 minutes. Serve them while hot, or set aside until needed and then reheat gently. Should the sauce become too thick, stir in a little milk or some chicken or beef stock.

BEEF STROGANOFF

Serves 4. This is one of the best and easiest versions of beef stroganoff that I have made. Serve with rice, plain or wild. Buttered carrots provide a vegetable of good color contrast.

BUY

1½ pounds round steak, cut in a slab about 1 inch thick
¼ pound fresh mushrooms
10¾-ounce can beef consommé
8-ounce container dairy sour cream

HAVE ON HAND	COOKWARE
Small onions	12-inch heavy skillet with
Flour	lid
Salt and pepper	
Butter	
Prepared mustard	
Tomato paste	

1. Slice *steak* slantwise into strips as thin as possible. If partially frozen, the meat will be easier to slice thinly.

2. Peel and thinly slice *2 small onions*. Wash and slice *mushrooms*. Set vegetables aside.

3. On piece of waxed paper combine *2 tablespoons flour, 1 teaspoon salt,* and *½ teaspoon pepper*. Toss the meat in this flour mixture. Reserve any flour mixture that is not absorbed by the meat slices.

4. In skillet melt *4 tablespoons butter,* and in it brown meat lightly and quickly on both sides. Add onion and mushroom slices, and cook over high heat until vegetables are lightly browned, stirring and shaking pan occasionally.

5. Stir *reserved flour mixture* into pan juices. Gradually stir in the *beef consommé* and *½ cup water;* cook, stirring, until sauce is smooth and thickened. Stir in *2 teaspoons prepared mustard* and *1 teaspoon tomato paste*. Cover and cook over very low heat for 1 hour, or until meat is tender. The liquid should not be allowed to boil.

6. Set aside until needed and then reheat, or finish and serve. To finish: Combine the *sour cream* with a little of the hot pan sauce. Stir this into remaining sauce, and heat just to serving temperature.

CHINESE PEPPER STEAK

Serves 3. Serve with rice, but be sure to have your rice cooked and steaming over low heat before starting to cook the steak, for the actual cooking takes only a few minutes once your preparation is made. Ice Cream Kona for dessert.

BUY

1-pound round steak cut in slab 1 inch thick
2 green peppers
Bunch of green onions
1-pound can bean sprouts
1-pound can tomatoes

HAVE ON HAND

Garlic
Cooking oil, preferably peanut oil
Salt and pepper

Soy sauce
Sugar
Cornstarch

COOKWARE

12-inch skillet, *or* wok, with cover

1. Slice *steak* slantwise into strips as thin as possible. If you have a freezer, put the steak into it for 1 hour before slicing. The meat is much easier to slice thinly if partially frozen.

2. Peel and mince *1 clove garlic*. Seed *green peppers* and cut into strips. Slice *4 green onions, including the green tops*. Set prepared vegetables aside.

3. Drain *bean sprouts* and measure out *1 cup*. Refrigerate remaining sprouts right in the can and add them to your next tossed salad.

4. In skillet or wok heat *¼ cup oil* until very hot. Add beef slices, and stir and toss them in the hot oil for 3 minutes, or until meat loses its red color. Sprinkle meat with *½ teaspoon salt* and *¼ teaspoon pepper*. Add the minced garlic, *4 tablespoons soy sauce*, and *1 teaspoon sugar*. Cover skillet and cook over high heat for 5 minutes.

5. Quickly drain *tomatoes* and add. Add bean sprouts and green pepper strips. Toss all together lightly, then cover and cook for 5 minutes longer. DO NOT OVERCOOK. The vegetables must be crisp and bitey.

6. While vegetables are cooking, combine *½ tablespoon cornstarch* and *2 tablespoons cold water* in small bowl or measuring cup. Stir this mixture into the liquid in skillet, and cook, stirring, until sauce is clear and slightly thickened. Empty into warm serving dish, and sprinkle with the *green onions*.

BRAISED STUFFED VEAL BIRDS

Serves 6. Buttered and parslied new potatoes and tiny carrots are excellent accompaniments to this delicate dish.

BUY

1½ pounds thinly sliced veal from the leg
Parsley
10½-ounce can beef consommé
8-ounce container cream

HAVE ON HAND	*COOKWARE*
Bread	Shallow oven-to-table casserole
Small onion	10-inch skillet
Salt and pepper	
Butter	
Celery	
Sage	
Flour	

1. Place the *slices of veal* between two pieces of waxed paper, and pound with the side of a heavy cleaver or with a meat pounder until very thin. Cut into 6 serving portions.

2. To make the stuffing, crumb *2 slices bread* into a mixing bowl; then add *1 minced small onion, 1 teaspoon salt, ¼ teaspoon pepper, ¼ cup melted butter, 2 tablespoons chopped parsley, ½ cup minced celery, ½ teaspoon crumbled sage,* and *2 tablespoons hot water.* Mix lightly. Place a spoonful of this stuffing on each slice of meat, roll up like small jelly rolls, and secure with wooden picks.

3. Melt *3 tablespoons butter* in the skillet. Roll the meat rolls in *flour;* sauté them gently in the butter until well browned on all sides, and then transfer them to the casserole. To the butter and juices remaining in the pan add the *can of consommé* plus an *equal amount of water.* Bring to a boil, stirring in all the nice brown bits from bottom and sides of pan. Stir in *½ cup cream,* and then pour the liquid over the rolls in the casserole. Set aside until ready to cook. Chop *2 tablespoons parsley* and set aside.

4. To cook: Preheat oven to 325° F. Cover the casserole and braise in the slow oven for 1½ hours.

5. Meanwhile combine *1 tablespoon flour* and *1 tablespoon soft butter.* Just before serving stir this paste into the pan liquid, bit by bit. Sprinkle with the chopped parsley and serve. If sauce is too thick, stir in *remaining cream.*

LOBSTER À L'AMÉRICAINE

Serves 4. For those who want a "fancy" lobster dish, here is the classic version of a famous one. Only the meat of live lobsters should be used, or fresh lobster meat—the canned won't make it. You can, if you wish though, substitute 1 pound fresh lump crabmeat for the lobster and then change the name of the dish to Crabmeat à l'Américaine. When seafood or chicken are braised they do not need the long cooking time required for meat. Serve with cooked rice. Go all the way and serve Crème Brûlée for dessert.

BUY

2 live lobsters (*or* 2 split-live by butcher, and ready-to-cook), each
   weighing about 1½ pounds
Shallots *or* green onions
1 stick sweet butter
Parsley
1-pound 12-ounce can whole tomatoes *or*
   small can tomato purée
Small bunch of fresh tarragon, if possible

HAVE ON HAND
Garlic
Salt and pepper
Cognac
Dry white wine
Fish stock *or* chicken broth
Dried tarragon
   (if you can't find fresh)
Cayenne pepper
Lemon

COOKWARE
Heavy 12-inch skillet with lid
Small saucepan

1. If they are *live whole lobsters,* split and prepare them for cooking as in recipe for Baked Lobster (see Index). Do not remove the shell. Reserve the coral and tomalley. Remove and crush the claws, and cut the tail into 1-inch sections. Peel and chop *2 shallots* or thinly slice *2 green onions,* including some of the tender green stalks. Peel, crush, and mince *1 clove garlic;* chop some *parsley.* Set vegetables aside.

2. In the skillet heat *2 tablespoons sweet butter.* Add the lobster claws and tail sections, sprinkle lightly with *salt and pepper,* and sauté until lobster meat firms and shells turn red. Sprinkle with *¼ cup Cognac* and set the Cognac aflame. When the flame burns out, add *the shallots or green onions, garlic, ⅔ cup dry white wine, ½ cup fish stock or chicken broth, 3 whole canned tomatoes or 2 tablespoons tomato purée,* and *a couple of sprigs of fresh tarragon or ¼ teaspoon dried.*

3. Cover skillet and braise the lobster for 20 minutes.

4. Transfer lobster pieces to a serving dish, remove the pieces of shell, and keep the meat warm.

5. Cook sauce remaining in the skillet until reduced by about one third or until thickened, stirring and mashing the whole tomatoes, if used, until they are blended with the sauce. Stir in the *tomalley* and *coral,* and correct the seasoning with *salt and pepper.* Add *a pinch of cayenne pepper* and a *dash of lemon juice* and cook, stirring, for 1 minute longer.

6. Strain the sauce into a small saucepan, pressing through as much of the tomato, coral, and tomalley as possible. Reheat to simmering. Add *2 tablespoons sweet butter,* raise pan, and swirl it above the heat until butter is just melted.

7. Pour the sauce over the lobster meat and sprinkle with chopped parsley.

CHICKEN FRICASSEES

Fricassees

Somewhere between a stew and a sauté lies a group of delicious sauced dishes, usually made of chicken and correctly known as fricassees. The chicken (or it can be veal) is first cooked in butter or oil, then liquid is added to barely cover, and the chicken is braised in it until tender. If the chicken is allowed to become brown before the liquid is added, the resulting dish is known as a brown fricassee. If, on the other hand, the chicken is first only firmed or plumped in the hot oil or butter and is not allowed to brown, the dish is known as a white fricassee.

Fricassees are easy to make and are always delicious. They are a good "company" dish, for they can be made in advance, in the morning or the day before, and actually improve in flavor on reheating. They are best served with plain rice, Rice Pilaf, or buttered noodles, but steamed Fluffy Bread-crumb Dumplings are also excellent with them.

COQ AU VIN

Serves 4. This is just the French and fancy name for a brown chicken fricassee made with red wine. I've made and tasted dozens of versions of this well-known dish, but the one described here is by far the best. Serve with cooked rice, or with buttered new potatoes sprinkled with chives, and *petits pois.*

BUY

3½-pound frying chicken,
   cut into serving pieces
¼ pound ham, sliced ¼ inch thick
8 small white onions
8 small mushrooms
Parsley

HAVE ON HAND

Garlic
Flour
Butter
Thyme
Bay leaves
Salt and pepper
Brandy or Armagnac
Dry red wine (preferably a Bordeaux)

COOKWARE

2½-to 3-quart top-of-
   stove casserole with cover

1. Soak *chicken pieces* in *cold water* for 30 minutes. Meanwhile dice the *ham,* and peel the *onions.* Trim stems of *mushrooms,* wash and dry on absorbent paper. Peel and chop *1 clove garlic.* Set vegetables aside.

2. Dry chicken pieces well, and roll in a *little flour.* Shake off any excess flour. Melt ¼ *pound butter* in the casserole, and in it brown pieces of chicken over moderate heat until nicely browned on all sides. Don't let the butter burn.

3. Add the diced ham, the onions, garlic, mushrooms, ⅛ *teaspoon thyme, 1 bay leaf, a few sprigs parsley, 1 teaspoon salt,* and ¼ *teaspoon pepper.* Let all cook together, so flavors will blend, for 2 to 3 minutes. Then pour over the chicken ¼ *cup brandy or Armagnac* and set the brandy aflame. When flame burns out, add *1 cup red wine,* cover, and cook over very low heat for 45 to 50 minutes, or until chicken is tender.

4. Combine ½ *tablespoon flour* and *1 tablespoon soft butter.* Mix this with a little of the juice from the casserole, then stir into liquid in casserole.

5. Discard parsley and bay leaf and serve, or cool and reheat when needed.

CHICKEN CACCIATORE
WITH RED WINE

Serves 8. Serve with buttered noodles or rice, a tossed salad, and garlic bread. Melon and *prosciutto* would make a good appetizer, and Refrigerator Cheesecake a suitable dessert.

BUY

2 chickens, about 3½ pounds each,
   cut into serving pieces
2 large onions
1 green pepper
1-pound 12-ounce can stewed tomatoes

HAVE ON HAND

Garlic
Olive oil
Butter
Dried tarragon
Salt and pepper
Dry red wine

COOKWARE

Heavy skillet
Large top-of-stove-
   casserole with cover

1. Soak *chicken pieces* in *cold water* for 30 minutes. Meanwhile chop *2 large onions* finely. Seed and chop the *green pepper. Peel and mince 4 cloves garlic.* Set vegetables aside.

2. Drain and dry chicken pieces well on absorbent paper.

3. In skillet, heat *4 tablespoons olive oil* and *¼ cup butter,* and in it sauté chicken pieces over moderate heat until nicely golden on all sides. As pieces brown, transfer them to the casserole.

4. Add to oil and juices remaining in skillet the onions, green pepper, and garlic, and cook over low heat for 6 to 8 minutes, or until onion is transparent but not brown. Sprinkle vegetables with *1 teaspoon dried tarragon, 2 teaspoons salt,* and *½ teaspoon coarsely ground black pepper.* Add *stewed tomatoes* and bring to a boil. Pour mixture over the chicken, cover the casserole, and simmer over low heat for 20 minutes, stirring occasionally.

5. Add *1½ cups dry red wine,* cover, and simmer for 20 minutes longer. Correct seasoning with salt, and then serve. Or turn off heat and partially remove cover; then reheat to steaming hot before serving.

CHICKEN CACCIATORE WITH WHITE WINE

Serves 6. Serve with rice.

BUY

6 to 8 serving portions frying chicken
1-pound can whole tomatoes
1 green pepper
Parsley

HAVE ON HAND

Flour
Salt and pepper
Butter
Olive oil
Onions, medium size
Garlic
Bay leaf
Dry white wine
Lemon

COOKWARE

Heavy 12-inch skillet
with lid

1. In paper bag combine *½ cup flour, 1 teaspoon salt,* and *½ teaspoon pepper.* Wash *pieces of chicken,* dry well, and put into bag with the flour mixture. Close bag and tip and shake, tossing the chicken pieces to coat them well with the seasoned flour. Remove and shake off excess flour.

2. In skillet, heat *¼ cup butter* and *2 tablespoons olive oil,* and in it brown pieces of chicken over moderate heat until golden on all sides.

3. While chicken is browning, drain *tomatoes* and cut into quarters. Peel and slice *2 onions.* Seed and slice *the green pepper.* Peel and mince *1 clove garlic.* Mince *¼ cup parsley.*

4. When chicken is nicely browned, add the tomatoes, onions, green pepper, and garlic, and *1 bay leaf* and *½ cup dry white wine.* Cover, and then simmer for 40 minutes.

5. Finish and serve, or set aside and reheat when needed.
To finish: Stir in *1 teaspoon lemon juice,* and sprinkle with the minced parsley.

CHICKEN FRICASSEE WITH WHITE WINE AND TOMATOES

Serves 6. Serve with Rice Pilaf.

BUY

3 small chickens, halved, *or* the equivalent in chicken parts
4 large ripe tomatoes *or* two 1-pound cans whole tomatoes
Chicken broth
Parsley

HAVE ON HAND

Onion
Garlic
Olive oil
Butter
Salt and pepper
Bay leaf
Dried tarragon
Dry vermouth *or* Chablis
Tomato paste
Cornstarch

COOKWARE

Heavy 12-inch skillet with lid

1. Soak *chicken* in *cold water* for 30 minutes. Meanwhile peel *tomatoes,* if fresh, cut each into 8 wedges, and squeeze out seeds. If tomatoes are canned, drain, squeeze out seeds, and chop coarsely. Set tomatoes aside, cover them lightly with waxed paper to keep them moist. Peel and chop *1 medium onion.* Peel and mince *2 cloves garlic.*

2. Drain and dry chicken pieces on absorbent paper.

3. In skillet, heat *1 tablespoon olive oil* and *2 tablespoons butter,* and in it brown chicken pieces a few at a time on all sides over moderate heat. As chicken pieces brown, remove from skillet to sheet of aluminum foil on side of stove. Reduce heat to low. Add onion and garlic to fat remaining in skillet, and cook until onion is transparent, but not brown.

4. Add *half the tomatoes* and all of the browned chicken. Sprinkle with *salt and pepper,* and add *1 bay leaf, 1 teaspoon dried tarragon, ½ cup dry vermouth or chablis, 1 cup chicken broth* and *1 tablespoon tomato paste.* Cover skillet, and simmer for 30 minutes.

5. Finish and serve. Or remove skillet from heat, partially remove cover, and let cool. Reheat to a simmer and proceed with last steps when ready to serve.
To finish: Chop a *little parsley* and set aside. Correct seasoning of the simmering sauce with *salt and pepper.* Remove chicken to serving dish and keep warm in a 200° F. oven.

6. Combine *1 tablespoon cornstarch* and *2 tablespoons cold water.* Stir into sauce and cook, stirring for 1 minute. Add *remaining tomatoes,* and cook over very low heat for 2 minutes, or until tomatoes are heated through. Spoon sauce and tomatoes over chicken, and sprinkle with chopped parsley.

CHICKEN BREAST WITH ALMONDS

Serves 6. This elegant fricassee calls for chicken breasts, but you may use any parts of chicken you wish, or quartered broiler-fryers. Again, rice is the best starch accompaniment. Fresh peas or canned *petits pois* are a colorful vegetable to serve.

BUY

6 breasts of chicken (ask butcher to bone them, please)
Scallions or shallots
Can blanched slivered almonds
13¾-ounce can chicken broth

HAVE ON HAND	*COOKWARE*
Butter	12-inch skillet with lid
Cognac	Small skillet
Tomato paste	
Flour	
Dry white wine *or* dry vermouth	
Salt and pepper	
Dried tarragon	

1. Wash *chicken breasts* well, and dry on absorbent paper.

2. In skillet melt *3 tablespoons butter* over moderate heat. Just as the butter starts to brown, place chicken breasts in the skillet, skin side down. Brown over gentle heat, being careful not to let the butter burn. When golden on one side, turn and lightly brown on the other.

3. While chicken is browning, mince *1 tablespoon scallions or shallots* and set aside.

4. When chicken breasts are browned, pour *2 tablespoons cognac* over them and set aflame. When flame burns out, remove chicken to a shallow pan or a sheet of aluminum foil. To juices remaining in skillet add *1 tablespoon butter.* Add shallots and cook, still over low heat, stirring, for 30 seconds. Add *½ cup of the almonds,* and cook, stirring, until almonds just begin to take on color. Stir in *1 teaspoon tomato paste* and *1½ tablespoons flour.* Gradually stir in *1½ cups chicken broth* and *¼ cup white wine,* and cook, stirring, until sauce is slightly thickened. Add *salt and pepper* to taste, remembering that the chicken broth has salt in it.

5. Return chicken breasts to skillet, then add *1 teaspoon dried tarragon.* Cover, and cook over low heat—25 minutes for chicken breasts; 35 to 40 minutes for legs or quarters.

6. Finish and serve, or set aside and reheat.
To finish: In small skillet melt *1 tablespoon butter.* Add *remaining almonds* and sauté, stirring constantly, until almonds are nicely browned.

7. Arrange chicken in serving dish, pour sauce over, and sprinkle with the sautéed almonds.

CHICKEN BIRIANNIE

Serves 4. This is an original curry inspired by a Pakistani dish known as *murghi biriani,* a great Mogul classic. But since this by no means follows the traditional recipe, I have changed the name as well as the ingredients.

Some markets carry ground blanched almonds in a 6-ounce bag (2 cups). If you cannot find these, you will have to grind blanched slivered almonds in your electric blender. A 4-ounce can will make enough. Serve with Rice Pilaf and strips of peeled cucumber.

BUY

3½-pound frying chicken, cut into serving pieces
2 large onions
4-ounce can blanched slivered almonds *or* a bag of ground almonds
1 pint half and half *or* light cream

HAVE ON HAND

Peanut *or* other cooking oil
Butter
Ground ginger
Ground coriander
Ground cumin
Fennel seeds
Poppy seeds
Turmeric
Salt
Coarse ground pepper
Chili pepper
1 lemon
Cloves
Stick cinnamon
Flour

COOKWARE

Heavy 12-inch skillet with lid

1. Wash and dry *chicken portions.* Peel and thinly slice *2 large onions.*

2. In large skillet heat *3 tablespoons peanut oil* and *3 tablespoons butter,* and in it sauté onions until soft, but not brown. Sprinkle with *1 teaspoon ground ginger, 1 tablespoon ground coriander, 1 teaspoon*

ground cumin, ½ *teaspoon fennel seeds, 2 tablespoons poppy seeds, 1 tea-*
spoon turmeric, 1 teaspoon salt, ¼ teaspoon coarse ground pepper, 1 dried
chili pepper, seeded and chopped, and *2 tablespoons finely ground*
blanched almonds. Add chicken pieces, and sauté on each side for 6 to 8
minutes, or until brown and well impregnated with the spice mixture.

3. Sprinkle chicken with *2 tablespoons lemon juice,* add *3 cloves* and
a *2-inch piece of stick cinnamon,* and gradually stir in the *2 cups half and*
half or light cream. Bring to a boil, cover almost completely, and cook
over low heat at barely a simmer for 20 to 30 minutes.

4. Finish and serve, or set aside and reheat when needed.
To finish: Just before serving stir in *1 tablespoon flour* combined with
2 tablespoons water, and cook, stirring, until sauce is slightly thickened.

CHICKEN IN SOUR-CREAM-
AND-WINE SAUCE

Serves 4. Serve with Rice Pilaf or wild rice and a colorful buttered vegetable.

BUY

3½- to 4-pound chicken, cut into serving pieces
½ pound mushrooms
Lemon
1 pint dairy sour cream
8-ounce container heavy cream
Chives *or* green onions

HAVE ON HAND

Butter
Flour
Dry white wine
Salt
Coarsely ground black pepper

COOKWARE

Heavy 12-inch skillet
with lid

1. Soak *chicken pieces* in *cold water* for 30 minutes. While chicken
is soaking, wash, dry, and slice the *mushrooms,* trimming stems if neces-

sary, and set aside. Grate the *rind of 1 lemon,* and combine this in a small bowl with *1½ cups sour cream,* the *heavy cream,* and the *juice of the lemon* that you just grated. Set this mixture, too, aside.

2. Dry chicken pieces well on absorbent paper.

3. In skillet heat *¼ cup butter (½ stick),* and in it sauté chicken pieces over moderate heat until golden brown on all sides. Remove chicken and set aside in a shallow pan or on a sheet of aluminum foil.

4. To the butter remaining in skillet, add mushrooms; cook, stirring occasionally, for 5 minutes. Stir in *2 tablespoons flour.* Gradually stir in *½ cup white wine,* and cook, stirring in all the brown bits from bottom and sides of pan. Stir in sour cream mixture, and continue to stir until sauce begins to simmer. Stir in *½ teaspoon salt* and *¼ teaspoon coarsely ground black pepper.*

5. Return chicken to skillet, and sprinkle with *1 tablespoon chopped chives or green onion tops.* Cover, and cook over low heat for 35 to 45 minutes, or until chicken is tender. Serve at once, or set aside, partially remove cover to cool, then refrigerate.
To reheat: Replace cover and bake in a preheated 325° F. oven for 30 minutes.

REAL HOT CHICKEN CURRY

In essence, this is a fricassee, but it is also a true Indian curry and hot as the hinges. This one does not include curry powder as it comes out of the can but uses individual aromatic spices and turmeric, a root indigenous to India, which gives curry its characteristic greenish-yellow color. So be sure to check your spice shelf, buy what you don't have, and replenish those which might have been on the shelf too long. Check sources in back of this book for canned ginger if you cannot buy the fresh at a local Chinese market. And if fresh coconuts are not in season, substitute milk for the coconut milk and heavy cream for the coconut cream. Your curry will still be good.

Serves 4. Rice and cooked lentils are traditional accompaniments to curry and, if you wish, you may serve a good chutney. Forget the usual chopped peanuts, toasted coconut and so on, and serve instead Turmeric

Cucumbers and Yogurt Cheese. Chilled melon or other fresh fruit is the best way to finish off a curry dinner.

BUY

1 fresh coconut
3½-pound broiler-fryer, cut into serving pieces
Fresh *or* canned ginger root

HAVE ON HAND	*COOKWARE*
Cheesecloth	12-inch heavy skillet with
Onions	lid
Garlic	
Butter	
Ground poppy seeds	
Ground cumin	
Ground turmeric	
Ground coriander	
Small red hot chilies	
Stick cinnamon	
Whole cardamom seeds	
Whole cloves	
Bay leaves	

THE COCONUT:

The easiest way to crack a coconut is to hold it in one hand with the end that does NOT have any eyes topside. With a hammer hit all around the top of the coconut with sharp glancing blows—they don't have to be very hard. Soon the top of the coconut will crack neatly all around and can be removed like the lid off a casserole. Remove all the meat from the shell and dice it coarsely. You don't have to peel off the thin brown skin, which is a great bore, but you should use an electric blender if you have one, otherwise you'll have to grate the coconut meat and that, too, is a bore.

So pile the *diced coconut meat* into the container of your blender, and add *2 cups boiling water*. If it all won't fit in safely, divide coconut and water and blend half at a time. Cover container and blend on high speed for 1 minute. Pour ground coconut and liquid into a sieve lined with cheesecloth and let the coconut milk drip through, pressing the coconut with the back of a wooden spoon to extract as much liquid as possible. Let the extracted milk stand undisturbed so that the cream will rise to the top. You should be able to spoon off *1 cup coconut cream* and have *1 cup coconut milk* left.

THE CURRY:

1. Soak *chicken pieces* in *cold water* for 30 minutes. Peel and thinly slice *4 small onions*. Peel and chop *5 large cloves garlic*. Set vegetables aside.

2. In skillet melt *6 tablespoons butter,* and in it sauté the sliced onion until golden brown. Remove most of the onion to a paper towel to drain, then set it aside for a garnish.

3. To butter remaining in pan add the garlic, *1¼ teaspoons ground poppy seeds, 1 teaspoon ground cumin, 1 teaspoon ground turmeric,* and *1 teaspoon ground coriander;* cook, stirring, for about 3 minutes to remove any raw taste from the spice.

4. Drain and dry chicken pieces, and place them in the skillet skin side down. Sauté chicken for about 5 minutes, then turn and sauté for about 5 minutes longer.

5. Add to skillet *2 cups water, 1½ teaspoons finely chopped ginger root, 6 small hot chili peppers,* a *3-inch stick cinnamon, 5 cardamom seeds,* husked, *5 whole cloves,* and *2 bay leaves.* Bring liquid to a boil, partially cover skillet, and simmer chicken for 30 minutes. The liquid should be reduced to almost nothing. If not, remove chicken and cook liquid over high heat until reduced to about ½ cup; then return chicken to skillet.

6. Skim the cream from the coconut milk and set aside. Add *coconut milk (about 1 cup)* to the chicken; cover and simmer for 20 minutes longer. Add *salt* to taste.

7. Finish and serve, or set aside and reheat when needed.
To finish: Bring sauce to a boil, then reduce heat to low. Stir in *coconut cream (about 1 cup),* turn off heat, cover skillet, and let the curry stand for 10 minutes. Sprinkle with the reserved fried onions before serving.

POULET MARENGO

Serves 6. This is an excellent brown fricassee which is prepared on top of the stove, then finished in a moderate oven. If you're not ready for dinner when it is, simply turn oven temperature to 200° F. and let it wait.

BUY

5-pound roasting chicken, cut into serving pieces
8 mushrooms
1-pound can tomatoes
Parsley

HAVE ON HAND	*COOKWARE*
Garlic	12-inch heavy skillet
Flour	3-quart casserole with cover
Salt	
Pepper	
Dried tarragon	
Olive oil	
Butter	
Dry white wine	

1. Soak *chicken parts* in *cold water* for 30 minutes. While chicken is soaking, peel and finely chop *1 clove garlic.* Wash *mushrooms,* trim stems, dry and slice.

2. In paper bag combine *½ cup flour, 1 teaspoon salt, ½ teaspoon pepper,* and *1 teaspoon dried tarragon.* Dry chicken parts between two pieces of absorbent paper, then drop into the bag. Close bag at top, then tip and shake to coat chicken with flour mixture. Remove chicken, shaking off excess flour, and reserve *remaining flour mixture.*

3. In heavy skillet heat *4 tablesoons olive oil* and *4 tablespoons butter.* Place chicken pieces in the hot fat, and sauté over moderate heat until golden brown on all sides. As pieces brown, transfer them to the casserole.

4. To fat remaining in skillet add reserved flour mixture and cook, stirring, until all flour in moistened with fat and mixture is bubbling. Gradually stir in *1 cup dry white wine,* and cook, stirring, until sauce is smooth and thickened. Pour sauce over chicken in casserole.

5. Add to casserole the chopped garlic and sliced mushrooms. Drain and add the *tomatoes.* Cover casserole and cook in a 350° F. oven for 20 minutes. Remove cover, stir sauce, and use some to baste chicken. Cover again, and cook for 20 minutes longer.

6. Serve sprinkled with a *little chopped parsley.*

CHICKEN WINGS MONACO

Serves 4. This is a really fun dish—easy and very economical. Serve with spaghetti and a tossed salad.

BUY

2½ pounds chicken wings
Carrots
1 quart tomato juice

HAVE ON HAND	*COOKWARE*
Onion	Heavy 12-inch skillet
Garlic	with cover
Flour	
Salt	
Cooking oil	
Cloves	
Dried basil	
Fresh *or* dried parsley	
Lemon	
Dry red wine	

1. Cut the wing tips from the *wings* and discard. Peel and chop *1 onion* and *1 clove garlic.* Scrape and slice *4 small carrots.*

2. Combine *⅓ cup flour* and *1 teaspoon salt,* and roll the wings in this mixture.

3. In skillet heat *¼ cup cooking oil,* add the wings, and sauté over moderate heat until nicely browned on all sides. Add the onion and garlic, *1 whole clove, ½ teaspoon dried basil, 1 tablespoon fresh or dried parsley, 1 tablespoon lemon juice,* and the carrots. Add *3 cups tomato juice* and *½ cup dry red wine.* Bring liquid to a boil, cover, and cook over low heat for 30 minutes.

4. Uncover, and cook for another 10 to 15 minutes, or until sauce thickens slightly. Serve immediately, or set aside and reheat when needed.

POLLO COMINO

Serves 4. For a typical Spanish dinner, serve Artichokes Vinaigrette as an appetizer and Caramel Flan for dessert.

BUY

1 chicken, about 3½ pounds, cut into serving pieces
1 large tomato
1 large sweet onion
1 large green pepper
3 medium zucchini

HAVE ON HAND	*COOKWARE*
Olive oil	Heavy 4-quart saucepan *or*
Bay leaves	deep skillet
Salt	
Garlic	
Cumin, ground	

1. Cut chicken breast into 4 pieces, making a total of *10 pieces of chicken.*

2. Peel and coarsely chop the *tomato* and *onion.* Seed and coarsely chop the *green pepper.* Trim the *zucchini,* slit lengthwise, and cut into 1-inch pieces.

3. Measure *6 tablespoons olive oil* into saucepan or skillet. Add chicken pieces and cook over low heat until chicken skin is puffed a bit and the flesh has stiffened. Add the tomato, onion, green pepper, zucchini, *3 bay leaves,* and *2 teaspoons salt.* Cover tightly and braise over low heat for 30 minutes, or until chicken and vegetables are tender.

4. Meanwhile peel and mince *1 large clove garlic,* then mash it with *1 teaspoon ground cumin.*

5. Stir the garlic-cumin mixture into chicken and vegetables, bring to a boil, then lower heat and simmer for 10 minutes.

CHICKEN SAUTÉS

Chicken Sautés

Sautéing is one of the simplest and quickest ways to cook chicken. Tender frying chickens are best to use, and one weighing 2½ to 3 pounds is usually sufficient to serve four. Always use fresh chickens when possible, and have them either quartered or cut into smaller serving portions.

The chicken is first sautéed in butter and oil over moderate heat. Spices and often vegetables are added after the chicken is browned, but liquid is used only after the chicken is completely cooked, when one makes the pan sauce. The sauce generally consists of a combination of shallots, wine, and perhaps tomatoes, in endless variations. *Larousse Gastronomique* lists over 70 different chicken sautés, but there are many more if we go beyond French cooking and encompass the chicken sautés of the world.

The secret of the pan sauce is the little brown bits of meat glaze remaining in the pan after the chicken is cooked. To capture these, the pan is deglazed with liquid. This is a fancy cooking term for a simple process.

Sautés are custom-made for those who enjoy demonstrating their culinary skills. However, they do not take kindly to reheating, and so should be served as soon as possible after they are made.

TO DEGLAZE A PAN:

Pour a little *wine* or *broth* into the hot skillet in which the chicken was cooked. Use a wooden spoon and scrape the brown bits from the bottom and sides of the skillet as the liquid cooks and reduces over high heat. Add a *tablespoon of butter,* turn off the heat, and swirl the pan until the butter is melted. Pour the sauce over the chicken and garnish as desired.

HOW DO YOU TELL
WHEN CHICKEN IS DONE?

Pierce the thickest part of the thigh with a two-tined fork. If the juice which runs out is clear with no tinge of pink, the chicken is done and ready to serve.

SIMPLE CHICKEN SAUTÉ

Serves 4

BUY

2½- to 3-pound frying chicken, quartered or cut into serving pieces
Parsley *or* chives *or* paprika

HAVE ON HAND	*COOKWARE*
Salt and pepper	Heavy 12-inch skillet, *or*
Butter	chicken fryer, with lid
Cooking oil	

1. Wipe *chicken parts* with a damp cloth, and sprinkle with *salt and pepper*.

2. In skillet heat *2 tablespoons each butter and oil.* Arrange chicken in the hot fat mixture, skin side down, and cook over moderate heat for 10 minutes. Turn chicken, cover, reduce heat to low, and cook for 20 to 30 minutes longer, or until chicken is tender. If you wish the chicken to be crisp, uncover during the last 10 minutes of cooking.

3. Just before serving, sprinkle with *chopped parsley or chives,* or dust with *paprika.*

ADD ALMONDS AND IT BECOMES
CHICKEN AMANDINE

Brown the chicken, turn, cover and cook for 10 minutes. Add *1 cup blanched, sliced almonds.* Cover, and continue to cook until chicken is tender.

ADD VEGETABLES IF YOU WISH—
CHICKEN JARDINIÈRE

After the chicken is browned and turned skin side up, add *1 small onion, minced, 1 green pepper,* seeded and chopped, and *½ cup sliced fresh or canned mushrooms,* or any other quick-cooking vegetable that you think would be good (sections of tomatoes, sliced zucchini or summer squash, etc.) Cover and continue to cook until chicken is tender. Sprinkle with *finely chopped parsley* before serving.

CHICKEN SAUTÉ SMITANE

Serves 4. This needs a colorful vegetable accompaniment, such as broccoli or asparagus.

BUY

¼ pound wild rice
2½- to 3-pound frying chicken, quartered or cut into serving pieces
8 mushrooms
Green onions *or* shallots
8-ounce container commercial sour cream
8-ounce container heavy cream
Watercress *or* parsley

HAVE ON HAND   *COOKWARE*

Salt and pepper   Heavy 12-inch skillet
Butter   with lid
Cooking oil
White wine *or* dry vermouth

1. Cook the *wild rice* (see Index) and keep warm.

2. Wipe *chicken parts* with a damp cloth, and sprinkle with *salt and pepper.*

3. In skillet heat *2 tablespoons each butter and oil,* and in it sauté the chicken, skin side down, over moderate heat for 10 minutes. Turn chicken, cover, reduce heat to low, and cook for 20 to 30 minutes, or until chicken is tender.

4. Meanwhile wash *mushrooms,* remove stems, and set stems aside. Dry mushroom caps well, and sauté in *2 tablespoons butter* for 2 minutes on each side or until lightly browned. Set aside. Chop the mushroom stems. Chop *2 tablespoons green onions or shallots.*

5. When chicken is tender, remove it from pan and arrange it on a warm serving platter around a center mound of the wild rice. Garnish with mushroom caps.

6. To butter and juices remaining in the pan, add onions or shallots and sauté for 30 seconds. Deglaze pan: Add *½ cup white wine,* and cook over high heat, stirring in all the brown bits from bottom and sides of pan. Continue to cook over high heat until wine is reduced by three-quarters.

7. Add the *sour cream* and *heavy cream* and the chopped mushroom stems; cook over high heat, letting the sauce boil (it won't curdle) until slightly thickened. Strain the sauce over chicken and mushroom caps, and garnish with a cluster of *water cress or parsley.*

CHICKEN HONGROISE

Serves 4. Buttered noodles are a must with this.

BUY

3-pound chicken, cut into serving pieces
8 medium mushrooms
8-ounce container heavy cream

HAVE ON HAND

Salt and pepper
2 medium onions
Butter
Cooking oil
Sweet paprika

COOKWARE

Heavy 12-inch skillet with lid

1. Wipe *chicken parts* with a damp cloth, and sprinkle with *salt and pepper*. Peel *2 onions* and slice thinly. Wash, dry, and thinly slice the *mushrooms.*

2. In skillet heat *2 tablespoons butter* and *2 tablespoons oil* and in it arrange chicken pieces, skin side down. Sauté over moderate heat for about 10 minutes, or until chicken is brown. Turn chicken pieces and sprinkle with *2 tablespoons sweet paprika,* the onions, and the mushrooms. Cover skillet, reduce heat to low, and cook for 20 to 30 minutes longer, or until chicken is tender.

3. Transfer chicken pieces to a warm serving dish, cover with aluminum foil and keep warm.

4. To vegetables and liquid remaining in skillet, add the *cream* and bring to a boil, stirring. Turn off the heat, add *2 tablespoons butter,* and swirl the pan until butter is melted. Pour the vegetables and sauce over the chicken and serve.

POULET MAXIM

Serves 4. Elegant, but very easy. Serve with buttered rice or wild rice.

BUY

3½-pound broiler-fryer, quartered
Carrots
8 small onions
12 small mushrooms
Chicken broth
Parsley
8-ounce container heavy cream

HAVE ON HAND

Butter
Salt and pepper
Cognac
Port wine
Dried tarragon
Paprika
Flour

COOKWARE

12-inch heavy skillet with cover
Oven-to-table serving casserole

1. Soak *chicken* quarters in *cold water* for 30 minutes. While chicken is soaking, scrape *2 large carrots* and slice thickly. If you want to be fancy, you may cut the carrots into 1-inch chunks, then with a vegetable peeler shave off any sharp edges, forming them into large olive shapes, as they do at Maxim's. Peel *onions*. Set vegetables aside.

2. Drain and dry chicken on absorbent paper. In skillet melt *4 table-spoons butter,* and in it sauté chicken over moderate heat until golden brown on both sides.

3. Sprinkle chicken with *½ teaspoon salt* and *¼ teaspoon ground pepper* (freshly ground is best). Pour over chicken *2 ounces (4 tablespoons) Cognac* and set Cognac aflame. Let flames die out. Then add *¼ cup Port wine* and *½ teaspoon dried tarragon*. Add prepared carrots and onions, then cover and cook over low heat for 45 minutes, basting chicken occasionally with liquid in pan.

4. Meanwhile trim stems from *mushrooms,* wash mushrooms and dry well. Chop *1 tablespoon parsley.*

5. When chicken is tender, remove chicken, onions, and carrots to the serving casserole; cover and set into a very low (200° F.) oven, where it will stay moist and warm for an hour or so if necessary.

6. To finish the dish: Add mushrooms to the juices remaining in the skillet. Stir in *½ cup chicken broth,* and simmer for 5 minutes. Stir in the *cream,* and bring to a boil. Correct seasoning with a *little salt* if necessary.

7. In cup or small bowl combine *2 tablespoons soft butter, 1 teaspoon paprika,* and *1 tablespoon flour.* Mix this to a smooth paste, then blend with 2 tablespoons liquid from skillet. Stir this mixture slowly into liquid remaining in skillet and cook, stirring, until sauce thickens slightly. If sauce is too thick, stir in a *little more chicken broth.*

8. Pour sauce and mushrooms over chicken in casserole. Sprinkle with the chopped parsley and serve.

CHICKEN SAUTÉED
WITH TOMATOES AND CREAM

Serves 4

   BUY

3-pound frying chicken, cut into serving pieces
½ pound medium mushrooms
Green onions *or* shallots
1-pound 12-ounce can whole tomatoes
8-ounce container heavy cream

   HAVE ON HAND   *COOKWARE*

Salt   Heavy 12-inch skillet with lid
Coarsely ground pepper   10-inch skillet
Butter
Olive oil
Dry vermouth
Dried tarragon

1. Wipe *chicken pieces* with a damp cloth, and sprinkle lightly with *salt and pepper.*

2. In skillet heat *3 tablespoons butter* and *1 tablespoon olive oil,* and in it sauté chicken, skin side down, over moderate heat for 10 minutes, or until brown. Turn chicken, reduce heat to low, cover, and cook for 20 to 30 minutes longer, or until chicken is tender.

3. While chicken is cooking wash, dry, and slice the *mushrooms.* Sauté mushrooms in smaller skillet in *2 tablespoons butter* until lightly browned on both sides. Set mushrooms aside. Chop ¼ *cup green onions or shallots.* Drain and chop the *tomatoes.*

4. When chicken is tender remove to a warm platter, cover with aluminum foil, and set in a warm place.

5. To oil remaining in skillet, add the onions or shallots and cook for 1 minute, stirring. Add the chopped tomatoes, ½ *cup dry vermouth,* the mushrooms, and *1 teaspoon dried tarragon.* Cook for 5 minutes, stirring frequently. Stir in the *cream,* and season to taste with *salt* and ½ *teaspoon coarsely ground pepper.* Cook, stirring, until sauce is steaming hot. Pour over chicken and serve.

CHICKEN SAUTÉ CHASSEUR

Serves 4

BUY

2½- to 3-pound chicken, cut into serving pieces
¼ pound mushrooms
Parsley
8-ounce can stewed tomatoes

HAVE ON HAND

Salt and pepper
Onion *or* shallots
Cooking oil
Butter
Flour
White wine *or* dry vermouth

COOKWARE

Heavy 12-inch skillet with lid

1. Wipe *chicken pieces* with a damp cloth, and sprinkle lightly with *salt and pepper*. Wash, dry, and slice the *mushrooms*. Chop *1 tablespoon onion or shallots*. Chop *1 tablespoon parsley*.

2. In skillet heat *2 tablespoons cooking oil*. Arrange chicken pieces in the hot oil, skin side down, and cook over moderate heat for about 10 minutes, or until nicely browned. Turn and cook for 10 minutes, or until browned on other side.

3. Add the mushrooms, cover and cook for 10 minutes longer, or until chicken and mushrooms are tender.

4. Remove chicken from skillet to a warm platter, cover with foil, and keep warm. Drain off excess oil from skillet, and add *2 tablespoons butter*. When butter is foaming add the onion or shallots and sprinkle with *1 teaspoon flour*. Cook and stir for 1 minute.

5. Add *¼ cup white wine or dry vermouth,* and cook until wine is reduced to half. Stir in *1 cup stewed tomatoes,* and cook for 5 minutes. Correct seasoning with *salt and pepper*.

6. Pour the sauce over the chicken, and sprinkle with the chopped parsley.

CHICKEN SAUTÉ GLORIA

Serves 4

BUY

2½- to 3-pound frying chicken, quartered or cut into serving pieces
½ pound medium mushrooms
8-ounce container heavy cream

HAVE ON HAND

Salt and pepper
Shallots *or* onion
Parsley
Butter

Flour
Dry white wine *or* Sauternes
Thyme
2 egg yolks
Lemon

COOKWARE

Heavy 12-inch skillet with lid

1. Wipe *chicken pieces* with a damp cloth, and sprinkle with *salt and pepper.* Chop *1 tablespoon shallots or onion.* Wash, dry, and slice *mushrooms.* Chop *1 tablespoon parsley.*

2. In skillet heat *2 tablespoons butter,* and in it sauté chicken pieces, skin side down, for 10 minutes over moderate heat, or until nicely browned. Turn and cook for 5 minutes longer. Add mushrooms, cover, and cook for 5 minutes. Add shallots or onion, and sprinkle with *1 tablespoon flour.* Cover and cook for 1 minute. Add *⅓ cup white wine, ½ cup heavy cream,* and a *pinch of thyme,* then partially cover and cook over low heat for 20 to 25 minutes.

3. When chicken is tender, remove pieces to a warm platter and keep warm. In small bowl or cup combine *2 egg yolks* with *juice of ½ lemon* and the *remaining ½ cup cream.* Move the skillet off the heat, and stir in the egg-cream mixture. Return skillet to low heat, and cook for 2 minutes, either shaking pan constantly or stirring to make sure the sauce does not curdle.

4. Correct seasoning of sauce with *salt and pepper,* then pour sauce over chicken and sprinkle with chopped parsley.

CHICKEN BREASTS VERMOUTH

Serves 4. This is a refinement—and there are many—of a classic sauté. If you wish, you can use chicken parts rather than breasts.

BUY

2 whole chicken breasts
Parsley
8-ounce container heavy cream

HAVE ON HAND   *COOKWARE*

Flour   Heavy 12-inch skillet
Salt and pepper
Onion *or* shallots
Butter
Cooking oil
Cognac
Dry vermouth
1 egg yolk

1. Skin the *chicken breasts*. Then with a sharp knife cut each fillet (one lies on each side) away from the bones, making 4 boneless pieces of solid white meat in all. You can have your butcher do this if you wish, but it's as easy as corn-meal mush. Place each fillet between two pieces of waxed paper, and pound with a meat pounder or the side of a heavy cleaver until they are very thin. Then coat them lightly on both sides with *flour,* and sprinkle lightly with *salt and pepper*. Chop *1 tablespoon onion or shallots*.

2. In skillet heat *2 tablespoons each butter and oil;* in it sauté the chicken breasts over moderate heat until golden on one side, then turn them over and continue to cook for about 10 minutes. Sprinkle the cooked breasts with *2 tablespoons cognac,* ignite it, and let the flames burn out.

3. Transfer the breasts to a heated platter. Pour off all but 1 tablespoon of the fat remaining in skillet, and add the shallots and *1 tablespoon of flour*. Cook, stirring, for 1 minute, or until onion or shallots are transparent. Then add *½ cup dry vermouth,* and cook over high heat until liquid is reduced to half its quantity.

4. Chop a *little parsley* and set aside.

5. In small bowl or cup combine *1 egg yolk* with *¾ cup cream*. Gradually stir this into liquid in skillet, and cook over VERY LOW HEAT until sauce is slightly thickened. DO NOT LET IT BOIL. Spoon the sauce over the chicken breasts, and sprinkle with parsley.

VEAL-SCALLOP SAUTÉS

Veal-Scallop Sautés

No other cut of meat lends itself to as many moods and manners of cooking as veal scallops. Known in France as *escalope,* in Italy as *scaloppine,* in Germany as *schnitzel,* and in Poland as *cielecy,* the veal scallop is a thin slice cut from a leg of veal on a slight slant, partly with and partly against the grain. The slices should be no more than ¼ inch thick when cut, then they must be pounded between sheets of waxed paper until they are very thin. Two to three minutes on each side is all the cooking they require; take another minute or two to make a quick pan sauce, and your dish is ready to serve. You couldn't ask for anything more simple or delicious. Just be sure that any platter garnishes or any vegetable you plan to serve with a scallop dish are ready before you start to cook the meat. Also before you begin, have your veal pounded, and see that all ingredients needed to complete the dish are at hand.

PREPARING THE SCALLOPS:

Place the slices of veal well apart between two pieces of waxed paper on a steady chopping block or work table. Pound with the side of a heavy cleaver or with a meat pounder (your butcher might sell you one) until they are stretched to at least twice their original size and are very thin. Some Italian meat markets will do this pounding for you, but usually the scallops still need a few good whacks when you get them home.

Artichokes Vinaigrette make a suitable appetizer to serve before a veal scallop sauté. Buttered noodles, small potatoes browned in butter, or rice are all appropriate starch accompaniments, and canned *petits pois,* steamed zucchini, or broiled tomatoes, Ratatouille, or mushroom caps make good vegetable garnishes.

ESCALOPES DE VEAU À L'ANGLAISE

Serves 4. We know these also simply as breaded veal scallops.

BUY

1½ pounds veal scallops *or* 4 thin slices cut from the leg
Lemons
Water cress *or* parsley

HAVE ON HAND	*COOKWARE*
Flour	Heavy 12-inch skillet
Egg	
Cooking oil	
Bread	
Salt and pepper	
Butter	

IN ADVANCE:

1. Pound *veal* according to directions on page 126. Keep covered with waxed paper until ready to cook.

2. Spread *a couple of tablespoons of flour* on another piece of waxed paper on work surface.

3. In a flat dish such as a pie plate lightly beat with a fork *1 egg, ¼ cup water,* and *1 tablespoon oil.* Cover with waxed paper until ready to use.

4. Crumb enough *fresh bread to measure 1 cup* (use an electric blender for this if you have one). Spread the crumbs on still another piece of waxed paper. Arrange all the above ingredients in assembly-line fashion from right to left on your work table.

WHEN READY TO COOK:

5. Sprinkle the veal with *salt and pepper* and coat it evenly on both sides with flour. Shake off excess flour. Dip the slices in egg, making sure that both surfaces are well moistened with the egg mixture. Then transfer each slice to the bread crumbs and coat both sides evenly, pressing the crumbs into the meat lightly with the flat side of a heavy knife.

6. In skillet heat *4 tablespoons butter.* Just as it starts to brown, place

the scallops in the butter, and cook over moderate heat for about 2 minutes, or until evenly browned on one side. Do NOT OVERCOOK. Turn with pancake turner, and cook for 2 minutes longer, or until lightly browned on other side.

7. Transfer veal to a warm serving platter.

8. To juices remaining in skillet, add *2 tablespoons butter*. Raise skillet over the heat and swirl the butter around to pick up any meat glaze. When butter is melted and foaming, pour it over the veal. Garnish platter with *lemon wedges* and *water cress*.

NOTE: By garnishing each scallop with a few rolled anchovy fillets stuffed with capers, you'll have the dish known as *escalopes de veau viennoise*. Try it, it's great!

BREADED VEAL SCALLOPS WITH MUSHROOMS

This recipe is like the one above, except for the sauce. Additional ingredients you will need to buy or have on hand are shallots or green onions, dried tarragon, 8 medium mushrooms, and some dry sherry. Buy parsley instead of water cress.

IN ADVANCE:

1. Follow steps 1 through 4 in the recipe above.

2. Mince *2 shallots or 4 green onions*. Wash, dry, and slice the *mushrooms*. Chop *a little parsley*.

WHEN READY TO COOK:

3. Cook scallops as in Step 6 in recipe above.

4. When scallops are cooked, transfer them to a warm serving platter.

5. To juices remaining in skillet add the shallots or green onions, *¼ teaspoon tarragon,* and the mushrooms. Sauté for 3 minutes, or until vegetables are tender, shaking pan occasionally. Add *½ cup dry sherry* and cook over high heat for 1 minute. Add *2 tablespoons butter,* raise skillet away from heat and swirl until the butter is melted.

6. Pour vegetables and sauce over meat, sprinkle with parsley, and garnish with lemon wedges.

ESCALOPES DE VEAU
SAUTÉES À LA CRÈME

Serves 4. Good with broiled mushroom caps.

BUY

1½ pounds veal scallops *or* 4 thin slices cut from the leg
8-ounce container heavy cream
Water cress *or* parsley

HAVE ON HAND	*COOKWARE*
Salt and pepper	Heavy 12-inch skillet
Flour	
Butter	
Cognac	

IN ADVANCE:

1. Pound *veal* according to directions on page 126. Keep covered with waxed paper.

WHEN READY TO COOK:

2. Sprinkle veal with *salt and pepper* and coat lightly with *flour.*

3. In skillet melt *4 tablespoons butter,* and in it sauté scallops for 2 to 3 minutes on each side, or until lightly browned.

4. Arrange meat on warm serving platter. Add *3 tablespoons cognac* to juices remaining in pan. Ignite and let flame burn out.

5. Stir in the *cream* and bring to a boil, stirring in all brown bits of glaze from bottom and sides of pan. Boil rapidly until cream is reduced and sauce is slightly thickened. Pour sauce over meat, and garnish with *parsley or water cress.*

SCALOPPINE ALLA MARSALA

Serves 4. You don't have to go to a fancy Italian restaurant to enjoy this well-known dish. It's better and a heck of a lot cheaper when made at home. Serve with broiled mushroom caps and broiled halved tomatoes, Tomatoes Provençale or Ratatouille.

BUY

1½ pounds veal scallops *or* 4 thin slices cut from the leg

HAVE ON HAND	COOKWARE
Salt and pepper	Heavy 12-inch skillet
Flour	
Butter	
Olive Oil	
Imported Marsala wine	

IN ADVANCE:

1. Pound *veal* according to directions on page 126. Keep covered with waxed paper.

WHEN READY TO COOK:

2. Sprinkle scallops with *salt and pepper*. Coat lightly with *flour*.

3. In skillet heat *3 tablespoons butter* and *1 tablespoon olive oil*, and in it sauté the scallops for 2 to 3 minutes on each side, or until lightly browned.

4. Transfer meat to a warm serving platter. Add ½ *cup Marsala* to juices in pan, and cook over high heat until wine is reduced to half, stirring in all brown bits of meat glaze from bottom and sides of pan. Add *2 tablespoons butter*, raise skillet above the heat, and swirl until butter is melted. Pour sauce over the veal. Garnish with mushroom caps and tomatoes, or as you wish.

PAPRIKA SCHNITZEL

Serves 4. Serve with hot buttered noodles and a tossed salad.

BUY

1½ pounds veal scallops *or* 4 thin slices cut from the leg
8-ounce container sour cream

HAVE ON HAND	*COOKWARE*
Shallots *or* green onions	Heavy 12-inch skillet
Salt and pepper	
Flour	
Olive oil	
Butter	
Good Hungarian paprika	
Dry white wine	
Chicken broth *or* stock	

IN ADVANCE:

1. Pound *veal* according to directions on page 126. Keep covered with waxed paper.

2. Mince *2 shallots or green onions.*

3. Remove *sour cream* from refrigerator.

WHEN READY TO COOK:

4. Sprinkle scallops with *salt and pepper.* Coat lightly with *flour.*

5. In skillet heat *3 tablespoons olive oil,* and in it sauté scallops for 2 to 3 minutes on each side, or until lightly browned.

6. Transfer meat to a warm serving platter. Pour off excess oil from skillet, and add *2 tablespoons butter.* When butter is foaming add shallots or green onions and *1 tablespoon paprika;* sauté, stirring, for 30 seconds.

7. Add ¼ *cup dry white wine,* raise heat, and cook until wine is almost completely evaporated. Add ¼ *cup chicken stock,* reduce heat to low, and gradually stir in the *sour cream.* When sauce is steaming hot, pour it over the scallops. Serve immediately.

CIELECY POLONAISE

Serves 4

BUY

1½ pounds veal scallops *or* 4 thin slices cut from the leg
2 fresh ripe tomatoes *or* a 1-pound can whole tomatoes
Parsley
8-ounce container sour cream

HAVE ON HAND	*COOKWARE*
1 small onion	Heavy 12-inch skillet
Salt and pepper	
Flour	
Butter	
Dry white wine	

IN ADVANCE:

1. Pound *veal* according to directions on page 126. Keep covered with waxed paper.

2. Mince *1 small onion*. Peel, seed, and chop the *fresh tomatoes*, or drain, seed, and chop the *canned*. Chop *1 tablespoon parsley*.

3. Remove *sour cream* from refrigerator.

WHEN READY TO COOK:

4. Sprinkle scallops with *salt and pepper*. Coat lightly with *flour*.

5. In skillet heat *4 tablespoons butter*, and in it sauté scallops for 2 or 3 minutes on each side, or until lightly browned.

6. Arrange meat on warm serving platter. Add minced onion to juice in pan, and sauté for 1 minute, or until onion is transparent. Add tomatoes, and cook, stirring, for 2 to 3 minutes.

7. Stir in ⅓ *cup dry white wine* and the chopped parsley. Raise heat and boil until liquid is reduced to half. Stir in ½ *cup sour cream* and heat to serving temperature. DO NOT BOIL. Pour sauce over meat, and garnish with parsley clusters.

ESCALOPES DE VEAU
SAUTÉES À L'ESTRAGON

Serves 4

   BUY

1½ pounds veal scallops *or* 4 thin slices cut from the leg
8 mushrooms (½ pound)

HAVE ON HAND	*COOKWARE*
Shallots *or* small onion	Heavy 12-inch skillet
Parsley	
Salt and pepper	
Flour	
Butter	
Dry white wine	
Dried tarragon	

IN ADVANCE:

   1. Pound *veal* according to directions on page 126. Keep covered with waxed paper.
   2. Wash, trim, and slice the *mushrooms*. Mince *2 shallots or ½ small onion*. Chop *1 tablespoon parsley*. Set vegetables aside.

WHEN READY TO COOK:

   3. Sprinkle scallops with *salt and pepper,* and coat lightly with *flour*.

   4. In skillet heat *3 tablespoons butter,* and in it sauté veal over moderate heat for about 2 minutes on each side, or until lightly browned.

   5. Transfer veal to a warm platter. To butter remaining in pan, add mushrooms; cook over low heat for 3 minutes, stirring frequently. Sprinkle mushrooms with the shallots or onion, and cook for 1 minute.

   6. Add ½ *cup dry white wine,* and cook over high heat until liquid is reduced to half. Correct seasoning with *salt*.

   7. Add *1 tablespoon butter,* and swirl pan above heat until butter is just melted. Add the parsley and ½ *teaspoon dried tarragon,* and pour sauce over the meat.

PAN BROILING: MEATS & FISH WITH QUICK PAN SAUCES

Pan Broiling
and Quick Pan Sauces

If you have a heavy cast-iron skillet, pan broiling on top of the stove—rather than broiling under the stove broiler—is usually the better home method of cooking steaks, chops, and hamburgers. Also, in pan broiling, a big advantage is that all the brown meat juices and glaze left in the pan at the end of the cooking can be used in the making of a quick pan sauce. In broiling on a grill, or under a stove broiler, any sauce served with the meat must be made separately.

There are two methods of pan or skillet cooking. The first is browning in butter over moderate heat; it is usually used for fish and veal, and for pork chops, which need slow cooking. In the second method, pan broiling, butter should not be used since it burns at the searing temperatures needed for red meats. Olive oil, or a little fat cut from the meat, is used instead. Otherwise, the two methods are the same and nobody needs a formal recipe for them.

A good pan sauce can change a chop or steak and even a hamburger from an ordinary food to something special. Such sauces are simple to make and they should be rather thin, not thick or gluey. When correctly made, they have an attractive sheen and a delicate flavor. Once you understand the basic principles of the pan sauce, you can take off on your own. Be sure, however, that you do use only a heavy skillet that is a good conductor of heat and cooks evenly over its entire surface.

STEAK OR HAMBURGERS
WITH PAN SAUCE

1. Use *very little olive or salad oil* in a heavy skillet, or rub the skillet with a little of the fat cut from the steak or chops. Heat to smoking hot, for you want the meat to cook quickly and yet get good and brown and crisp on the edges.

2. Place the *steak or hamburgers* in the hot fat and cook over high heat until very brown on one side. Turn and brown the other side and cook until done to taste.

FOR RARE MEAT: A good rule to use in timing the cooking is *5 minutes per side per inch of thickness.* A 1-inch-thick steak or hamburger will be cooked rare if pan-broiled for 5 minutes on each side.

FOR MEDIUM RARE MEAT: After cooking meat to rare stage, reduce heat to moderate, and cook for 2 to 3 minutes longer on each side.

3. Transfer meat to a warm serving platter and pour off all excess fat from skillet. Don't wash the skillet.

4. Return skillet to moderate heat and add *a chunk of butter* and *a little finely chopped shallot or onion.* You need proportions, honest? Okay, about ½ tablespoon butter and ½ teaspoon shallots or onions PER SERVING. Cook for 1 minute, without letting onions or shallots brown.

5. Now add *a splash of dry red or white wine or meat broth* (about 2 tablespoons per serving) and let it boil, stirring rapidly and scraping bottom and sides of skillet with a wooden spoon. Sprinkle with *a little salt and freshly ground pepper, some chopped parsley,* and finally—here's the trick to a glossy sauce—add *another chunk of butter.* Don't let this butter cook. Raise the pan a little above the heat and swirl it until the butter is just melted. Pour the sauce over steak or hamburgers.

FRENCH AND FANCY

If your steak just happened to be thick slices of fillet of beef, and you used a *dry red wine* for the liquid, you've just made *entrecôte bordelaise!*

VARIATIONS AD INFINITUM

Add *a few sliced mushrooms* along with the shallots, plus *a spoonful of heavy cream*—or cream sauce, or leftover gravy. Sprinkle with *chives or tarragon* instead of parsley.

LAMB CHOPS WITH BERCY SAUCE

Same procedure as above, including the timing for rare or medium rare, but use *tomato juice*—or, better still, a little fresh tomato, peeled, seeded, and finely chopped—instead of wine or other liquid.

PORK CHOPS WITH SAUCE PIQUANTE

In cooking pork chops, low heat is needed, for the meat must be cooked thoroughly, that is, until no pink juice runs out when chops are pierced with a two-tined fork. When chops are done, transfer them to a warm platter and discard excess fat from skillet.

Return skillet to moderate heat. For each 2 chops, proceed as follows: Add *1 tablespoon butter* and *1 teaspoon finely chopped shallots or onion.* Cook for about 1 minute. Add *¼ cup vinegar,* and cook, stirring in all brown bits from bottom and sides of pan, until vinegar is reduced to half. Add *1 cup chopped fresh or canned tomatoes* and boil for 5 minutes. Add *1 tablespoon minced parsley, 3 tablespoons chopped sour pickles,* and *a little dried tarragon,* and swirl in *1 tablespoon butter* until melted. Never let a sauce containing pickles boil after they have been added. It makes them rubbery.

CRAIG CLAIBORNE'S FAVORITE HAMBURGERS

Serves 4. Top-notch hamburgers without even a pan sauce.

BUY

2 pounds freshly ground round steak
Parsley

HAVE ON HAND	*COOKWARE*
Salt	Large heavy skillet
Freshly ground black pepper	
Butter (at room temperature)	
Tabasco	
Worcestershire sauce	
Lemon	

1. Shape the *meat* lightly into 4 large cakes about 1-inch thick. Chop *a little fresh parsley.*

2. Sprinkle bottom of the skillet lightly but evenly with *salt.* Place skillet over high heat until salt begins to brown. Place meat cakes in skillet and brown well on one side. This will take about 3 minutes. Reduce heat to medium, turn cakes, and cook for 3 minutes longer. Reduce heat to low and cook to the desired degree of doneness, no more than a total of 10 minutes for rare.

3. Transfer cakes from skillet to a warm serving platter, and sprinkle generously with *black pepper.* Top each cake with *½ tablespoon soft butter,* and sprinkle with a *drop or two of Tabasco, Worcestershire sauce,* and *lemon juice,* and the chopped parsley.

LONDON BROIL

Serves 4. This cut of meat is especially good cooked over hot coals (see page 157), but pan-broiled it is good, too, especially if you serve a little wine sauce with it. Good with Swiss Fried Potatoes or Pommes Anna.

BUY

2 pounds prime beef top round, cut 2½ inches thick. It should
   measure 3 inches wide and about 8 inches long.
Parsley

HAVE ON HAND	*COOKWARE*
Salad oil	Large heavy skillet
Salt	
Coarsely ground black pepper	
Red wine *or* beef consommé	
Butter	

1. Brush the *meat* generously on both sides with *salad oil,* and sprinkle with *salt* and *lots of black pepper.* Chop a little *fresh parsley* and set aside.

2. Place skillet over high heat until smoking hot. Place steak in skillet, and cook over high heat for 5 minutes on each side. Reduce heat to medium, turn steak, and pan broil 15 minutes longer for rare, turning once or twice.

3. Transfer the steak to a hot serving platter. Pour off any excess fat from pan, and return pan to low heat. Add *½ cup red wine or beef consommé,* and cook, stirring in all the brown glaze from bottom and sides of pan with a wooden spoon. Turn off heat, add *2 tablespoons butter* to sauce in pan, and swirl pan until butter is melted.

4. Pour sauce over steak and sprinkle with the parsley. Carve meat in thin slices, across the grain, and serve with a spoonful of the sauce.

BUTTERFLIED SIRLOIN

Serves 2

BUY

12-ounce piece of boneless sirloin, cut about 1-inch thick
10¾-ounce can beef consommé

HAVE ON HAND	*COOKWARE*
Salt	Large heavy skillet
Freshly ground black pepper	
Butter	
Worcestershire sauce	
Prepared mustard (preferably Dijon)	
Chili sauce	

1. Place *steak* on wooden board. Trim excess fat from steak, and, with a sharp knife, cut it horizontally almost, but not quite in half. Open it, and then pound it to flatten it with the side of a heavy cleaver or knife. Sprinkle steak on both sides with *salt and pepper.*

2. Place skillet over high heat, and rub bottom with a piece of *beef fat.* When pan is smoking hot, place steak in it and pan-broil for 3 minutes on each side for rare.

3. Transfer steak to a warm serving platter. Pour off all excess fat from pan, and add to pan *1 tablespoon butter, 1 teaspoon Worcestershire sauce, 1 teaspoon mustard, ¾ cup beef consommé, a dash of pepper* and *a dash of chili sauce.* Stir with a wooden spoon over moderate heat until sauce boils. Mix in all brown bits from bottom and sides of pan, then reduce heat to low. Add *another tablespoon butter* and swirl pan until butter is just melted.

4. Pour sauce over steak. Cut meat in half and serve with the sauce.

STEAK DIANE

Serves 2. This is a quick entrée, and one which has become popular at many New York restaurants, where it is prepared at the table by the *maître d'hôtel.* There are many variations, including flaming the meat with cognac. Below is how the dish is made at Quo Vadis, where they use a 12-ounce sirloin steak to serve one person. At home a steak of this size should be sufficient for two.

BUY

12-ounce boneless sirloin steak,
   or substitute 2 minute steaks

HAVE ON HAND	COOKWARE
Salt	Large electric skillet
Freshly ground pepper	
Shallots *or* onion	
Chives	
Parsley	
Butter	
Worcestershire sauce	
A-1 sauce	

1. If using *sirloin,* trim away all the fat. Then put the steak between two pieces of waxed paper, and pound it with a meat pounder or with side of a heavy cleaver until it is about ¼ inch thick. Sprinkle well on one side with *salt and pepper.*

2. Chop *a good teaspoon shallots or onion* and the *same amount of chives.* Mince about *1 tablespoon parsley.* Put these ingredients in little dishes on a tray along with the steak, *2 tablespoons butter,* and the bottles of *Worcestershire and A-1.* When ready to cook, take your electric skillet and your tray set-up to the table. Plug in the skillet.

3. Put *half the butter* in the skillet and turn heat to high. As the butter begins to brown, add the shallots or onion and sauté for 1 minute. Add the steak and sear it quickly on both sides until lightly browned. Remove steak to a plate. Reduce skillet heat to moderate.

4. To juices remaining in pan, add *remaining butter* and the chives and cook for a few seconds. Add *a good dash of Worcestershire sauce* and

about 1 tablespoon A-1 sauce. You're not supposed to measure these ingredients, for that would take the *savoir* out of your *savoir faire!* Cook, stirring, until the sauce thickens, being careful NOT to let the sauce BOIL.

5. Return the steak to the pan and sprinkle one side with *half the parsley.* Turn and sprinkle the other side with the *remaining parsley.*

6. Place steak on serving platter and pour sauce over it. If desired, sprinkle with *about 2 tablespoons cognac* and set the cognac aflame.

THE TIMID COOK'S STEAK DIANE

Serves 4. Here is the kitchen method. A good winter-time appetizer to serve before this entrée would be broiling hot cups of Onion Soup. In summer switch to gazpacho.

BUY

4 boneless sirloin steaks, each about 6 ounces;
  or substitute 8 chicken steaks

HAVE ON HAND	COOKWARE
Shallots *or* onion	Small saucepan
Parsley	Heavy 12-inch skillet
Butter	
Worcestershire sauce	
Salt	
Peppermill with black peppercorns	

1. If *sirloin steaks* are used, put them between two pieces of waxed paper and pound with meat pounder or heavy cleaver until about ¼ inch thick. Chop *2 tablespoons shallots or onion* and the *same amount of parsley.* Set aside.

2. In small saucepan heat *2 tablespoons butter,* and in it sauté shallots or onion for a couple of minutes, or until lightly browned. Add *2 tablespoons Worcestershire* and heat to bubbling. Keep hot over very low heat.

3. In skillet heat *6 tablespoons butter.* When it begins to brown, add steaks and cook on one side for 3 minutes. Turn and cook for 2 to 3 minutes longer, or until done to taste.

4. Transfer steaks to warm serving platter and sprinkle with *salt* and *freshly ground black pepper*. Pour the sauce over the meat, and sprinkle with the chopped parsley.

STEAK DIJONNAISE

Serves 4

BUY

4 minute steaks *or* 8 chicken steaks
8-ounce container heavy cream
Parsley

HAVE ON HAND

Salad oil
Salt
Coarsely cracked pepper
Sage
Rosemary
Cognac
Butter
Dijon mustard
Paprika

COOKWARE

Heavy 12-inch skillet

1. Chop *a little fresh parsley*. In skillet heat *1 tablespoon oil,* and in it pan-broil *steaks* over high heat for 2 minutes. Turn steaks, sprinkle with *salt and pepper* and *a pinch each of crumbled sage and rosemary,* and pan-broil for 2 minutes longer.

2. Pour excess oil from pan, leaving steaks in the pan. Sprinkle steaks with ¼ *cup cognac,* ignite, and let the flame burn out. Transfer meat to a warm serving platter.

3. Reduce heat to moderate. Then to juices remaining in skillet, add *1 tablespoon butter, 2 tablespoons mustard,* and *1 teaspoon paprika.* Gradually stir in the *heavy cream,* and cook, stirring constantly, for 1 minute. Add *another tablespoon butter* and swirl pan until butter is just melted. Pour sauce over the steaks, and sprinkle with the chopped *parsley.*

STEAK AU POIVRE

Serves 4. Pommes Anna are a perfect starch accompaniment.

BUY

2 pounds lean sirloin steak, cut 2 inches thick
Parsley
Can of beef consommé

HAVE ON HAND	*COOKWARE*
Coarsely cracked black pepper	Large heavy skillet
Olive oil	
Prepared mustard (preferably	
Dijon)	
Worcestershire sauce	
Butter	

1. With the heel of one hand, press *1 tablespoon coarsely cracked pepper* onto each side of the steak. Let steak stand at room temperature for about 1 hour before cooking. Chop *¼ cup parsley* and set aside.

2. In skillet heat *⅓ cup olive oil* until smoking. Brown steak quickly on both sides. Reduce heat to moderate, and cook meat for 6 to 8 minutes longer on each side, or until done to taste. Do not overcook.

3. Transfer steak to warm serving platter.

4. Pour off oil from skillet, return skillet to heat, and add *½ cup consommé.* Bring to a rapid boil, stirring in all the meat glaze from bottom of pan. Stir in *1 teaspoon mustard, 1 tablespoon Worcestershire,* and the chopped parsley. Add *2 tablespoons butter* and swirl pan above the heat until butter is just melted.

5. Pour pan juices over steak and serve immediately.

Pan Broiling or Sautéing Fish

Boneless fillets or small whole fish are the best choice for cooking in this manner. If the skin on a whole fish is tough, remove it completely; if it is thin, slash it diagonally with a sharp knife in several places on both sides.

The fish either is pan-broiled in a little oil over high heat, as with steaks and chops, or is browned on both sides in a small quantity of butter over moderate heat. The fish is then transferred to a warm serving platter. If oil is used, it should be poured off; then butter (about 1 tablespoon per serving) is added to the skillet for making a quick pan sauce. If butter is used initially, it should not be allowed to brown and a little additional butter is added to the skillet. As soon as this melts and foams up in the pan, a few drops of lemon juice are added, and the sauce is quickly poured over the small fish or fillets. A light sprinkling of salt and pepper, some chopped parsley, or chopped parsley mixed with chopped chives, and a few lemon slices for garnish complete the dish.

FILLETS, SMALL FISH, OR SCALLOPS SAUTÉ MEUNIÈRE

Use a large skillet so the fish or fillets won't be crowded. If too many are put into one pan, they steam rather than sauté. Coat the fillets or fish lightly with *flour,* and sauté quickly in a *small amount of hot oil* until golden brown on one side. Turn, and continue to cook until golden brown on the other side. When fillets or small fish or scallops are brown, they have cooked through and are ready to serve. Remove them to a warm serving platter, and sprinkle lightly with *salt and pepper.*

Pour off any oil remaining in the skillet. Return skillet to moderate heat, and add *1 tablespoon butter for each serving.* Let the butter melt but do not let it brown, then add *fresh lemon juice* (about 1 teaspoon per serving), and sprinkle with *chopped parsley, chervil,* or *chives.* Swirl pan over the heat until butter foams, then pour the sauce over the fish.

FILLETS, SMALL FISH, OR SCALLOPS SAUTÉ BEURRE NOISETTE

The fish is cooked in the same way as above, except that the additional butter is allowed to cook until it takes on a good hazelnut-brown color. Pour this over the fish while it is still foaming, and garnish the platter with *lemon wedges* and sprays of *parsley* or *water cress.*

FILLETS OF SOLE AMANDINE

Serves 4. When we speak of "sole," we are generally referring to certain species of flatfish that frequent American waters, such as lemon sole, gray sole, fluke or flounder, for there is no true sole in this country. Imported genuine sole from the English Channel is called Dover Sole in fish markets and restaurants to distinguish it from the Yankee impostors. Fresh asparagus in season is the perfect vegetable accompaniment.

BUY

4 fillets of sole (about 1½ pounds)
4-ounce can blanched slivered almonds
Water cress or parsley for garnish

HAVE ON HAND	*COOKWARE*
Flour	Heavy 12-inch skillet
Butter	
Salt and pepper	
Lemon	

    1. Carefully remove the fine line of bones that run down the center of each *fillet.* Keep fish cold until ready to cook. Measure ½ *cup almonds* and set aside.

2. Spread *¼ cup flour* on a piece of waxed paper. Coat the fillets with flour evenly, and shake off all excess.

3. In skillet *melt 2 tablespoons butter,* and in it sauté the fillets over moderate heat for 2 to 3 minutes on each side, or until lightly browned.

4. Remove fillets from pan to a warm serving dish, and sprinkle lightly with *salt and pepper.*

5. To skillet add *2 tablespoons butter.* As soon as it foams up in the pan, add the almonds; shake skillet back and forth until the almonds are lightly toasted. Add the *juice of ½ lemon,* then pour the almonds and lemon butter over the fish. Garnish with *water cress or parsley.*

SKILLET SHRIMP BOURGUIGNONNE

Serves 4. If you like *escargots bourguignonne*—or even if you don't—you'll adore this dish, for who doesn't like shrimp? Hot Italian bread and a tossed salad are a must and quite sufficient to serve with it.

BUY

1½ pounds raw shrimp

HAVE ON HAND	*COOKWARE*
Garlic	Attractive oven-to-table
Parsley	12-inch skillet
Cooking oil, preferably olive	
Butter (1 stick)	
Salt	
Coarsely cracked black pepper	

1. Clean and devein the *shrimp* (see Index). Keep them cold until ready to cook. Peel and finely chop *2 cloves garlic.* Chop *¼ cup parsley.* Set vegetables aside.

2. Heat *¼ cup oil* and *4 tablespoons (½ stick)* butter in skillet. Add shrimp, and sauté over moderate heat for 5 minutes, or until shrimp turn pink, shaking skillet often to turn shrimp and cook them on all sides—this is why you need a large skillet.

3. Sprinkle shrimp with *½ teaspoon salt* and *¼ teaspoon black pepper*. Add *the remaining ½ stick of butter,* and cook, shaking pan, until butter begins to foam. Sprinkle with the garlic and parsley, and continue to shake pan vigorously for 30 seconds to coat the shrimp with the pungent butter.

4. Take the skillet right to the table, and serve the shrimp with hot bread to dunk in the juices.

SOFT-SHELL CRABS

The Dr. Jekyll and Mr. Hyde of piscatorial fame is the edible blue crab which frequents Atlantic waters from New Orleans to Maine. During most of the year, he is the hard-shell crab, and as such he is dormant and lazy, not even eating. He does, however, provide a great delicacy when simply boiled, cracked, and served hot with lemon butter or cold with garlic mayonnaise. When the spring sun warms the coastal waters, the crab begins to eat vociferously, making up for his winter's abstinence. He begins to grow and his hard shell that once fit him comfortably begins to pinch, so he sheds it and, at this point in his life, he becomes the tender, succulent soft-shell crab, so soft that every bit of him, including his claws, may be eaten. For a period of 48 hours, before his new shell begins to form, the hard crabby creature is a softy.

Your fish dealer will prepare soft-shell crabs for you, ready for the skillet, broiler, or deep-fat fryer, and pack them on a bed of crushed ice. If, however, you catch them yourself or wish to bring them home alive from the market, here is how to dress them:

To CLEAN SOFT-SHELL CRABS: Cut off the head of each crab just behind the eyes. Squeeze out the green bubble which lies behind the eyes. Raise the soft shell where it comes to a point on each side and cut out the spongy white gills with kitchen scissors. Turn crab on his back, peel the "apron" back, and cut it off.

Count on two to three soft-shell crabs per person, depending on size, and keep them very cold until ready to cook. Then wash in cold salted water, and dry well on absorbent paper.

Sautéing is the best method of cooking soft-shell crabs, as it is with most tender fish. If you MUST broil them, use gentle heat and keep the crabs a good 5 inches away from the source of heat. A few minutes' cooking on each side is all they take.

SAUTÉED SOFT-SHELL CRABS

Serves 4. Serve with tartar sauce—buttered fresh asparagus and it *will* be in season—and a water cress salad.

BUY

8 soft-shell crabs, cleaned
Parsley

HAVE ON HAND	*COOKWARE*
Salt and pepper	Heavy 12-inch skillet
Flour	
½ cup (1 stick) butter	
Lemon	

1. Wash and dry *crabs.* Sprinkle lightly with *salt and pepper,* and coat lightly on both sides with *flour.* Mince *about ¼ cup parsley* and set aside.

2. Heat *½ cup butter (1 stick)* in skillet. When it begins to foam, place the crabs, back side down, in the skillet, and sauté over moderate heat for 5 minutes, or until lightly browned. Turn and sauté for 5 minutes longer.

3. Transfer crabs to a warm serving platter.

4. To juices in skillet add the minced parsley and the *juice of 1 lemon.* Heat to bubbling and pour over the crabs.

SOFT-SHELL CRABS
SAUTÉ AMANDINE

Follow recipe above, omitting parsley and lemon juice. Add *½ cup blanched shredded almonds* to juices in pan, and sauté until golden, stirring constantly. Pour almonds and pan juices over the crabs.

BROILING IN THE STOVE
& CHARCOAL BROILING

Broiling in the Stove

Indoor broiling is best left up to restaurant chefs—unless you have a semi-professional stove, that is, a stove with a broiler that really gets hot enough to char a steak or chop, and with a good exhaust fan. That's my opinion, even though you didn't ask for it! With adequate facilities and an eye-level broiler (not one where you have to lie on your stomach to see what's going on), broiling can be a quick method of cooking, but it requires your undivided attention. It's not a good method at all for pork or veal, for these meats should be cooked slowly.

Broiling steak or chops less than 1 inch thick must be done quickly or they will be dry and tough no matter how much butter or sauce you put on them. So remember, the thicker the meat, the slower the broiler heat. For steaks or lamb chops, *count on 5 minutes on each side per inch of thickness* as a general rule for timing. Have your broiler really hot. Rub the grill with a little oil, or with fat from the meat. Brush the meat itself on both sides with melted butter or salad oil. Sprinkle with a little salt and pepper. And begin to broil. It's as simple as that.

Small whole fish or thick fish fillets may be broiled, but they should be well floured and then dipped into melted butter or salad oil before being placed on the grill. Even so, fish and seafood take much more kindly to the lower heat of the oven or the sauté pan than to the higher heat of the broiler.

One of the most successful meats for home-broiling is chicken. A simple switch from one spice or herb to another, or a generous dash of wine, fruit juice, or vinegar added to Basic Broiled Chicken can result in flavor changes to keep the palate interested in having broiled chicken frequently on the menu. Good garnishes are broiled mushroom caps and tomatoes and a cluster of water cress.

BASIC BROILED CHICKEN

Sprinkle broiler-fryer chickens, halved or quartered, with salt and pepper, and then brush them with melted butter or salad oil. Place the pieces skin side down on a greased broiler rack. Cook them 3 to 6 inches from the heat in a gas range; 6 to 9 inches from the heat in an electric range. Broil for 20 to 25 minutes on one side, then turn them over and broil for 15 to 20 minutes longer on the other side, or until golden brown, basting occasionally with melted butter, salad oil, or a good French dressing.

LEMON-BUTTER BASTING SAUCE
FOR CHICKEN

In a small saucepan combine *¼ pound butter, grated rind and juice of 2 lemons, 1 minced clove garlic, 1 tablespoon chopped parsley, 1 teaspoon dried dill weed, ½ teaspoon salt,* and *¼ teaspoon pepper.* Place over low heat until butter is melted.

BROILED CHICKEN
WITH TARRAGON BUTTER

Serves 6

BUY

3 broiler-fryers, about 1½ pounds each, split

HAVE ON HAND   *COOKWARE*

½ cup (1 stick) butter   Small saucepan
Dried tarragon
Salt and pepper

1. In saucepan melt *1 stick butter* with *1 teaspoon dried tarragon.*

2. Brush *chicken* on both sides with *some of the tarragon butter,* and sprinkle with *salt and pepper.* Arrange on broiler rack, and cook according to recipe for Basic Broiled Chicken, basting frequently with the tarragon butter.

3. Arrange chicken on warm serving platter, and over it pour *remaining butter.*

BROILED CHICKEN TEXAS STYLE

Serves 8

BUY

2 broiler-fryers, about 3½ pounds each, quartered
Chives

HAVE ON HAND

Salad oil
Dry white wine
Lemon
Garlic
Dried dill weed
Parsley
Salt and pepper

COOKWARE

Shallow broiling pan

1. Early in the day combine *½ cup salad oil, ¾ cup dry white wine, 1 tablespoon lemon juice, ¼ cup chopped chives, 1 minced clove garlic, 1 teaspoon dill weed, 2 tablespoons chopped parsley, ½ teaspoon salt,* and *¼ teaspoon pepper.*

2. When ready to cook, arrange chicken in a shallow broiling pan and pour the wine mixture over it. Place pan with chicken under broiler heat and broil slowly, turning chicken pieces and basting frequently for 30 to 40 minutes, or until chicken is well browned.

BROILED CHICKEN DIABLE

Serves 2

> BUY

1½- to 2-pound broiler chicken

HAVE ON HAND	*COOKWARE*
Butter	Small saucepan
Salt	Small shallow baking pan
Prepared mustard (preferably Dijon)	
Worcestershire sauce	
Bread	

1. Split the *broiler* down the back, spread it open on a work surface, and flatten it with the palm of one hand, or with a heavy cleaver.

2. Melt *4 tablespoons butter*. Place the broiler, skin side up, in a shallow baking pan and brush with *a little of the butter*. Sprinkle with *salt*. Bake in a preheated 425° F. oven for 15 minutes, or just long enough to firm the flesh and give a golden color to the skin. Remove from oven, and leave in baking pan.

3. While bird is in the oven, combine *remaining melted butter* with *1 teaspoon mustard, 1 teaspoon Worcestershire sauce,* and *1 cup fine fresh bread crumbs.* Spread this mixture over the skin of the chicken, then set meat aside until ready to continue the cooking.

4. To finish: Preheat broiler. Take chicken in baking pan and place in broiler under medium heat for 20 to 25 minutes, or until crumbs are crisp and browned and chicken is done. Do keep chicken far enough away from heat to keep the crumbs from burning.

HERB-STUFFED BROILERS

Serves 6

BUY

3 broiler-fryers, about 1½ pounds each, split
Parsley (preferably Italian)
Chives *or* green onions

HAVE ON HAND	*COOKWARE*
½ cup (1 stick) butter	Small saucepan
Dried tarragon	
Salt and pepper	

1. Mash *1 stick butter* to a smooth paste, and blend with *1 cup chopped parsley, ¼ cup chopped chives or the tops of green onions,* and *1 teaspoon dried tarragon.*

2. Loosen skin covering the breast areas of the *chickens* by inserting the fingers between skin and breast meat, and stuff the pocket generously with *some of the savory butter.* Melt the *remaining butter* over low heat.

3. Sprinkle chicken with *salt and pepper,* and broil according to basic recipe, basting frequently with the hot melted butter throughout the cooking.

Charcoal Grilling

No cookbook would be complete without a few pages devoted to charcoal grilling. Far too much good food is sacrificed year in and year out on the altar of the barbecue grill, charred offerings served in the name of good eating. A properly barbecued steak nevertheless can be excellent, and so can broiled chicken, swordfish, and lamb.

Whether you use a real charcoal broiler or one of the new gas grills, true grilling or barbecuing should impart a mild smoky flavor to the food and this cannot be achieved with charcoal alone. Green hardwood twigs or dampened hardwood chips should be added to the fire bed when you are ready to start cooking. Avoid pine or any woods containing tars and resins, for these give an undesirable flavor.

A GOOD CHARCOAL-BROILED STEAK

Choose prime beef—porterhouse, T-bone, sirloin, or top round, and have it cut at least 1½ inches thick (preferably 2 inches thick), allowing at least ½ pound per serving. Cut off excess fat, and score remaining fat with a sharp knife to prevent the edges from curling. Rub the steak well on both sides with good oil.

When the fire bed is just right, take a piece of the excess beef fat and rub it over the grill; then place the steak over the hot coals. Sear it quickly on both sides, then lower the coal bed, or spread out the coals to reduce the intensity of heat. For rare meat broil the steak as follows: 1½ inches thick, 8 minutes on each side, or a total of 16 minutes; 2 inches thick, 10 minutes on each side, or a total of 20 minutes. Set a bowl of water by the side of the grill; if fat drips into the coals causing too much flaming, sprinkle the fire with water.

When the steak is done to taste (it's quite permissable to make a small slit in the meat close to the bone to see if the steak is cooked as you want it), remove it to a hot platter or wooden cutting board. Sprinkle generously with salt and coarsely cracked pepper, and spread it with Steak Butter. Slice across the grain as the butter melts.

STEAK BUTTER TO SERVE 4

¼ cup (½ stick) butter
1 clove garlic, crushed
1 tablespoon Worcestershire sauce
1 tablespoon minced parsley *or* chives
3 dashes Tabasco
1 tablespoon red wine *or* lemon juice

1. Cream the *butter* and add the *crushed garlic*. Let stand at room temperature for 1 hour.

2. Discard garlic and beat in *remaining ingredients*.

CHARCOAL-ROASTED HERBED CHICKEN

Serves 6. Frequent basting with a simple herb butter is one of the best ways to enhance charcoal-roasted chicken. The chicken remains moist and tender as it barbecues.

BUY

3 broiler chickens, 2 to 2½ pounds each, split

HAVE ON HAND

½ cup (1 stick) butter
1 lemon
Fresh *or* dried tarragon;
   or dill weed
Salt and freshly ground pepper
   (white is super)

1. Dry *broiler halves* on absorbent paper, and trim off any loose skin and fat.

2. Melt the *butter* over low heat either on stove or at one side of grill. Stir in *juice of 1 lemon* and *1 tablespoon chopped fresh tarragon; or 1 teaspoon dried tarragon or dill weed.*

3. Brush chicken on both sides with *some of the herb butter* and sprinkle lightly with *salt and pepper.* Place on grill, skin side down, and cook over a bed of very low coals for 25 to 35 minutes, turning once or twice and basting frequently with *remaining herb butter.*

BARBECUED BUTTERFLIED LAMB

Serves 8. Lamb is one of the best meats for the barbecue. Lamb chops, shish kebab, ground lamb patties, and rack of baby lamb are all delicious, but a butterflied leg is my favorite. It takes well to a savory marinade prior to grilling. Delicious with Curried Fresh Corn and Green Peppers and Pommes Dauphinoise.

BUY

6-pound leg of lamb, boned and butterflied (see below)

HAVE ON HAND

Coarsely cracked pepper
Lemon
Garlic
Red wine
Olive oil
Bay leaves
Dried tarragon *or* oregano
Salt

1. Have the butcher bone the leg and split the *meat* almost—but not quite—through so that the meat can lie flat in one large piece.

2. Spread the lamb out flat in a glass, enamel, or porcelain-lined container. Sprinkle with *1 teaspoon pepper, 2 tablespoons lemon juice,* and *4 cloves garlic,* peeled and sliced. Add *½ cup red wine, ½ cup olive oil, 2 bay leaves, ½ teaspoon dried tarragon or oregano,* and *2 teaspoons salt.*

Marinate in refrigerator for 6 to 8 hours before cooking, turning meat occasionally in the marinade.

3. Remove meat from the marinade, reserving marinade, and barbecue over very hot coals for 6 minutes on each side until well browned and charred, basting generously with the marinade before and after turning. Lower the fire bed, or spread the coals to reduce heat intensity, then continue to barbecue for 6 to 7 minutes longer on each side. A total of 25 to 30 minutes is required here for medium rare. Cook the lamb longer if you wish, but take care NOT to OVERCOOK it.

4. Transfer meat from grill to warm serving platter. Slice thinly on a slight slant, across the grain.

POACHING & BOILING

Poaching & Boiling

Many epicurean dishes fall into the category of poached foods. Poaching is a method used primarily for cooking delicate-fleshed fish and chicken. The liquid—water, stock, or a combination of water or stock and white wine—is seasoned with onion or shallots, a little chopped carrot and celery, a bay leaf, and a pinch of thyme. This poaching liquid, known as a *court-bouillon*, is later used to make a rich sauce.

The food to be poached is barely covered with liquid; the liquid is brought just to a simmer, and is never allowed to do more than simmer throughout the entire cooking period. When bubbles start to rise from the bottom to the top of the liquid, that is poaching. The liquid barely moves—just smiles.

Boiling is simply a matter of turning the heat up a few degrees higher than for simmering, but when you come right down to it, a "boiled" tongue or a New England "boiled" dinner is generally more tender and flavorful if the liquid is kept at a simmer rather than an active boil.

FILLETS OF SOLE
IN VERMOUTH SAUCE

Serves 4

BUY

4 medium fillets of sole *or* flounder
8-ounce container heavy cream

HAVE ON HAND

Butter, soft
Shallots *or* green onions
Salt
White pepper
Dry vermouth
Flour
Parsley

COOKWARE

Heavy 10-inch skillet with lid

1. Place *fillets* on work table. Run finger down center of each one and you will find a line of tiny bones. Remove bones with sharp knife, and discard them. Cut fillets in half lengthwise. Roll each half fillet like a tiny jelly roll and secure with a wooden pick.

2. Arrange rolls curled side up in a generously buttered skillet, and sprinkle with *1 tablespoon minced shallots or green onions, ¼ teaspoon salt, a good dash of white pepper,* and *½ cup dry vermouth.* Cover and keep cold until ready to cook.

3. When ready to cook, combine *1 tablespoon flour* and *3 tablespoons soft butter.* Set aside.

4. Bring liquid in skillet to a boil. Reduce heat, cover skillet, and cook for 5 minutes. Turn each fillet with a slotted spoon, cover skillet again, and cook for 5 minutes longer. Arrange fillets on a warm serving platter, and discard wooden picks.

5. Cook liquid remaining in skillet over high heat until reduced to half its quantity. Add *cream* and boil rapidly for 3 to 4 minutes, or until sauce becomes the consistency of light syrup.

6. Reduce heat to moderate, and gradually stir in butter-flour mixture bit by bit.

7. Pour the velvety sauce over the fillets and sprinkle with *chopped parsley.*

NOTE: Scallops may be used in place of sole or flounder.

FILLETS OF SOLE DUGLÈRE

Serves 4

BUY

4 fillets of sole *or* flounder
Parsley
2 large ripe tomatoes *or* 1-pound can whole tomatoes
Chicken broth

HAVE ON HAND	*COOKWARE*
Onion	Heavy 12-inch skillet with lid
Garlic	
Butter	
Dry white wine	
Flour	
Salt and pepper	

1. Remove the fine line of bones which runs down the center of each *fillet*. Cut fillets in half lengthwise. Roll each half fillet like a tiny jelly roll and secure with a wooden pick. Mince *2 tablespoons onion*. Peel and mince *1 clove garlic*. Chop *2 tablespoons parsley*. Peel, seed, and chop the *ripe tomatoes;* or drain *canned tomatoes* well, squeeze out seeds and excess liquid, and chop the flesh. Set vegetables aside.

2. When ready to cook, melt *1 tablespoon butter* in the skillet. Arrange the fillets in the pan, curled side up. Add *¼ cup chicken broth* and *½ cup dry white wine,* the chopped onion, garlic, and parsley, and the tomatoes.

3. Bring liquid to a simmer. Cover skillet and let the fish poach for 5 minutes. Turn and poach for 5 minutes longer.

4. Transfer the fillets with a slotted spoon to a warm serving platter and discard the wooden picks.

5. Bring liquid remaining in skillet to a rapid boil. Combine *1 tablespoon butter* and *1 tablespoon flour* and stir this paste into the liquid bit by bit. Season the sauce with *salt and pepper* to taste, and cook, stirring, for 2 minutes.

6. Pour sauce over the fillets and tuck a sprig of parsley into the center of each one. Serve immediately.

SHAD ROE

Fresh shad roe is available only in the spring months and is always a great treat for its admirers. The roe is a delicate sac of eggs, so delicate, in fact, that it should be cooked only by low-heat methods. The brisk heat of the broiler shrivels and destroys its sweetness, and bacon, the usual accompaniment, is too highly flavored to complement the roe.

Shad roe is sold by the pair, and separately from the fish itself, each pair coming from one shad. A pair, if good size, will generally serve two persons. The two lobes of each pair are attached by a thick blood vessel; it should be removed carefully, so as not to tear the fragile membrane covering and holding together the millions of shad eggs within.

SHAD ROE POACHED IN BUTTER

Serves 6. For a really exquisite meal, try hot cornbread squares, fresh buttered asparagus, and a salad of Bibb lettuce with the shad roe; have Strawberries Romanoff for dessert. A chilled white Graves would be perfect with both the fish and the dessert.

BUY

3 large pair shad roe
Parsley
Water cress

HAVE ON HAND	*COOKWARE*
½ pound butter	Heavy 12-inch skillet with lid
Flour	
Salt	
Pepper	
Lemons	

1. Rinse the *roe* in cold water, dry on absorbent paper, and separate the lobes by gently removing the vessel between them. Cover with waxed paper and keep cold until ready to cook. Chop *½ cup parsley* and set aside.

2. When ready to cook melt *1 cup butter (2 sticks)* in the skillet over low heat. Roll each roe gently in *flour* and place it in the pan. Turn the roe so that all sides are coated with the warm butter. Cover skillet and cook over very low heat for 10 minutes. Turn roe, sprinkle with the parsley, cover, and poach for 10 minutes longer.

3. Sprinkle the roe with *salt* and *freshly ground pepper* and the *juice of ½ lemon,* and transfer to heated serving platter. Pour pan juices over them and garnish with *water cress* and *lemon wedges.*

SOLE LANARD

Serves 6. This is a lovely dish that involves quite a number of steps. Some of them must be done ahead, and some will need undivided attention. The result, however, is well worth the time and care. Serve with rice and with buttered canned *petits pois,* or fresh garden peas or asparagus in season.

BUY

1 pound fresh mushrooms
Large head Boston lettuce
6 small fillets of gray sole
2 containers heavy cream (8 ounces each)

HAVE ON HAND	COOKWARE
Shallots *or* green onions	Small skillet
Butter	Shallow baking dish
White wine (preferably a sauterne)	2-quart saucepan
Salt and pepper	
Flour	
Lemon	

1. Wash *mushrooms,* trim stems evenly with the underside of the cap, and dry thoroughly. Then spread the caps out on a chopping board. Hold a chef's knife by the handle with one hand, and hang onto the tip with the other hand. Begin cutting the mushrooms. Chop, chop, chop, scraping the bits of mushrooms back into a pile in the center of

the work area until chopped ultra fine. You can do this same job by putting the mushrooms through a meat grinder with the fine blade, if you have one in your kitchen. Put the chopped mushrooms into a piece of cheesecloth or a kitchen towel and squeeze out as much excess liquid as possible. Chop *2 tablespoons shallots or white part of green onions.*

2. In small skillet melt *2 tablespoons butter.* Add *half the shallots or onion,* the mushrooms, *2 tablespoons of white wine,* and *a sprinkling of salt and pepper.* Cook, stirring frequently, until mixture is fairly dry. This is called a "duxelles." Remove it from the stove and set aside to cool.

3. Cut out and discard the heart of the *lettuce.* Carefully remove as many of the large outside leaves as possible without tearing them. Wash them well. Stack leaves on top of one another and put into the saucepan. Cover with *water* and bring to a boil. Then cover the saucepan and steam the lettuce over very low heat for 5 minutes. Drain and squeeze lettuce lightly to remove excess moisture.

4. Place fish *fillets* on a flat surface. Remove the fine line of tiny bones which runs down the center of each one, and separate each fillet into two long sections. Sprinkle sections with *salt and pepper,* and spread each with an equal portion of the duxelles. Roll each half fillet, beginning at the narrow end, into a fat jelly roll; this is called a "paupiette," if you want to be correct about it. Stand each paupiette upright on work surface. Spread 2 lettuce leaves (or 3 if small) on the work surface, overlapping them slightly at stem ends. Stand a paupiette on the overlapping edges and pull up the free edges of the lettuce leaves to completely enclose the fish.

5. Butter bottom of the baking dish and sprinkle with *remaining half of shallots or onion.* Arrange the lettuce packages in the dish, and top each one with *1 tablespoon butter.* Cover with foil and keep cold until needed.

6. When ready to cook, preheat oven to 375° F. Remove foil from fish and set the dish directly over medium heat. Add *1 cup wine* and bring it to a boil, basting the fish occasionally. Set dish into preheated oven and bake for 15 minutes.

7. Remove baking dish from oven, and drain as much of the liquid as possible into saucepan. Cover fish with foil, return to oven, turn off heat, and leave door ajar.

8. Place the saucepan over high heat, bring liquid to a boil, and boil rapidly for 5 minutes to reduce it to about half its original quantity.

Remove fish from oven and you will find that more liquid has accumulated in the dish. Drain this into the saucepan, and again return fish to oven.

9. Add the *heavy cream* to liquid in saucepan and again bring to a boil. Cook, watching carefully, for this mixture can boil over the second you take your eyes off the pot. Adjust heat accordingly to keep mixture from bubbling up too high in pan. Boil rapidly for 5 minutes. The cream will become slightly thickened—about the consistency of syrup.

10. Blend *2 tablespoons flour* with *2 tablespoons butter,* and stir into the sauce, bit by bit. When sauce is thickened, remove from heat. Taste, and correct seasoning with *salt and pepper.* Add *juice of ½ lemon* and another *2 tablespoons butter.* Swirl pan until butter is melted.

11. Arrange the paupiettes on a warm serving platter and pour the sauce over them.

SHRIMP CREOLE

Serves 2. A dish with a lot of character which is very simple to make. Unlike the other recipes in this chapter, this one calls for poaching the shrimp in a finished sauce. Serve with Saffron Rice and a green salad.

BUY

¾ pound raw shrimp
Bunch green onions
1 green pepper
1-pound can whole tomatoes

HAVE ON HAND

Carrot
Celery
Garlic
Dried hot red peppers
Cooking oil
Flour
Salt

Coarsely ground black pepper
Bay leaves
Thyme
Dry white wine (optional)

COOKWARE

Heavy 10-inch skillet with lid

1. Prepare *shrimp:* Wash well, remove shell, slit lightly down back, and rinse out sand vein. Dry on absorbent paper and refrigerate until ready to cook.

2. Chop *½ cup green onions, ½ green pepper, 1 small carrot,* and *2 stalks celery with leaves.* Mince *2 cloves garlic* and *1 small dried red pepper.* Set aside.

3. In skillet heat *2 tablespoons oil,* and in it sauté the green onions for 3 minutes, without letting them brown. Stir in *1½ tablespoons flour.* Cook, stirring, until mixture bubbles.

4. Add the other prepared vegetables, the *1-pound can tomatoes including liquid, ½ teaspoon salt, ¼ teaspoon coarsely ground black pepper, 1 bay leaf, ⅛ teaspoon thyme* and *½ cup white wine or water.* Bring to a simmer, then cover and cook over low heat for 20 minutes, stirring occasionally. If necessary, add *a little more wine or water.* Set dish aside, partially covered, until ready to serve.

5. When ready to serve, remove cover and reheat sauce to a simmer. Add the prepared shrimp, and cook for 5 minutes, stirring and turning the shrimp over until they become pink on both sides. Don't let sauce boil after shrimp are added. Correct seasoning of sauce with *salt* if needed.

POACHED CHICKEN MAYFAIR

Serves 4. This is an original recipe, patterned after the renowned Greek chicken dish with lemon sauce, known as chicken *avgolemono.* Rice, or Rice Pilaf, is the best accompaniment. A green vegetable and a tossed salad complete a delicious meal.

BUY

3½-pound fresh frying chicken, quartered

HAVE ON HAND	*COOKWARE*
Salt	Heavy kettle, *or* skillet, large
Peppercorns	enough to hold chicken
Garlic	Saucepan
Medium onion	
Celery	
Dried hot red peppers	
Bay leaves	
Thyme	
Lemons	
Butter	
Flour	
2 egg yolks	

1. Put *chicken* into the kettle and add *enough water to barely cover.* Add *1 teaspoon salt, ½ teaspoon peppercorns, 1 clove garlic,* halved, *1 medium onion,* peeled and coarsely sliced, *3 stalks celery with leaves,* coarsely cut, *1 hot red pepper pod, 1 bay leaf, ½ teaspoon thyme,* and *½ lemon,* sliced. Bring liquid to a boil, turn heat very low, partially cover pot, and let chicken poach for about 45 minutes, or until very tender. The liquid should barely bubble, not boil. Set kettle aside if you wish and reheat when ready to serve.

2. To FINISH: Remove hot chicken from broth to a warm serving platter and cover with foil to keep moist and warm. Correct seasoning of broth with *salt,* seasoning it rather highly, then strain into a bowl. There should be at least 3 cups.

3. In saucepan melt *3 tablespoons butter.* Stir in *3 tablespoons flour* and cook, stirring, until mixture bubbles. Remove from heat. Add *3 cups of the hot broth,* return pan to heat, and stir rapidly until sauce is smooth and slightly thickened.

4. In small bowl beat *2 egg yolks* with *juice of 1 lemon* and a little of the hot sauce. Stir into remaining sauce, and cook, stirring, for 1 minute, without letting sauce boil. Remove immediately from heat and pour over chicken.

POACHED CHICKEN D'AURIA

Serves 6. Serve with cooked rice or noodles.

BUY

3 pounds chicken parts, *or* 12 pieces
13¾-ounce can chicken broth
8-ounce container heavy cream

HAVE ON HAND

Medium onion
Celery
Garlic
Butter
Bay leaves
Thyme
Salt
White pepper
Flour
Dry white wine *or* dry vermouth
Lemon
2 egg yolks

COOKWARE

12-inch deep skillet *or*
    chicken fryer

1. Soak *chicken parts* in cold water for 30 minutes.

2. Peel and mince *1 medium onion.* Wash and finely chop *4 stalks celery.* Peel and mince *1 clove garlic.*

3. In skillet, heat *2 tablespoons butter,* and in it cook the onion and celery over low heat for 10 to 15 minutes, or until vegetables are soft but not brown. Add the minced garlic, *1 bay leaf,* ⅛ *teaspoon thyme,* ½ *teaspoon salt,* and ¼ *teaspoon white pepper.* Stir in *2 tablespoons flour.*

4. Drain chicken, and arrange the parts, one layer deep, on the bed of vegetables. Add the *chicken broth,* ½ *cup dry white wine or vermouth,* and ½ *cup water or enough so that liquid barely covers* the chicken pieces. Cover skillet and simmer over low heat for about 45 minutes, or until chicken is tender. Correct seasoning of the sauce with *salt,* and stir in *juice of* ½ *lemon.* Finish, or set aside and reheat when ready to serve.

5. To FINISH: Remove hot chicken to a warm serving dish. Combine

2 egg yolks and *½ cup cream* with a few tablespoons of the hot sauce from the skillet. Gradually stir this mixture into the skillet, and cook the sauce over low heat, stirring constantly, for 2 or 3 minutes, without letting it boil. Pour sauce over chicken in serving dish and serve immediately.

NOTE: If you want to make a really elegant dish out of this one, you can strain the sauce before adding the egg yolks and cream. But why bother? It's delicious as is.

LUXURIOUS CHICKEN

If you don't try any other recipe in this book, DO TRY THIS ONE. It originated in China, but you don't have to serve it with a Chinese meal. Luxurious Chicken is excellent either as a summer salad luncheon or as a buffet dish, and is always a provocative appetizer served before any meat or fish. For it to be truly authentic, you should use fresh ginger root available in Chinese markets or the canned product found in specialty shops; otherwise you may substitute ground ginger.

The Chinese method of cooking the chicken is fascinating, and completely contrary to the French method of poaching a chicken very slowly in wine and seasoned water in order to extract all the flavor from the chicken into the broth, with which they make a fabulous sauce. France is a country of sauces, and the French would sooner have the chicken flavor in the sauce than in the chicken itself. The Chinese, on the contrary, want to seal all the flavor in the chicken meat, and they do so most successfully by an unusual method. They boil the hell out of it—and it really works! They don't even add salt to the cooking water; moreover, when the chicken has finished cooking the water is *still* flavorless. The bones slip easily out of the chicken without a trace of flesh adhering to them.

If you want to enjoy your Chinese chicken and have a French broth, too, you can return the skin and bones of the cooked chicken to the water, add a little salt, peppercorns, herbs, and chopped vegetables, and simmer it all down to about 4 to 6 cups. When the liquid is strained, you have an excellent broth for soups or sauces.

LUXURIOUS CHICKEN SALAD PLATTER

Serves 6

BUY

3½- to 4-pound whole fresh chicken, ready to cook
1 head iceberg lettuce
Green onions *or* scallions
Fresh *or* canned ginger root; *or* ground ginger
Cherry tomatoes

HAVE ON HAND	*COOKWARE*
Soy sauce	4- to 5-quart heavy kettle
Honey	with cover
Salt	
Monosodium glutamate	
Garlic	
Dried red-hot chili peppers	
Peanut oil	

CHINESE METHOD OF COOKING A WHOLE CHICKEN:

1. Wash the *chicken* under cold running water and clean inside very carefully, removing any blood clots or bits of lung or liver which might remain in the carcass.

2. In a large heavy kettle bring *3 to 4 quarts water* to a boil. There should be enough to completely cover the chicken. When it is boiling rapidly, lower the chicken into the water, breast down. Let the water come back to a rapid boil, then cover the kettle, and boil the chicken as hard as possible for 18 to 20 minutes (this method requires only 5 minutes' boiling per pound of chicken). Immediately turn off the heat, and let the chicken cool in the water, still covered, until cool enough to handle.

3. Remove the chicken from the water. Cut off wing tips. Then slit the chicken up the back with scissors or a sharp heavy knife. Remove the skin and pull out all the bones, leaving the meat in large pieces.

4. Put the chicken pieces in a bowl and cover with some of the cooking liquid. Refrigerate until ready to serve.

IF YOU WISH TO MAKE BROTH:

Return wing tips, skin, and bones to the liquid and bring to a simmer. Add *1 bay leaf, 1 onion,* coarsely cut, *1 carrot,* coarsely cut, *a couple of stalks of celery, a small bunch of parsley, ½ teaspoon peppercorns,* and *½ teaspoon salt.* Boil rapidly until the liquid is reduced to about 1 quart. Strain into a bowl and you have a flavorful broth.

TO PREPARE LUXURIOUS CHICKEN FOR SERVING:

1. Wash and core the *head of lettuce.* Shred the lettuce and spread on a serving platter.

2. Remove chicken from the liquid and slice into 2-inch pieces, about ½ inch wide. Arrange the chicken pieces in regimental fashion on the lettuce. Cover with transparent plastic wrap and return to the refrigerator.

3. In a small mixing bowl combine *½ cup soy sauce, 4 tablespoons honey, 1 teaspoon salt,* and *⅛ teaspoon monosodium glutamate.* Add *2 cloves garlic,* minced. Set aside.

4. Chop *4 green onions,* including as much of the green stalks as is tender. Put these in a small saucepan, and add *8 slices ginger root,* finely chopped, or *½ teaspoon ground ginger.* Then add *1 teaspoon crushed dried red chili peppers,* and *6 tablespoons peanut oil.* Place saucepan over low heat until mixture begins to simmer. Stir the contents of the saucepan into the soy sauce mixture. Set aside until needed.

5. Spoon the pungent dressing over the chicken 5 to 10 minutes before serving to let the flavors blend. Garnish platter with *cherry tomatoes.*

CURRIED CHICKEN SALAD

Serves 4 to 6. Here is another delicious luncheon or buffet salad made with cooked chicken meat. At one time I always poached the chicken in the French manner, but now I boil it in accordance with the Chinese method so that it retains *all* its flavor.

BUY

3½- to 4-pound whole fresh chicken, ready to cook
1 sweet apple

Small jar sweet watermelon rind
5-ounce can water chestnuts
Green onions
3½-ounce can shredded coconut
Chicken broth
Lettuce *or* romaine
Small box candied ginger

HAVE ON HAND

Chutney
Celery
Parsley
Salt
Curry powder
Mayonnaise

COOKWARE

4- to 5-quart heavy kettle with lid
Small saucepan

1. A DAY IN ADVANCE: Cook *chicken* according to the Chinese method in preceding recipe. Let cool, remove flesh from the bones, cover with cooking liquid, and refrigerate.

2. NEXT DAY: Reserve the *breast meat* of the chicken for slicing and garnishing the salad. Dice *2 cups dark meat.* Combine this with *1 apple,* peeled and diced; *½ cup diced watermelon rind;* and *4 tablespoons chopped chutney, including the syrup.* Add *½ cup shredded water chestnuts, 3 green onions, including tender green stems,* sliced, *½ cup thinly sliced celery, 2 tablespoons chopped parsley, ½ cup shredded coconut,* and *½ teaspoon salt.*

3. In a small saucepan combine *1 tablespoon curry powder* and *2 tablespoons chicken broth.* Cook over low heat, stirring constantly, for 2 minutes, or until the mixture becomes a smooth paste. Combine this paste with *1 cup mayonnaise,* and stir the curry mayonnaise into the chicken mixture.

4. Pile the salad onto a chilled serving platter lined with *lettuce or romaine leaves.* Cover the mound with slices of chicken breast, and sprinkle with *2 tablespoons chopped candied ginger* and *remaining shredded coconut.*

NOTE: The secret of this salad lies in the cooking of the curry powder to a paste before it is mixed into the mayonnaise. If you add raw curry powder to salads or sandwich fillings it gives an unattractive, bitter taste.

POACHED SALMON

Fresh salmon is at its best in July, but it is available in fish markets during most of the summer months. For 6 to 8 people, select a nice *thick center cut of a large salmon* weighing from 3 to 4 pounds. For a party buffet buy a *small whole salmon* weighing from 8 to 10 pounds. If there is any left over, you're lucky—it's just as good the second or third day.

When you buy your salmon, make sure that you have a pan big enough to cook it in. A fish poacher is best. This is a long narrow pan fitted with a removable rack for lifting the fish in and out of the cooking liquid. If you don't want to buy one to add to your *batterie de cuisine,* perhaps you can borrow one from a cookin' friend.

If the salmon is whole, leave on the head and tail, but cut away and discard the pink gills from each side of the head. Whether whole or a chunk, it should be washed well in cold water, care being taken that all the scales are removed from the skin. Scrape away any blood clots that may lie along the backbone inside the fish. Then wrap the fish in cheesecloth, and tie it at both ends, leaving cheesecloth tails to help remove the fish from the pan.

Into the fish poacher or a kettle large enough to hold your fish, put *about 2 quarts of cold water or part cold water and dry white wine.* Add *¼ cup vinegar or lemon juice, 1 tablespoon salt, 1 coarsely cut onion, 1 coarsely chopped carrot, a few stalks of celery, a few sprigs of parsley, 1 teaspoon peppercorns,* and *1 bay leaf.* Set the kettle over high heat and bring the liquid to a boil. Then reduce the heat and simmer for 15 minutes. You now have a court bouillon in your kettle. Carefully lower the salmon into the hot liquid, which should barely cover the fish. If it doesn't, add *a little more water.* Bring the liquid again to a boil, then turn the heat to very low so that the court bouillon barely simmers. Cover the kettle and poach the salmon for 5 minutes per pound. Turn off the heat, partially remove the cover, and let the fish cool in the flavored liquid.

When the salmon is cool enough to handle, lift it out onto a chopping board or work table and remove the cheesecloth. Discard the skin and, with a dull knife, scrape away the dark fatty flesh that lies directly under the skin. Transfer the fish to your serving platter, turning it over so that the skinned side is down. Now remove the skin and dark flesh from the uppermost side. Cover fish with transparent plastic wrap, and chill until needed.

When ready to serve, lay salmon on platter and garnish it imaginatively with thin slices of lemon and clusters of parsley or water cress. Another nice garnish is small tomatoes stuffed with cooked vegetables dressed with mayonnaise. Serve the salmon with thinly sliced cucumbers and either warm Blender Hollandaise Sauce or cold Sauce Aurorian.

BLENDER HOLLANDAISE

Makes 1½ cups. This is a variation of the quick hollandaise that I originated in an electric blender and that has been adopted even by French chefs. It is made with the amounts of eggs and butter used in the classic recipe.

HAVE ON HAND	*COOKWARE*
½ pound (2 sticks) butter	Heavy saucepan
4 egg yolks	
Salt	
1 lemon	
Tabasco	

1. In saucepan heat *2 sticks butter* until melted and very hot, but do not let the butter brown or even begin to brown.

2. Into container of an electric blender put the *4 egg yolks, ¼ teaspoon salt, 2 tablespoons lemon juice,* and *3 to 4 drops Tabasco.*

3. Cover container of the blender and turn on low speed. Remove cover and pour in the hot butter in a steady stream. When all the butter is added, switch blender to high speed and blend for 5 seconds.

4. Set the container into a saucepan containing a few inches of hot, but not boiling, water, where it will keep warm until ready to serve. Should sauce become too stiff, add *a few drops (no more than 1 teaspoon) hot water* and blend again briefly.

NOTE: This sauce will keep in the refrigerator for several days and may be reheated over hot water. It may also be frozen for future use.

SAUCE AURORIAN

Makes about 1 cup

HAVE ON HAND	COOKWARE
Butter	Heavy saucepan
4 egg yolks	
Lemon	
Salt	
Cayenne pepper	
Mayonnaise	
Cream	

1. Put into saucepan *4 tablespoons butter* and *4 egg yolks.* Stir well together with a wooden spoon. Set mixture aside until it reaches room temperature.

2. Stir in *2 tablespoons lemon juice,* *½ teaspoon salt,* and *a good dash cayenne.* Beat with a wire whip over hot water vigorously for about 3 minutes, or until thickened. Set aside to cool.

3. Stir in *3 tablespoons mayonnaise* and *enough (about ⅓ cup heavy cream* to make the desired consistency. It will keep for a week or more in the refrigerator, but should be removed and allowed to come to room temperature, and whipped briefly, before serving.

GERMAN MEAT BALLS
WITH CAPER SAUCE

Serves 4. Serve with noodles.

BUY

1½ pounds ground raw veal
¼ pound ground fat pork
2 cans beef consommé, 10½ ounces each
Small jar of capers

¼ pound (1 stick) butter
Bread
Onion
Eggs
Salt and pepper
1 lemon
Worcestershire sauce
Parsley
Flour

Heavy 12-inch skillet with lid
Small skillet

1. In the small skillet melt *2 tablespoons butter* over low heat. In large mixing bowl combine the melted butter with the *ground veal and fat pork*. Set remainder of stick of butter aside to soften.

2. Soak *2 slices bread* in *½ cup water* until soft. Squeeze out excess water, add bread to meat, and mix.

3. Re-use small skillet to sauté *2 tablespoons minced or shredded onion* in *1 tablespoon butter* until golden, but not brown. Add onion and pan juices to the meat mixture, along with *3 eggs, 1 teaspoon salt, ½ teaspoon pepper, ½ teaspoon grated lemon peel, 1 tablespoon lemon juice, 1 teaspoon Worcestershire sauce,* and *¼ cup chopped parsley*. Mix thoroughly with your hands and shape into 12 large balls. Place meat balls on plate and refrigerate until ready to cook them and make the sauce. *Make ½ cup fresh bread crumbs* and set aside until needed.

4. To cook the meat balls: Pour the *2 cans consommé* into the large skillet and add *2 cans full of water*. Bring liquid to a boil, then reduce heat. Place the meat balls, one at a time, on a slotted spoon and lower them gently into the simmering liquid. Cover, and simmer for 10 minutes. Turn the balls over with the slotted spoon, cover and simmer for 10 minutes longer.

5. Meanwhile mix *3 tablespoons butter* with *5 tablespoons flour* to a smooth paste. Remove the meat balls from the hot consommé to a warm serving dish, and stir the flour paste, bit by bit, into the consommé. Cook, stirring, until sauce is slightly thickened. Stir in *2 tablespoons drained capers, 2 tablespoons chopped parsley,* and *1 tablespoon butter*. Turn off heat but keep sauce warm.

6. Melt the remaining *1 tablespoon butter* in the small skillet. Add

the bread crumbs and stir over moderate heat until crumbs are golden brown.

7. Pour the gravy over the meat balls and sprinkle with the golden crumbs.

POACHED TONGUE DINNER

Serves 6. Serve with horseradish or mustard and sour pickles.

Beef or ox, veal, lamb or pork tongues, fresh or smoked, may be prepared in many delicious ways. All should be cooked slowly in moist heat—that is, simmered or braised—to make them tender. Smoked tongues these days are, like hams, lightly smoked, and need no presoaking to refresh them or to remove excess salt.

BUY

3½- to 4-pound beef tongue, fresh *or* smoked
6 carrots
6 medium potatoes
8 medium onions
1 medium cabbage
Parsley *or* chives

HAVE ON HAND

Bay leaves
Peppercorns
Juniper berries (optional)
Lemon
Vinegar
1 large onion
Cloves

COOKWARE

Heavy kettle large enough to hold tongue
Steamer *or* saucepan for cabbage

1. Remove the transparent casing from the *tongue*. Wash tongue well in cold water, and put it into a pot large enough to accommodate it comfortably. Add *water just to cover.* Add *2 bay leaves, 1 teaspoon peppercorns, 1 teaspoon juniper berries, ½ lemon,* sliced, *¼ cup cider vinegar,* and *1*

large onion stuck with 4 cloves. Bring liquid to a simmer, cover partially with pot lid, and simmer for 3 hours. The water should not boil hard or the tongue will be toughened.

2. Meanwhile trim and scrape the *carrots,* and peel the *potatoes* and *onions.* Drop the vegetables into a bowl of cold water. When the tongue has cooked for 3 hours, drain the vegetables and arrange them around the tongue in the kettle. Continue to simmer for 1 hour longer.

3. Discard any coarse or discolored leaves from the *cabbage,* cut out most of the core, and slice the remainder into 6 wedges. Half an hour before tongue is cooked, steam the cabbage wedges (if you have a vege-table steamer), or cook them in a little salted water in a separate sauce-pan, tightly covered, until they are just fork tender.

4. Remove the tongue from the broth and let it cool a little. Then slit the skin at the base of the tongue; peel off and discard the skin. Also cut off the fat and gristle at the butt end. Slice the tongue on a slight slant, and arrange the slices on a warm serving platter. Surround them with the cooked vegetables. Spoon a little broth from the kettle over the vegetables, and sprinkle with *chopped parsley or chives.*

NOTE: Always save the liquid in which tongue was poached in case there is any tongue left over. Put the leftover tongue into a bowl and cover with some of the cooking liquid. Refrigerate for a day or so, then reheat in the broth until heated through. Never boil leftover meat or you will toughen it. Just bring the broth to steaming temperature. Serve leftover tongue with Sweet-sour Sauce, tiny cooked peas or string beans, and mashed or candied sweet potatoes.

SWEET-SOUR SAUCE
FOR POACHED TONGUE

In saucepan combine *1 teaspoon dry mustard, 2 tablespoons cornstarch, ½ cup light brown sugar, ¼ cup vinegar,* and *½ cup golden seedless raisins.* Gradually stir in *2 cups of the broth in which tongue was cooked,* and cook over moderate heat, stirring constantly, until sauce is clear and thickened.

NEW ENGLAND BOILED DINNER

Serves 8. If you are one of those people who shudder at the very idea of eating tongue, then you'd better stick with what we have here—corned beef and cabbage. This dish is usually served with horseradish. Blueberry Pie for dessert if you want to go New England all the way.

BUY	*COOKWARE*
4 pounds best quality corned beef brisket	Saucepan
	Large heavy kettle with lid
8 small carrots	
8 medium potatoes	
8 medium onions	
8 beets	
1 medium head cabbage	

1. Wipe the *meat* with a damp cloth and place it in the kettle. Add *cold water just to cover.* Bring water to a boil, cover and simmer for 3½ to 4 hours, adding *more water* from time to time to keep the meat covered with liquid.

2. Meanwhile trim and scrape the *carrots,* and peel the *potatoes* and *onions.* Drop these vegetables into cold water until 1 hour before meat is cooked. Then drain and add them to the kettle with the meat.

3. One hour before the brisket is cooked, put the *beets* into a saucepan, cover with boiling water, and boil for 45 minutes, or until beets are fork tender. Drain; peel whole while they are hot; and keep them warm.

4. Meanwhile remove coarse outer leaves from the *cabbage,* and cut out the core. Cut the cabbage into 8 wedges. Half an hour before the brisket is cooked, steam the cabbage wedges, or cook them in a little salted water in a separate saucepan, tightly covered, for 15 minutes, or until just fork tender. Remove cover and keep cabbage hot.

5. Remove brisket from the kettle, drain, and place in the center of a large heated platter. Surround the brisket with the cabbage, onions, carrots, potatoes, and beets.

6. To serve, slice the meat thinly across the grain. Place a wedge of cooked cabbage in center of each serving plate. Place slices of the hot brisket over it, and surround with the other vegetables.

BAKED & AU GRATIN DISHES

Baked Dishes

This chapter begins with a personal collection of really easy—really quick —baked dishes. Most of them can be prepared in the morning and then baked about an hour and a half before you want to serve them. Most of them, too, are inexpensive family dishes but good enough to serve to guests, who by this time you have convinced that you are a pretty great impresario at the range.

Then we progress to a few *au gratin* dishes which also can be made ahead of time.

Many people think that *au gratin* means a dish with crumb or crumb-and-cheese topping. Tain't necessarily so. It can mean crumbs, but it can also mean any sauced dish, covered with a blanket of sauce, which is browned under a hot broiler or in a hot oven. Such dishes are great for "come over for supper" occasions. The *au gratin* dish comes out of the refrigerator and goes right into a hot oven along with a loaf of French or Italian bread. By the time you have tossed a green salad, and opened a bottle of wine, all's done and you're ready to serve.

BAKE-AND-SERVE LEMON CHICKEN

Serves 4. Good with curried rice.

BUY

3½-pound broiler-fryer, cut into serving portions

HAVE ON HAND

Olive oil
1 lemon
Garlic

Dried tarragon
Salt and pepper
Butter
Parsley

COOKWARE

10 x 6-inch oven-to-table shallow
baking dish

IN ADVANCE:

1. In baking dish combine *¼ cup olive oil, juice and grated rind of 1 lemon, 1 minced clove garlic, ½ teaspoon dried tarragon, 1 teaspoon salt, and ¼ teaspoon pepper.* Mix well with a wooden spoon.

2. Roll the pieces of *chicken* in the lemon mixture, coating them on all sides. Cover the dish with foil, and refrigerate for at least 4 hours, turning the pieces once.

TO FINISH:

3. Preheat oven to 350° F.

4. Dot chicken pieces with *4 tablespoons butter.* Bake in the preheated oven for 1 hour, basting occasionally with juices in the dish.

5. Sprinkle chicken with *2 tablespoons minced parsley,* and serve right in the baking dish.

CHICKEN WINGS RICHARD

Serves 4. Fingers are a must for eating this dish, and, if you don't like wings, you can substitute chicken legs. Add a tossed salad and some garlic bread for an easy and delicious meal. A cheap one, too

BUY

12 large chicken wings

HAVE ON HAND

½ cup (1 stick) butter
Garlic
Coarsely cracked pepper
Dried tarragon *or* oregano
Salt
2 lemons

COOKWARE

13 x 9-inch oven-to-table shallow
baking dish

IN ADVANCE:

1. Cut and discard the wing tips from the *chicken wings*.

2. Place the baking dish over low heat. Put *1 stick of butter* in it and let the butter melt.

3. Roll the chicken wings one by one in the melted butter, and line them up side by side in the pan.

4. Sprinkle the wings with *1 minced clove garlic, ¼ teaspoon coarsely cracked pepper, ½ teaspoon tarragon or oregano, 1 teaspoon salt,* and *¼ cup lemon juice.* Cover with foil and refrigerate until about 1 hour before serving.

TO FINISH:

5. Preheat oven to 425° F. Remove foil from chicken wings and bake in the hot oven for 25 minutes. Then turn each wing over and bake for 25 to 30 minutes longer, or until most of the liquid in the pan has evaporated. Serve from the baking dish.

SWEET-AND-SOUR GLAZED ROAST CHICKENS

Serves 4 to 6. Serve with plain rice or Rice Pilaf.

BUY

2 broiler-fryers, about 2½ pounds each

HAVE ON HAND	*COOKWARE*
2 lemons	Shallow roasting pan
Butter	Small saucepan
Honey	
Salt	
Paprika	

IN ADVANCE:

1. Wash the *broilers* inside and out in cold running water and dry well on absorbent paper. Fold the wing tips under the backs. Place the chickens breast side up in a roasting pan.

2. In saucepan combine *¼ cup lemon juice, 4 tablespoons butter, 4 tablespoons honey, 1 teaspoon salt,* and *½ teaspoon paprika.* Heat until butter melts and mixture is hot. Pour sauce over the chickens, cover with foil, and refrigerate until 1½ hours before serving time.

TO FINISH:

3. Preheat oven to 325° F. Place the chickens in the hot oven and bake for 1 hour and 15 minutes, basting every 10 to 15 minutes with liquid in pan. Now increase oven temperature to 375° F. and bake for about 15 minutes longer, basting and watching carefully, for the sauce can burn very easily at this point.

4. Place chickens on warm serving platter and pour pan juices over them. Carve at table.

QUICK POPPY CHICKEN

Serves 4. Here's another cheap and easy chicken dish. Check to make sure you have poppy seeds on your spice shelf. If you wish you can substitute chicken breasts or legs for the quarters.

BUY

3½- to 4-pound chicken, quartered
Italian flavored bread crumbs

HAVE ON HAND	*COOKWARE*
Poppy seeds	13 x 9-inch oven-to-table shallow
1 lemon	baking dish
½ cup (1 stick) butter	

IN ADVANCE:

1. Arrange the *chicken pieces* skin side up in baking dish. Sprinkle with *½ cup Italian flavored bread crumbs, 1 tablespoon poppy seeds,* and the *juice of 1 lemon.* Dot with *½ cup butter.* Cover and refrigerate until 1½ hours before serving.

TO FINISH:

2. Preheat oven to 350° F. Remove foil from baking dish, place in oven, and bake for 1½ hours, basting every 20 to 30 minutes with liquid in pan. What could be easier!

QUICK MEXICAN DINNER

Serves 10 to 12. Serve with cooked rice and a tossed salad. Barbara Wolferman, my partner in breeding and showing Mayfair Yorkshire Terriers, gave me this recipe to try. Having a good-size aversion to most canned meat products, I was inclined to look down my nose at it, but it turned out to be great—if you like chili and tamales, and who doesn't!

BUY

4 cans tamales in chili gravy, 15 ounces each
2 cans chili con carne without beans, 15 ounces each
3 cans chili con carne with beans, 15 ounces each
½ pound sharp cheddar *or* Monterey Jack cheese

HAVE ON HAND

Peanut *or* olive oil
Onions
Oregano
Cumin seeds

COOKWARE

3- to 4-quart oven-to-table casserole

IN ADVANCE:

1. Heat *½ cup peanut or olive oil* in the casserole over direct heat. Add *2 large onions,* chopped, and cook slowly for 10 minutes, or just until onions are tender. Remove casserole from heat.

2. Remove and discard the corn husks from the *tamales.* Arrange half of the tamales over the onions in the casserole. Add the *5 cans of chili con carne* and sprinkle them with *1 teaspoon oregano* and *1 teaspoon cumin seeds.* Top with the remaining tamales. Cover and refrigerate until about 1 hour before serving time.

3. Meanwhile shred the *cheese* and set aside. You should have about 2 cups.

TO FINISH:

4. Preheat oven to 350° F. Remove cover from casserole and bake in the moderate oven for 30 minutes, or until bubbling. Sprinkle the cheese over the top and bake for 15 minutes longer. If you're not ready to serve, go ahead, have another Marguerita. Turn oven down to 250° F. and the Mexican Dinner will be ready for you when you are ready for it.

STEAK IN CHEESE CRUST
WITH TOMATO SAUCE

Serves 6

2½-pound slab of top round, cut 1 inch thick
8-ounce can tomato sauce

HAVE ON HAND	*COOKWARE*
Flour	Heavy skillet
Eggs	2-quart baking dish with
Corn flake crumbs	cover
Grated Parmesan cheese	
Salt and pepper	
Salad oil	
Fresh *or* dried parsley	
Garlic	
Onion	

1. Cut the *steak* into 3-inch squares. Coat all sides evenly with *flour*.

2. In a shallow dish or pie plate beat *2 eggs* and *½ cup water* lightly with a fork. In another shallow dish combine *1 cup corn flake crumbs, ½ cup grated Parmesan cheese, ½ teaspoon salt,* and *½ teaspoon pepper.* Dip the meat in the egg mixture, again making sure that the pieces are coated evenly, then roll in crumb mixture to coat completely.

3. In the skillet heat *1 cup salad oil,* and in it fry the meat pieces, a few at a time, until brown on all sides. As the pieces brown, transfer them to the baking dish. Sprinkle the browned pieces in the baking dish with *1 tablespoon chopped parsley, 1 minced clove garlic,* and *1 tablespoon finely chopped onion.*

4. Empty the *tomato sauce* into the skillet and bring to a boil, stirring in all the nice brown bits from bottom and sides of pan. Pour over the meat. Cover the casserole and bake in a 300° F. oven for 1½ to 2 hours, or until you are ready to serve. Extra baking time won't hurt, but check to make sure that all the liquid in the casserole has not evaporated. If it has, add *½ cup hot water.*

BAKED SPARERIBS

Serves 4

BUY

4-pound slab of medium-size meaty spareribs

HAVE ON HAND	*COOKWARE*
Heavy-duty aluminum foil	Large shallow roasting pan
Monosodium glutamate	
Salt	
Coarsely cracked pepper	
Garlic	
Soy sauce	
Honey	
4 lemons	
Ground ginger	
Cayenne pepper	

1. Preheat oven to 350° F. Line the roasting pan with a sheet of foil long enough that you can bring it up over the ribs and seal it with a double fold. Place the *ribs* on the foil and sprinkle with *½ teaspoon monosodium glutamate, 1 teaspoon salt, ½ teaspoon coarsely cracked pepper,* and *4 large cloves garlic,* minced.

2. Bring the foil up and over the ribs and seal tightly with a double fold. Place the ribs in the moderate oven and let them bake and steam for 1 hour.

3. Meanwhile combine *½ cup soy sauce, ½ cup honey, ½ cup lemon juice, ½ teaspoon ground ginger,* and *¼ teaspoon cayenne pepper.* Set aside.

4. Remove roasting pan from oven and open the foil. Increase oven temperature to 375° F. Transfer the ribs to a chopping board or work table. Discard the aluminum foil, and pour off all but a couple of table-spoons of the fat and liquid in the pan. Cut the slab into individual ribs and arrange these in the roasting pan. Spoon the soy-sauce mixture over them and bake for 1½ hours, basting several times with the sauce and liquid in the pan. The ribs should be well-browned and glossy (even so, they will be juicy and tender). If the ribs are not sufficiently glazed, increase

oven temperature to 400° F. and bake them 15 minutes longer, watching carefully so they do not burn.

Note: If you prefer a Mexican flavor for your spareribs rather than a Chinese one, make your basting sauce as follows: In a small saucepan combine *3 tablespoons chili powder, 1 tablespoon lemon juice, 3 tablespoons tomato paste,* and *1 cup water.* Bring to a boil, and stir until well blended. Pour over ribs and bake as in above recipe.

VEAL PARMIGIANA

Serves 4. Serve with fried eggplant and a tossed salad.

BUY

8 small slices leg of veal (about 1 pound)
12-ounce jar marinara sauce
8 ounces mozzarella cheese

HAVE ON HAND

Egg
Milk
Bread
Olive oil
Parmesan cheese

COOKWARE

Heavy 12-inch skillet
4 individual au gratin dishes
  or 1½-quart baking dish

IN ADVANCE:

1. Pound *veal slices* between two pieces of waxed paper until paper thin. Use a wooden mallet or the flat side of a cleaver for pounding.

2. In a shallow dish or pie plate beat with a fork *1 egg with 2 tablespoons milk.* Make *2 cups of bread crumbs,* first removing the crusts from the bread. Crumbs are a cinch to make if you have an electric blender. Spread the crumbs on a piece of waxed paper.

3. Dip veal slices into the egg mixture, coating them completely on both sides; then coat with crumbs, gently pressing them into the meat with the flat side of a knife.

4. Heat ¼ *cup olive oil* in a skillet, and in it sauté the veal slices for

about 2 minutes on each side, or until lightly browned. Add *a little more oil* if needed.

5. Arrange 2 pieces of veal in each au gratin dish, overlapping them if necessary, or overlap them in the large baking dish. Spoon *half of the jar of marinara sauce* over the meat.

6. Slice the *mozzarella cheese* thinly, and place 2 slices in each au gratin dish on top of the sauce, or 8 slices in the large dish. Spoon over the *remaining marinara sauce.* Cover the dish and refrigerate until ready to bake. Meanwhile grate *enough Parmesan cheese to measure ½ cup.* Set aside until needed.

TO FINISH:

7. Preheat oven to 375° F.

8. Sprinkle the Parmesan cheese over the veal, using about 2 tablespoons for each dish. Bake for 20 minutes, or until cheese is lightly browned. Serve when the sauce is bubbling hot.

VEAL SCALLOPS ITALIENNE

Serves 4. Serve with Gnocchi Italienne or Polenta and a tossed salad.

BUY

4 medium zucchini
5 medium-size ripe tomatoes
½ pound Gruyère cheese
8 veal scallops, pounded until very thin
1 can chicken broth

HAVE ON HAND

½ pound butter
Salt
Black peppercorns in peppermill
Garlic
Flour
Brandy
Dry sherry
Grated Parmesan cheese

COOKWARE

Saucepan
Large skillet
12 x 8-inch shallow baking
  pan *or* lasagne dish

IN ADVANCE:

1. Wash and trim the *zucchini*. Cut in half lengthwise, then slice ½ inch thick.

2. In saucepan melt *2 tablespoons butter*. Add the zucchini, and sprinkle with *½ teaspoon salt and some freshly ground black pepper*. Cover tightly and braise the zucchini for 15 minutes, shaking pan occasionally. Empty contents of saucepan into the baking dish and spread the zucchini evenly over the bottom.

3. Peel *tomatoes* and slice thickly. Chop 2 teaspoons *garlic*.

4. In skillet melt *4 tablespoons butter,* and in it sauté *half the tomatoes* for 2 minutes; then turn slices, sprinkle with *half the garlic,* and sauté for 2 minutes longer. Arrange tomato slices on top of zucchini. Repeat with *remaining tomatoes and garlic*. Add any juices remaining in skillet to baking dish.

5. Cut *Gruyère cheese* into 8 thin slices. Set aside.

6. Dust the *veal scallops* with *flour* and sprinkle with *salt and pepper*. In same skillet heat *2 tablespoons butter,* and in it sauté *2 or 3 slices veal* at a time for 2 to 3 minutes on each side, or until lightly brown. Add *butter* to the skillet as needed, arrange meat and cheese on top of vegetables, overlapping the slices so that they cover the vegetables.

7. To all the brown bits and juices remaining in skillet add *3 tablespoons brandy*. Tip pan so that the brandy ignites or light it with a match; let the flame blaze and die out. Add *2 tablespoons butter,* and when this melts, stir in *2 tablespoons flour*. Gradually stir in *1 cup chicken broth* and cook, stirring, until sauce is slightly thickened. Stir in *2 tablespoons dry sherry,* and correct seasoning with *salt and freshly ground black pepper*.

8. Spoon the sauce over meat and cheese. Sprinkle with *½ cup grated Parmesan cheese*. Cover dish loosely with aluminum foil and refrigerate until ready to heat and serve.

TO FINISH:

9. Remove foil. Place dish in a preheated 350° F. oven, and bake for 35 minutes.

VEAL SCALLOPS MONTE CARLO

Serves 4. Serve with Mushrooms Estragon or Braised Cauliflower.

BUY

8 thin slices veal from leg, pounded until paper thin
8 thin slices prosciutto ham
8 ounces mozzarella cheese
10¾-ounce can beef gravy
Parsley

HAVE ON HAND

Flour
Salt and pepper
Butter
Grated Parmesan cheese

COOKWARE

Shallow baking *or* au gratin
  dish
Heavy 12-inch skillet

IN ADVANCE:

1. Coat the *veal scallops* with *flour*, shake off excess flour, and sprinkle with *salt and pepper*.

2. In large skillet heat *4 tablespoons butter* until foaming. Cook the scallops, one at a time, in the hot butter for about 3 minutes on each side, or until nicely browned.

3. Arrange veal in baking dish. Top each slice of veal with *a slice of prosciutto*. Cover the prosciutto with *a slice of mozzarella cheese*. Top each slice of cheese with *1 tablespoon of the beef gravy*. Sprinkle generously with *chopped parsley* and *½ cup grated Parmesan cheese*. Cover dish with aluminum foil and refrigerate until ready to cook.

TO FINISH:

4. Preheat oven to 350° F. Remove foil cover from dish and bake for 15 to 20 minutes, or until cheese is bubbly and melted. Serve very hot.

BAKED BASS STUFFED
WITH CRABMEAT

Serves 4. I first tasted this marvelous fish dish at a party given for Jim Beard in honor of the publication of his *Fish Cookbook.* The recipe is from that book, of course.

BUY

A 3- to 4-pound very fresh striped bass, ready to cook
1 pound fresh lump crabmeat
Chives *or* green onions
Parsley
Water cress (optional)

HAVE ON HAND

Salt
Pepper
Butter
Celery
Bread *or* bread crumbs
¼ cup heavy cream
Salad oil
Lemons

COOKWARE

Shallow baking pan large enough to hold the fish

IN ADVANCE:

1. Make Sauce Rémoulade 2 hours ahead (see next recipe).

2. Wash the *fish* thoroughly under cold running water, making sure all the scales are off the skin and scraping out any blood clots along the backbone inside the fish. Dry on absorbent paper, and sprinkle lightly inside and out with *salt and pepper.*

3. Reserve *½ cup crabmeat* for the sauce. Combine the *remaining crabmeat with ¼ cup chopped chives or green onion, ¼ cup chopped parsley, 3 tablespoons finely chopped celery, 4 tablespoons melted butter, ½ cup bread crumbs, ¼ cup heavy cream,* and *salt and pepper to taste.*

4. Stuff the fish with the crabmeat mixture, then sew up the opening or close it with a skewer. Line the baking pan with a double fold of heavy aluminum foil, letting the ends come up and out of the pan—these will

facilitate removing the fish from pan after it is baked. *Oil* the fish and place it in the pan; now oil the topside of the fish. Cover with additional foil and refrigerate until ready to bake.

TO FINISH:

5. Preheat oven to 400° F. Remove foil covering, place fish in the hot oven and bake for 25 to 35 minutes.

6. Fold the *reserved half cup of crabmeat* into the Sauce Rémoulade. Keep sauce at room temperature until serving time.

7. When fish is baked, remove from pan by grasping each end of the foil and transfer fish to warm serving platter. Slip foil out from under fish. Garnish with *water cress or parsley* and *lemon wedges*. Serve with the Rémoulade.

SAUCE RÉMOULADE

Combine *2 cups mayonnaise* and *2 cloves garlic,* minced, *1 tablespoon finely chopped tarragon, 1 teaspoon dry mustard, 2 hard-cooked eggs,* chopped, *1 tablespoon each capers and finely chopped parsley,* and *1 teaspoon anchovy paste.* Let stand at room temperature for 2 hours before serving.

BAKED LOBSTER

This is THE PERFECT way to cook a freshly split live lobster. You don't even need the familiar side dish of butter sauce with it. Your fish man will split live lobsters for you and pack them on a bed of crushed ice, where they will keep cool until you get them home. Put them in the refrigerator in their package of crushed ice and they will remain live-fresh for half a day. Naturally you'll cook them as soon as possible. If you can split them yourself (I can't), here's how:

Place a live lobster back side up on a board. With a large, strong, sharply-pointed knife, pierce through the shell behind the eyes at the point where the head joins the body to sever the spinal cord. Firmly cut down through body and on down to the end of the tail. Turn the halves meat side up, and remove and discard both the black intestinal vein that runs down the tail and the sac, or bubble, that lies in the head. The grayish-white gills just back of the head are tough and also should be discarded. Everything else is not only edible but delicious. The coral-colored roe and the green tomalley, or liver, are particularly good.

Serves 2. Serve with very thin home-made French fries, a tossed salad, and lavishly buttered toasted pilot biscuits.

BUY

2 live, or split-live ready-to-cook, lobsters, about 1½ pounds each

HAVE ON HAND	*COOKWARE*
Salt	Shallow baking pan large
Peppercorns in pepper mill	enough to accommodate
1 stick butter	the lobsters
2 lemons	

1. Preheat oven to 350° F.

2. Arrange the *lobster halves,* side by side, meat side up, in a baking pan. Fold the large claws in front of the eyes of the lobster.

3. Sprinkle lightly with *salt* and generously with *pepper*. Arrange thin slices of *butter* on claws and down tail meat of the lobsters, using ¼ pound, or 1 stick, for 2 lobsters. Sprinkle with the *juice of 1 lemon.*

4. Bake in the preheated oven for 30 minutes, basting half way through the baking period with juices in the pan.

5. Serve one lobster per person, transferring each two halves to an individual serving plate. Spoon over the lobsters any melted butter remaining in the baking pan, and garnish with *lemon wedges.*

GRATIN OF CRABMEAT MORNAY

Serves 4

BUY

1 pound fresh lump crabmeat *or* 2 cans Alaska king
   crab (6¾-ounces each)

HAVE ON HAND	COOKWARE
Swiss *or* Gruyère cheese	2 two-quart saucepans
Parmesan cheese	
2 cups milk	
Butter	
Flour	
Salt	
White pepper	
Prepared mustard (preferably Dijon)	

FIRST MAKE MORNAY SAUCE:

1. Shred *6 tablespoons Swiss or Gruyère cheese*. Grate *6 tablespoons Parmesan cheese*. Combine cheeses on a piece of waxed paper; measure and set aside *¼ cup*. In one saucepan heat *2 cups milk* until steaming hot.

2. In the other saucepan melt *¼ cup butter*. When it foams stir in *4 tablespoons flour, ½ teaspoon salt* and *¼ teaspoon white pepper*. Cook, stirring, until this mixture, or roux, is smooth and bubbling. Remove saucepan from heat and pour in the hot milk. Stir rapidly with wooden spoon, or whip with a wire whisk, until sauce is smooth and thickened. Return sauce to heat and cook, stirring, for 2 minutes. Add *all but the ¼ cup of the mixed cheeses* and stir until they are melted and sauce is again smooth. Set aside.

MAKE CRABMEAT MIXTURE:

3. Pick over crabmeat and discard any cartilage. In a saucepan melt *3 tablespoons butter*. Add the crabmeat and cook over low heat just until heated through. Stir in *1 teaspoon mustard* and *1½ cups of your Mornay sauce*.

4. Divide crab mixture among 4 individual au gratin dishes or put in a 1½-quart baking dish. Spread *remaining Mornay sauce* over the surface and sprinkle with the *reserved ¼ cup cheeses*. Dot with *1 tablespoon butter*. Cool, then cover with transparent plastic film and, if necessary, refrigerate until ready to bake and serve.

BAKE AND SERVE:

5. Preheat oven to 425° F. Place dishes or dish in upper one-third of the oven and bake for 15 to 20 minutes, or until top is nicely browned and sauce is beginning to bubble.

DEVILED CRAB

Serves 6

BUY

1 pint light cream
1½ pounds fresh lump crabmeat *or* 3 cans Alaska king
  crab (6¾ ounces each)
Parsley

HAVE ON HAND	*COOKWARE*
Butter	Small saucepan
Flour	2-quart saucepan
Salt	6 individual au gratin dishes,
Dry mustard	*or* 10 x 6-inch shallow baking pan
Paprika	
Nutmeg	
Lemon	
Bread	

IN ADVANCE:

1. In small saucepan heat the *light cream* until steaming hot.

2. In another saucepan melt *4 tablespoons butter*. Stir in *4 tablespoons flour* and cook, stirring, until mixture bubbles. Stir in *½ teaspoon salt, 1 teaspoon dry mustard, ½ teaspoon paprika,* and *a pinch of nutmeg.* Remove saucepan from heat and add the hot cream. Stir rapidly with wooden spoon or wire whisk until sauce is smooth and thickened. Return to moderate heat and cook, stirring, for 3 minutes. Set aside.

3. Drain *crabmeat*. Pick over and discard any cartilage. Add crabmeat to sauce and stir in *1 tablespoon lemon juice* and *2 tablespoons chopped parsley.*

4. Empty mixture into baking dish, or divide among individual au gratin dishes. Sprinkle with *½ cup fresh bread crumbs* and dot with *2 tablespoons butter*. Cool, then cover and refrigerate until ready to cook.

TO FINISH:

5. Preheat oven to 375° F. Place dish or dishes in upper one-third of the oven and bake for 20 minutes, or until crumbs are lightly browned and sauce is bubbling around the edges.

GRATIN OF SCALLOPS IN VERMOUTH SAUCE

Serves 4

BUY

1½ pounds fresh scallops
Shallots *or* green onions
2 containers heavy cream (8 ounces each)

HAVE ON HAND

Parmesan or Gruyère cheese
Parsley
Salt
White pepper
Dry vermouth
Butter, at room temperature
Flour

COOKWARE

2-quart saucepan
1½-quart shallow baking dish
   or 4 individual au gratin dishes

IN ADVANCE:

1. Grate *¼ cup cheese;* chop *1 tablespoon parsley*. Set aside. Wash *scallops* carefully under rapidly running cold water to remove any sand. If they are large, cut them into quarters.

2. Put scallops into the saucepan with *1 tablespoon chopped shallots or green onions, ¼ teaspoon salt, ⅛ teaspoon white pepper,* and *½ cup dry vermouth*. Bring liquid to a simmer and cook over low heat for just 2 minutes. DO NOT OVERCOOK or scallops will be tough. Remove scallops with slotted spoon to a buttered au gratin dish or 4 individual ramekins.

3. Cook liquid remaining in saucepan over high heat until it is reduced to ¼ cup. Add *1½ cups of the cream* and boil rapidly until mixture is reduced to the consistency of a thin cream sauce. Watch carefully to prevent sauce from boiling over.

4. Meanwhile combine *3 tablespoons soft butter* and *1 tablespoon flour*. Stir this butter mixture, bit by bit, into the hot cream; cook, stirring, until sauce is smooth and thickened.

5. Pour sauce over scallops. Sprinkle with the grated cheese and set aside. If necessary, cover lightly and refrigerate until ready to bake.

TO FINISH:

6. Preheat oven to 425° F. Place dish or dishes in upper one-third of oven and bake for 15 minutes, or until cheese is lightly browned and sauce is bubbling. Sprinkle with the chopped parsley before serving.

COQUILLES ST. JACQUES

Serves 6. In this au gratin recipe, the liquid in which the scallops are poached is combined with a butter-and-flour *roux* to make a classic sauce known as *fish velouté*. When this sauce is enriched with eggs and cream it becomes one of the most famous of all French sauces, *sauce parisienne,* which is used as the basis of many great fish dishes. It is no more difficult to make than a cream or Mornay sauce as long as you keep in mind the fact that eggs DO CURDLE at near boiling temperatures.

As with other au gratin dishes in this chapter, it may be prepared in advance and reheated when needed.

BUY

2 pounds fresh scallops
½ pound fresh mushrooms
8-ounce container heavy cream
¼ pound Swiss *or* Gruyère cheese

HAVE ON HAND	COOKWARE
Butter	Saucepan
Shallots *or* green onions	Skillet
Dry white wine *or* dry vermouth	1½-quart shallow baking dish
Bay leaves	NOTE: This dish must be able to
Flour	resist both the heat of the oven
Salt	and top of the stove heat.
White pepper	
3 egg yolks	
Lemon	
Parsley	

IN ADVANCE:

1. Wash *scallops* under rapidly running cold water to remove any sand. If scallops are large, cut them into quarters.

2. In saucepan melt *2 tablespoons butter,* and in it cook *2 teaspoons minced shallots or green onions* for 2 minutes. Add scallops, *1 cup dry white wine or dry vermouth,* and *1 bay leaf.* Bring liquid to a boil, cover and simmer for 2 minutes only. Set aside, away from heat.

3. Wash and finely chop the *mushrooms.* In skillet heat *4 tablespoons butter,* and in it cook mushrooms over low heat for 5 minutes, or until tender. Stir in *4 tablespoons flour, ½ teaspoon salt,* and *¼ teaspoon white pepper.* Remove skillet from heat. Strain the liquid from the scallops into the skillet, and cook over moderate heat, stirring rapidly with a wooden spoon all over bottom and sides of pan until sauce is thickened. It will be quite thick.

4. In a small bowl, combine the *1 cup cream* with *3 egg yolks, 1 tablespoon lemon juice,* and *1 tablespoon chopped parsley.* Stir in a little of the hot sauce, then gradually stir egg mixture into sauce in skillet. Place skillet over low heat, and stir rapidly for 2 to 3 minutes, being careful not to let the sauce boil.

5. Stir in scallops. Spoon scallops and sauce into the baking dish. Sprinkle with *6 tablespoons grated Swiss or Gruyère cheese* and dot with *2 tablespoons butter.* Set aside or refrigerate until ready to reheat.

TO FINISH:

6. Preheat oven to 425° F.

7. If dish was refrigerated, place it over low heat and bring just to serving temperature, taking care not to let sauce boil. Place the baking dish on top of a shallow pan containing cool water and bake in the upper two-thirds of the hot oven for 10 to 15 minutes, or until nicely browned. Since the pan of water prevents the oven heat from penetrating the bottom of the dish, the sauce will not curdle while the top is browning.

NOTE: Individual au gratin dishes may be used instead of the larger baking dish; if so, they should NOT be refrigerated, but should be finished and served as soon as convenient. Place the smaller dishes on a baking sheet, and then set the baking sheet over a shallow pan of cool water in the hot oven.

GRATIN OF SOLE, SAUCE PARISIENNE

Make as above, in a baking dish, substituting *fillets of sole or flounder* for the scallops.

ROASTS & A FEW
LEFTOVER DISHES

Roasting

Originally roasting meant cooking on a revolving spit before the dry, hot heat of an open fire. Modern methods recommend moderate temperatures in a closed oven, where humidity from the roast can build to a point where the meat is practically steamed.

There is less shrinkage by modern methods, but proportionately less flavor, and high-temperature roasting is still used and preferred by professional chefs. The meat browns on the outside quickly, sealing inside all the good juices and flavor. However, there is always room for compromise; for, while the professional chef and his assistants can stand by the stove or spit, ready to baste and turn a roast as needed, the average home cook has more to attend to than the roast in the oven. So wherever possible I have developed new techniques, combining oldfashioned high-heat roasting with modern-day ease.

The most popular of these new methods is one I perfected for people who like their rib roasts rare. If you are one who likes his roast beef well-done, you might just as well skip what comes next and stick to pot roasts rather than waste your money overcooking an expensive rib roast.

The method was published by Craig Claiborne in the *New York Times* in 1966. It turned out to be the most requested recipe of any published that year in the *Times,* and was repeated again early in 1967. I think its success has been due to the fact that no oven thermometer and no basting are needed. The roast is taken from the refrigerator, put directly into a preheated 500° F. oven, and roasted for AN EXACT TIME. (See roasting chart.) Then the oven heat is turned off, and the door to the oven is NOT OPENED for at least 1 hour. What's more, the roast can remain in the closed oven for as long as 2 to 4 hours—long enough for a round of golf or an appointment at the hair-dresser—yet it will still be hot and perfectly cooked from first to last slice, brown and crusty on the outside, juicy and evenly rare on the inside.

Rib roasts are expensive and many cooks are nervous about roasting one. The beautiful part of this method is that the roast may be cooked well in advance of slicing, and the host or hostess may relax, knowing that the beef is done to perfection, ready whenever he is. So pour another martini—the roast will keep.

RARE ROAST BEEF

Serves 2 persons per rib

BUY

A 2- to 4-rib roast of beef, without the short ribs

HAVE ON HAND   *COOKWARE*

Flour   Shallow open roasting pan
Salt
Coarsely cracked black pepper

1. Preheat oven to 500° F.

2. Remove *roast* from refrigerator and place it in a shallow roasting pan. Sprinkle with *a little flour* and rub the flour into the fat lightly. Season generously with *salt and pepper.*

3. To protect your oven from spattering fat, place a tent of aluminum foil loosely over the top of the meat.

4. Put the roast in the preheated oven and roast according to the roasting chart below, timing the minutes EXACTLY. If you have a timer, set it to remind you, for a few minutes' overcooking can mean disaster.

5. When cooking time ends, turn off oven heat. Do NOT OPEN OVEN DOOR. Allow the roast to remain in the oven for at least 1 hour, or until the oven is lukewarm, which occurs in about 2 hours. The roast will retain a crunchy outside, and an internal heat suitable for serving for as long as 4 hours.

ROASTING TIME

This works out to 15 minutes per rib, or approximately 5 minutes' roasting time per pound of trimmed, ready-to-cook roast.

No. of Ribs	Weight without Short Ribs	Roasting time at 500° F.
2	4½ to 5 lbs.	25 to 30 minutes
3	8 to 9 lbs.	40 to 45 minutes
4	11 to 12 lbs.	55 to 60 minutes

FILLET OF BEEF WITH PORT OR MADEIRA SAUCE

Serves 12. A fillet of beef is the most expensive cut of beef, so is seldom cooked at home except for very special occasions. Like a rib roast it should be served rare or medium rare, but rare is best. This is the time to bring out the caviar and serve Crème Brûlée for dessert.

BUY

A well-trimmed fillet of beef (about 8 pounds)
6 medium mushrooms
10¾-ounce can beef gravy

HAVE ON HAND

Butter
Salt
Peppercorns and pepper mill
Shallots *or* onion
Port *or* Madeira wine
Lemon

COOKWARE

Shallow open roasting pan
Small skillet

1. Heat *4 tablespoons butter* in roasting pan set over direct heat. Place the *fillet* in the hot butter and brown it lightly on all sides. Sprinkle

with *salt* and *freshly ground pepper,* and set aside until half an hour before serving time, lightly covered with a foil tent.

2. Wash, dry well, and slice the *mushrooms.* Peel *shallots or onion* and chop *enough to measure 2 tablespoons.*

3. To make Port or Madeira Sauce: In skillet melt *1 tablespoon butter.* Add mushrooms and cook over medium heat for about 5 minutes, stirring occasionally. Sprinkle with *salt and pepper.* Add shallots or onion; cook, stirring frequently, until most of the liquid is cooked away. Add the *can of beef gravy* and ½ *cup Port or Madeira wine.* Cook, stirring, until sauce is hot. Correct seasoning and add *a squeeze of lemon juice.* Set aside.

4. Preheat oven to 450° F. while you get ready to roast the meat. Place the browned fillet in the preheated oven and roast for 25 to 30 minutes for rare. To test for doneness: Pierce the meat to the center with a two-tine kitchen fork. If the juice which runs out is red, the meat is rare; if pink, the meat is medium rare.

5. Remove roast from oven and transfer it to a large serving dish. Keep roast warm and allow it to rest—or, as the French would say, "reposer"—while you finish the sauce.

6. Pour off most of the fat from the pan. Add to pan the Madeira or Port Sauce; cook over direct heat, stirring in all the brown bits from sides and bottom of pan. Add *2 tablespoons butter* and stir until butter is barely melted. Spoon a little of the sauce over the beef, and pour the rest into a sauceboat to serve with the meat as it is sliced.

A LAMB OF A MEAL— OR FOUR OF THEM

One of the most economical meats for a family, whether it consists of two, four or six people, is a leg of lamb. It may be served roasted for one meal with enough left over for two or more meals, depending on the number of servings required each time.

Let's assume you serve roast lamb to four people with normal appetites. There will be enough left over for two more dishes, each of which will serve four. This means you get twelve servings from a 6½- to 7-pound leg of lamb, and that's hard to beat in this day of rising food costs.

ROAST LEG OF LAMB
WITH TARRAGON CREAM GRAVY

Serve as many as 12. How about that Cold Lemon Soufflé for dessert?

BUY

6½- to 7-pound leg of lamb
8-ounce container heavy cream

HAVE ON HAND	*COOKWARE*
Garlic	Shallow open roasting pan
Flour	
Salt	
Coarsely cracked pepper	
Dried tarragon	
2 medium onions	

1. Preheat oven to 450° F.

2. Place *lamb* in the roasting pan, fat side up. Peel *2 cloves garlic*. Make deep incisions in the meaty parts of the leg, and in each one insert a thin sliver of garlic. Tuck any remaining pieces of garlic under the roast. Sprinkle the leg and the roasting pan with *2 tablespoons flour*. Sprinkle the meat with *1 teaspoon salt, ½ teaspoon coarsely cracked pepper,* and *1 teaspoon dried tarragon*. Quarter *2 onions* and arrange pieces around the roast.

3. Place the lamb in the hot oven and roast for 20 minutes. Then reduce oven heat to 350° F. and continue to roast for a total roasting time of 1½ hours. This will give you meat that is just nicely rare, and lamb is best eaten rare, believe it or not. Roast 15 minutes longer for medium rare, and a total of 2 hours for well-done, dried-out, and strong-tasting lamb!

4. Remove roast to a warm serving platter and let it rest for a few minutes while you make the gravy. But, first, put some water on to boil.

5. Pour off all but 4 tablespoons of the fat in the pan, leaving the dark meat juices and the charred onion and flour. Place roasting pan on stove—with heat off—and stir in *6 tablespoons flour*. Add *2 cups boiling*

water and stir rapidly with whisk or wooden spoon until smooth. Now turn heat on to medium. Cook the gravy, stirring in all the brown bits of meat glaze from bottom and sides of pan. When gravy has thickened, let it boil rapidly for a few minutes, then gradually stir in the *heavy cream*.

6. Correct seasoning of the gravy with *salt and pepper* and, if it is too thick to suit you, stir in *a little more boiling water*. Strain gravy through a sieve into a sauce boat and serve separately from the roast.

GOOD DISHES FROM LEFTOVER LAMB

After a dinner of roast lamb, let remainder of the leg cool, then wrap in foil and chill in refrigerator overnight. Save any leftover gravy, too.

Next day cut all meat off bones. Slice the best parts about ½ inch thick and then cut them into cubes, making 4 cups cubed lamb. Put all remaining bits and pieces through medium blade of a meat grinder, or chop finely. You should have from 3 to 4 cups ground lamb. Both the diced lamb and the ground lamb can be frozen in plastic freezer bags for future use. You can also freeze any leftover gravy.

Now, here are some good ways to prepare these valuable leftovers, whether used immediately or after they have been frozen and thawed.

LAMB HASH

Serves 4. Serve with chili sauce.

HAVE ON HAND	COOKWARE
1 large onion	Heavy skillet with lid
3 large potatoes	
Butter	
3 cups ground cooked lamb	
Dried thyme	
Salt and pepper	

1. Peel and chop *1 large onion*. Peel and dice *3 large raw potatoes*.

2. In the skillet heat *5 tablespoons butter,* and in it sauté the onion for 5 minutes, or until transparent. Add the potatoes, the *ground lamb, ¼ teaspoon dried thyme,* and *salt and pepper to taste.* Mix lightly.

3. Cover skillet and cook over moderate heat for 15 minutes, or until · potatoes are tender and bottom of mixture is brown and crusty.

4. Turn mixture over with a spatula. Smooth top and cook, uncovered, for 15 to 20 minutes longer, or until hash is brown and crusty again on the bottom.

CURRIED LAMB

Serves 4. Serve with cooked rice and additional chutney.

BUY

1 tart cooking apple
8-ounce container heavy cream
2 cans chicken *or* beef broth
Chutney

HAVE ON HAND

Onion
Garlic
Butter
Curry powder
Flour
Leftover lamb gravy (optional)
4 cups diced lamb
Lemon

COOKWARE

2-quart heavy saucepan
1-quart saucepan

1. Peel and chop *1 medium onion* and *2 cloves garlic.* Peel, core, and chop the *apple.*

2. In large saucepan melt *4 tablespoons butter,* and in it sauté onion, garlic, apple, and *2 tablespoons curry powder* over moderate heat for about 10 minutes, or until onion is tender. Stir in *6 tablespoons flour,* then set aside.

3. In small saucepan combine any *leftover gravy* with enough *chicken*

or beef broth to make a total of 3 cups liquid, or use 3 cups broth. Heat to boiling.

4. Pour the hot liquid into the curry mixture and stir rapidly with whisk or wooden spoon over moderate heat until sauce is thickened. Then cook over low heat for 10 minutes, stirring occasionally. Add the *diced lamb,* and cook for 5 minutes longer without letting the sauce boil.

5. Stir in the *cream,* the *juice of ½ lemon,* and *¼ cup chopped chutney.* Heat just to serving temperature, or set aside and reheat before serving.

GIGOT À LA BRETONNE

Serves 6 to 8. In many parts of France, but especially in Brittany, gravy or sauce seldom accompanies a roast of lamb, but the pan juices remaining after the excess fat is removed are used to give flavor to a dish of green shell beans known as *flageolets.* This dish is the traditional accompaniment to a leg of lamb. Small dried lima beans or navy beans may be substituted for the *flageolets.*

BUY

1 pound dried flageolets *or* other
   dried beans
Parsley
1-pound can whole tomatoes
6-pound leg of lamb

HAVE ON HAND	COOKWARE
Bay leaves	Shallow open roasting pan
Thyme	Skillet
Salt	2-quart saucepan
Coarsely cracked black pepper	
Garlic	
1 large onion	
Butter	

1. Day before, wash and pick over the *beans.* Cover with *plenty of cold water* and let soak overnight.

2. Next day, drain the beans, cover with *fresh cold water*, add *1 bay leaf, ¼ teaspoon thyme, 1 teaspoon salt* and *½ teaspoon coarsely cracked pepper*. Bring to a boil and simmer for about 1½ hours, or until beans are tender. Do not overcook. Add water from time to time, if necessary, to keep the beans barely covered with liquid.

3. When you start to cook the beans, turn on oven heat and set at 450° F. Place *leg of lamb* in roasting pan, fat side up, and insert slivers of *garlic* into deep slashes made in the meat. Sprinkle with *salt and pepper* and roast in the hot oven 20 minutes; then reduce oven temperature to 350° F. and roast for 1 hour longer. Turn off heat, open oven door slightly, and let roast rest while you complete the dish.

4. Peel and chop *1 large onion* and *1 large clove garlic*. Chop *2 tablespoons parsley*. Set aside.

5. In skillet heat *2 tablespoons butter,* and in it sauté the onion and garlic for 10 minutes, or until onion is tender but not brown. Drain *tomatoes* and chop them coarsely. Add tomatoes to the onion mixture and cook for 2 minutes, stirring constantly.

6. Drain liquid from the beans, but leave them quite moist. Add the tomato mixture to the beans, mix lightly, and cook for 10 minutes, stirring frequently. Empty beans into serving dish.

7. Place lamb on warm serving platter. Remove all excess fat from roasting pan, and pour the *remaining pan juices* over the beans. Sprinkle with the chopped parsley.

ROAST LOIN OF PORK WITH WHITE WINE

Serves 6. Serve with Sweet Potato Casserole and hot French or Italian bread. Apple Brown Betty is a good dessert if this is a cold-weather dinner.

BUY

6-pound pork loin roast
10¾-ounce can beef consommé

HAVE ON HAND   *COOKWARE*

Carrots   Shallow open roasting pan
Medium onions
Garlic
Celery
Bay leaves
Cloves, whole
Thyme
Salt and pepper
Olive oil
Dry white wine
Lemon

1. Preheat oven to 475° F.

2. Scrape and thickly slice *2 carrots*. Peel and thinly slice *2 medium onions,* peel and mince *2 cloves garlic,* and chop *2 stalks celery.*

3. Sprinkle the carrots, onions, garlic, and celery over the bottom of the roasting pan. Add *1 bay leaf* and *2 whole cloves*. Place the *roast,* fat side up, on the bed of vegetables. Sprinkle with *1 teaspoon dried thyme* and *a generous amount of salt and pepper*. Dribble *¼ cup olive oil* over the roast, and add *½ cup each of consommé and white wine* to the roasting pan.

4. Roast in the hot oven for 20 minutes. Reduce oven temperature to 350° F. and continue to roast for about 3 hours longer, basting occasionally with juices in the pan. Pork must be cooked until well done, or 30 to 35 minutes per pound when roasted at the above temperatures. To test whether roast is well cooked, pierce the thickest part of the meat with a two-tined kitchen fork. The juices that run out must be clear with no tinge of pink.

5. A few minutes before serving, remove the roast to a warm platter and squeeze the *juice of ½ lemon* over it. Turn off oven heat and return roast to it while making the gravy.

6. Pour off all the fat from the roasting pan and place pan over direct heat. Stir in the *remaining consommé, 1 cup dry white wine* and *¼ cup water*. Boil rapidly, stirring and scraping the bottom and sides· of the pan, until only about 1 cup slightly thickened sauce remains.

7. Strain the sauce into a bowl and serve separately from the roast.

ROAST CHICKEN

Serves 4. There's not much better eating than a tender chicken roasted in butter and served with a pan gravy. Here, again, I go along with professional chefs, prefer an initial high temperature for roasting, otherwise steam forms and the chicken is apt to taste more stewed than roasted.

BUY

3½- to 4-pound chicken, ready-to-cook

HAVE ON HAND	*COOKWARE*
Salt and pepper	Shallow open roasting pan
Small onions	
Parsley	
Celery	
Bay leaves	
Tarragon *or* thyme	
Butter	
Carrots	
Water *or* white wine	
Chicken stock *or* water	

1. Wash inside of *chicken* and scrape out any blood clots lying along the backbone and any remaining bits of viscera. Sprinkle the cavity with *a little salt and pepper,* and insert into it *1 small onion,* quartered, *a few sprigs parsley, 1 stalk celery with leaves, 1 bay leaf,* a *pinch of tarragon or thyme,* and *1 tablespoon butter.*

TRUSS THE CHICKEN—IT'S EASY!

It really is easy, though the instructions don't sound as if they make much sense unless you actually have a bird in front of you to practice on:

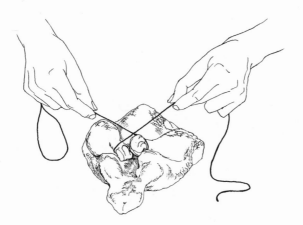

2. You need only a piece of white kitchen string about 1 yard long. Set the chicken on its back with the drumsticks pointing away from you. Slip the center of the string under the two tips of the drumsticks, then cross the two ends over them.

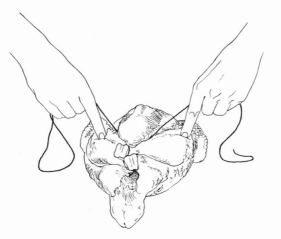

Push both drumsticks, hard, downward and against the breast, so that the ends of the drumsticks are *below* the tip of the breastbone. Pull the strings tight, pushing them, too, well under the tip of the breastbone. Draw the two ends toward you on each side, between the legs and body of the chicken.

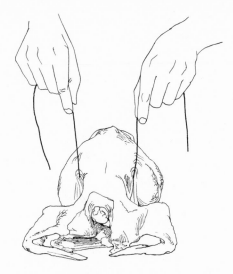

Hang on to the strings, flip the chicken over, and pull the strings upward toward you. The tail of the bird is now toward you, and the strings have come up on each side between the body and legs.

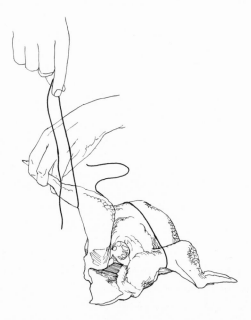

Hook a wing around each string, and pull them tightly again.

Pull the neck skin over the neck opening onto the back, and hold it in place by tying the string firmly over it.

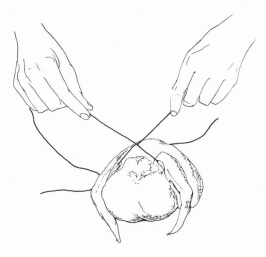

Now twist each wing tip inward over the back, which will give a nice support to the bird in the roasting pan.

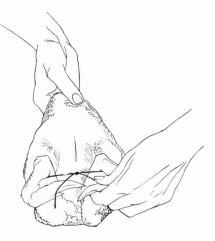

Turn the chicken over onto his back again. The great thing about this system is what happens when you remove the string from the roasted bird. Cut it just once, at the point where it is wrapped around the tips of the drumsticks, and pull one end— it will all come off in one piece!

3. Rub the roasting pan with *a little butter* and sprinkle it with slices of *1 small onion* and *1 small carrot*. Place the chicken, breast side up, on the bed of vegetables. Rub the breast with *2 tablespoons butter* and sprinkle with *salt and pepper*. Add *¼ cup water or white wine* to roasting pan.

4. Roast in a preheated 400° F. oven for 30 minutes. Reduce oven temperature to 375° F. and roast for 1 to 1½ hours longer, or until chicken is done. Baste bird occasionally, adding, if necessary, just enough liquid to keep the pan juices from burning and drying out.

TEST FOR DONENESS:

Pierce second joint deeply with a two-tined kitchen fork. If the juices which run out when fork is withdrawn are clear and colorless, with no tinge of pink, the chicken is done.

5. Remove the trussing string, place the bird on a warm serving platter, and let it rest for 10 minutes while making the pan gravy.

MAKE PAN GRAVY:

6. Pour off all fat from surface of the pan liquid and place roasting pan over direct heat. Add *½ cup water or chicken stock;* cook for a few minutes over moderate heat, stirring in all the brown bits from bottom and sides of pan. Correct seasoning with *salt,* and add *1 tablespoon butter.* Remove pan from heat before the butter has completely melted. Serve separately from the chicken.

ROAST LEMON-AND-TARRAGON CHICKEN

Serves 6

BUY

5-pound roasting chicken, ready to cook

HAVE ON HAND

½ cup (1 stick) butter
Dried tarragon
Garlic

Salt
Coarsely ground black pepper
Lemon

Shallow open roasting pan

1. Prepare and truss *chicken,* as in previous recipe.

2. In roasting pan melt *½ stick butter.* Sprinkle with *1 tablespoon dried tarragon* and *1 minced large clove garlic.*

3. Place chicken ON ITS SIDE in the pan, and sprinkle with *1 teaspoon salt, ½ teaspoon pepper,* and *juice of 1 lemon.* Dot with *½ stick butter.*

4. Roast in preheated 400° F. oven for 20 to 30 minutes, or until nicely browned. Turn ON OTHER SIDE and roast for 30 minutes longer. Turn chicken BREAST UP, reduce oven temperature to 375° F. and roast for a total roasting time of 2 to 2½ hours, basting occasionally with juices in the pan.

5. Place chicken on warm serving platter, and pour the flavorful roasting butter over it.

POULET RÔTI VALLÉE D'AUGE

Serves 4. Serve with artichoke bottoms filled with tiny buttered peas. This gorgeous chicken dish comes from the Valley of Auge in Normandy. It makes the most of the local produce—the apples from the orchards and the rich cream and butter from the dairy herds.

BUY

2 small (2½-pound) chickens, ready to cook
Calvados (apple brandy)
Cider
8-ounce container heavy cream

HAVE ON HAND

Salt
Peppercorns and pepper mill
Butter
Onion *or* shallots
Parsley
Dried thyme

COOKWARE

Shallow open roasting pan

1. Sprinkle *chickens* inside and out with a little *salt* and *freshly ground black pepper*. Truss chickens and rub all over with *4 tablespoons butter*. Place them on their sides in the roasting pan and roast in a pre-heated 400° F. oven for 20 minutes. Baste, turn chickens to their other side and roast for 20 minutes longer.

2. Meanwhile chop enough *onion or shallots to measure 3 table-spoons*. Chop *1 tablespoon parsley*. Set aside.

3. Remove chickens from oven and arrange them breast side up in the pan. Pour over them ⅓ *cup Calvados* and set the brandy aflame. When flame burns out, sprinkle pan with the chopped parsley and onions or shallots, and with ¼ *teaspoon dried thyme*. Return chickens to the oven and roast for 45 minutes, or until golden brown all over.

4. Remove chickens from roasting pan, and discard trussing strings. Cut birds into quarters, and arrange them on warm serving platter.

5. Place roasting pan over direct heat and add ½ *cup apple cider*. Cook for a few minutes over moderate heat, stirring in all the brown bits from bottom and sides of pan. Stir in *1 cup heavy cream* and bring sauce to a boil. Boil rapidly until sauce is slightly thickened. Correct seasoning with *salt and pepper,* add *2 tablespoons butter,* and swirl pan until butter is barely melted. Pour sauce over chickens and serve immediately.

DUCKLING OF THE FOUR SEASONS

Serves 2. Sweet Potato Casserole is a good accompaniment. You need a simple dessert, without fruit, such as ice cream with Hot Chocolate Rum Sauce.

BUY

5-pound frozen Long Island duckling
Fresh *or* candied *or* preserved ginger
2 large ripe peaches *or* other fresh fruit
Water cress

HAVE ON HAND

Salt and pepper
Garlic
Onion

Sugar

Stick cinnamon

Lemon

COOKWARE

Shallow roasting pan with rack

Saucepan

1. Defrost *duckling* at room temperature overnight, or in refrigerator for 24 hours. Remove package of gizzard from inside the duck.

2. Prick the skin of the duckling all over with a two-tined fork, especially in the fatty areas under the leg joints. This will allow the fat under the skin to escape, so the skin will be crisp and well browned. Sprinkle duckling inside and out with *salt and pepper*. Insert into the cavity *3 cloves garlic,* sliced, *1 medium onion,* cut into 8 sections, and *two 2-inch pieces of ginger*.

3. Place duckling on its back on a rack in roasting pan and roast at 400° F. for 1 hour. Remove duck from oven, then tip it over, or raise it up by the wings, to allow all fat accumulated in the cavity to drain into the pan. Either pour or syphon off all fat from roasting pan. Reduce oven temperature to 350° F. Return duck to the oven and continue to roast for 1 hour, or until skin is crisp and brown.

4. While duckling is roasting, peel, pit, and halve *two fresh peaches*. In saucepan combine *1 cup water, 1 cup sugar, 1 stick cinnamon,* and *1 sliced lemon*. Bring liquid to a boil and boil rapidly for 3 minutes. Add peaches and poach for 2 minutes on each side. Turn off heat and let peaches steep in the hot syrup until ready to serve.

5. When duckling is cooked, transfer it to a warm serving platter, surround it with the peach halves, and garnish with water cress.

NOTE: If peaches are not in season, use other fresh fruit, such as apples, pears, cantaloupe or honeydew melon, or pineapple.

HOW TO CARVE A DUCK:

On each side of the breast bone, slit the flesh from one end of the duck to the other in one continuous cut. On one side and then the next, insert a serving spoon, bowl up, in the slit and loosen flesh from breast bone.

Insert a fork close to wing joint and, using a strong knife, disjoint wing from body. Remove wing and breast meat together.

Insert fork close to upper thigh joint and use knife to disjoint leg from body.

Serve a breast-wing and a leg to each person.

DUCKLING BIGARADE

Serves 2

BUY

5- to 5½-pound duckling, ready to cook
2 large oranges
10¾-ounce can beef gravy

HAVE ON HAND

Lemon
Sugar
Wine vinegar
Grand Marnier *or* Cointreau
Salt
Cognac

COOKWARE

Shallow roasting pan
Small saucepan
Small heavy saucepan *or*
  skillet

1. Put the *duckling* on a rack in a shallow roasting pan. Roast in a preheated 350° F. oven for 2 hours, basting occasionally and also pouring off excess fat as it accumulates in pan.

2. Meanwhile, strip off the *thin yellow rind from one of the oranges* with a vegetable peeler. Cut the rind into thin julienne strips. Put the rind into a small saucepan and cover generously with *water*. Bring water to a boil and simmer for 10 minutes. Drain off bitter liquid and set rind aside.

3. Combine the *juice from the peeled orange* with the *juice of 1 lemon*. Set aside.

4. Remove sections from *second orange*. An easy way to do this is to take a sharp knife and peel the orange right down to the juicy part, removing not only the rind but the white pulp that lies beneath. Then slip knife against the dividing membranes, and cut out the sections. Do this over a small bowl in order to catch any juice which drains out. Set bowl of sections aside.

5. In a small heavy saucepan or skillet combine *4 teaspoons sugar* and *1 tablespoon wine vinegar*. Cook over moderate heat until sugar turns light caramel in color. Set aside.

6. When duckling is golden brown and skin is crisp, remove from pan to a flameproof serving platter. Surround by the orange wedges and keep warm.

7. Drain off all fat from the roasting pan, retaining the clear dark pan juices. Place pan over direct heat and add the sugar-vinegar mixture. Add *beef gravy* and bring to a boil, stirring constantly. Boil briskly for 5 minutes, stirring frequently. Stir in the combined orange and lemon juice and *3 tablespoons Grand Marnier or Cointreau* and *salt to taste*. Heat gently to serving temperature, pour into a sauceboat, and stir in the reserved orange rind.

8. Pour *2 tablespoons Grand Marnier or Cointreau* and *2 tablespoons cognac* over the duckling and serve flaming.

9. Carve duck, circle each portion with orange sections, and spoon a little sauce over the duck.

ROAST DUCKLING DINNER FOR FOUR

Prepare *Savory Baked Beans* and have them in the casserole ready to bake. They require three hours' cooking. Preheat oven to 350° F. Bake the beans covered during the first hour.

Meanwhile, with a two-tined fork, prick the skin of *two 5-pound ready-to-cook ducklings* to allow fat to escape. Place on rack in a shallow roasting pan, and sprinkle with a little salt. When beans have cooked for 1 hour, slip the ducks in beside the covered casserole and cook beans and ducks together for 1 hour.

Remove cover from beans. Pour off all fat from roasting pan. Continue to bake beans and ducks for another hour.

During the last hour of cooking make a *tossed salad*, ready to be dressed, and set aside.

Serve half a duckling per person along with the baked beans, a sliced loaf of *dark pumpernickel bread*, and a fine bottle of imported *red Bordeaux wine*.

Dress the salad, and serve it as a separate course with a hunk of *good aged cheese* and what's left of the bottle of red wine.

Lemon Sherbet makes an appropriate dessert.

ROCK CORNISH GAME HENS

Somewhere along the line the Dark Cornish of English fame was crossed with a game bird—pheasant, perhaps, or the partridge or the quail. Nobody quite knows, or will tell, its origin. The result, however, was a pleasant one, and Rock Cornish game hens are available across the country in frozen and sometimes fresh form. If you live in an area where Rock Cornish are raised, buy them fresh, by all means; otherwise make sure you buy them from a store which has a large turn-over of the frozen birds, for if carelessly frozen or frozen for too long, they can be hopelessly flavorless and stringy. Better to settle for small fresh-killed chickens, which may be prepared in the same way as the game hens in the following two favorite recipes of mine.

GAME HENS VÉRONIQUE
WITH PORT WINE SAUCE

Serves 6 (½ bird per serving)

BUY

3 Rock Cornish game hens, fresh or frozen
8¼-ounce can light seedless grapes
8-ounce container heavy cream
Water cress

HAVE ON HAND

Salt and pepper
Butter
Bacon
4 green onions *or* 1 small onion
Port wine
Cognac
Cayenne pepper
Lemon

COOKWARE

Shallow open roasting pan
Saucepan

1. If *hens* are frozen, defrost them, in their pliofilm wrapping, in cold water. This will take from 1 to 2 hours. Remove the bag of giblets from inside the birds, and then dry birds well with paper towels.

2. Preheat oven to 350° F.

3. Sprinkle birds generously inside and out with *salt and pepper*. Arrange them in *a lightly buttered roasting pan*. Cut *3 slices bacon* in half crosswise and arrange 2 pieces over each breast. Bake in the preheated oven for 1 hour, basting occasionally with juices in roasting pan.

4. Meanwhile finely chop *4 green onions; or enough mild onion to measure 2 tablespoons*. In saucepan melt *2 tablespoons butter* and in it sauté the onion for 2 minutes. Drain the *can of grapes* and add the grapes to the saucepan. Add *½ cup Port wine* and bring to a boil. Simmer for 2 minutes. Set aside.

5. Remove birds from roasting pan and discard bacon. Cut each bird in half with poultry shears or a heavy knife. Arrange the halves on a warm serving platter.

6. Pour off fat from roasting pan and place pan over direct heat. Add *¼ cup Cognac* to liquid remaining in pan, and cook, stirring, until Cognac is reduced to half. Add the *heavy cream* and boil rapidly until mixture is reduced to the consistency of a thin cream sauce.

7. Strain the sauce in the roasting pan into the grapes and Port wine and heat to serving temperature. Season with *salt, cayenne,* and *1 teaspoon lemon juice*.

8. Pour sauce and grapes over the birds, and garnish with *water cress*.

ROCK CORNISH GAME HENS DIABOLO

Serves 6 (½ bird per serving)

BUY

3 Rock Cornish game hens, fresh *or* defrosted
1 can chicken broth
8-ounce container heavy cream

HAVE ON HAND	COOKWARE
Butter	Shallow open roasting pan
Prepared mustard (preferably	
Dijon)	
Salt	
Peppercorns and pepper mill	
Lemon	
Flour	

1. Defrost *hens* if necessary, remove bag of giblets from inside the cavity, and split each hen in half lengthwise.

2. Preheat oven to 400° F.

3. Combine *3 tablespoons butter* with *1 tablespoon mustard* and *1 teaspoon salt*.

4. Arrange game hens in roasting pan, skin side up. Spread skin with the butter-mustard paste, and sprinkle generously with *pepper*. Roast in the preheated oven for 50 minutes, basting occasionally with juices in pan.

5. Meanwhile remove the *thin yellow rind from ½ lemon* with a vegetable peeler. Shred the rind with a sharp knife into thin julienne strips. Put the shreds into a small saucepan and cover well with *water*. Bring water to a boil and simmer the rind for 10 minutes. Drain off the bitter liquid and set rind aside.

6. Remove birds from oven and arrange them on a warm serving platter. Place roasting pan over direct heat. Stir *3 tablespoons flour* into fat and juices remaining in the pan, and cook, stirring, until mixture bubbles. Stir in *1 tablespoon mustard*. Gradually stir in *1 cup chicken broth*. Cook, stirring constantly, until sauce is smooth and thickened. Gradually stir in the *cream*. Bring sauce to a boil and correct seasoning with *salt and pepper* to taste. Add the strips of lemon peel, and swirl in *1 teaspoon butter*.

7. Pour the sauce over the birds and serve.

ROAST TURKEY
WITH ALL THE TRIMMINGS

Roast turkey is only as good as the turkey was to begin with, so don't settle for anything less than a fresh bird. During the holiday season, when you're most apt to be called upon to roast a turkey for a crowd, almost every butcher shop has fresh ones available, but you should place your order well in advance of the day you want it.

And let's go all the way and stuff our turkey. Present-day home economists recommend cooking the stuffing in a casserole beside the bird rather than IN it, but I like my stuffing moist and nicely flavored with turkey juices. And kids like it better that way. And, honestly, don't most people prefer roast turkey with old-fashioned stuffing?

I also like to brown my turkey at a good high starting temperature, and I like to baste it, and I like to smell the wonderful aroma of roast turkey emanating from the kitchen and to watch the turkey get shinier and browner each time the juices from the roasting pan are ladled over the breast. A good fresh bird, a hot oven, lots of butter, and loads of basting make the perfect roast turkey. So if you don't belong to the basting school, don't bother to read any further. Simply buy a roll of heavy-duty aluminum foil and follow the directions on the box. Happy steamed turkey!

BEGIN A DAY OR TWO IN ADVANCE AND MAKE THE STUFFING; then keep it cold in the refrigerator, and don't put it in your turkey until the day of roasting.

You should count on 1 cup crumbled bread for each pound of ready-to-cook turkey. If there are any helping hands around the house, turn this job over to them, for it can be a bore. I have no short cuts to offer except to make it fun. Many years ago I used to go to a ski lodge at Lake Placid for Christmas. All the guests would sit around a tremendous two-story fireplace in the central lounge on Christmas Eve and crumble the bread for the roast turkey the next day. It was part of the tradition of the lodge—and everyone enjoyed it!

ROAST STUFFED TURKEY
WITH GIBLET GRAVY

Serves 12

BUY

12- to 14-pound fresh tom turkey, ready to cook
2-pound loaf white *or* whole wheat bread
Onions
Celery
1 pint freshly shucked oysters with liquor (optional)
Poultry skewers
½ pound butter

HAVE ON HAND

Salt and pepper
Poultry seasoning
Sage
Peppercorns
Thyme
Parsley
Flour

COOKWARE

Shallow open roasting pan
Skillet
3-quart saucepan

PREPARING AND STUFFING THE BIRD

1. A day or two in advance make the stuffing. Crumble *enough bread to measure 12 cups (3 quarts)*. Set aside. Peel and chop *1 large or 2 medium onions*. Chop *2 cups celery and a few celery leaves*. Remove all fat from body cavity and around giblets; chop *enough turkey fat to measure 1 cup*. In skillet sauté the turkey fat until it is rendered and the bits of tissue are brown and crispy. Add onion and celery; sauté for about 10 minutes, or until vegetables are tender but not brown. Combine mixture of vegetables and fat with the crumbs. Add *3 teaspoons salt, 1 teaspoon pepper, 1 teaspoon poultry seasoning, and 1 teaspoon sage*. Moisten with about *1½ cups warm water,* or stir in *oysters along with their liquor*. Mix lightly, cool, and refrigerate until needed.

2. Scrape out any bits of blood and viscera left in the turkey and rinse it out with cold water. Dry well with paper towels.

3. Stuff the neck opening lightly with stuffing. Fold neck skin over

the back of the turkey and fasten it to the back with a poultry skewer or "nail." These are available at most hardware stores. Fold wing tips back under the bird.

4. Stuff the body cavity lightly, allowing room for the stuffing to expand, and insert skewers at intervals across the opening. Lace the opening together with heavy string (quite a long piece) much as you would lace a boot, starting from the part nearest the breast bone and lacing down to the tail, leaving long ends of string hanging.

5. Turn turkey over and insert a poultry skewer through the base of the tail. Turn turkey breast side up again. Press legs close to the body, then tie the ends of the drumsticks together and fasten to the skewer. Now bring the two ends of the string between the body and thighs on each side, then under the bird and up around the main joint of the wings. Finally run the strings under the wing tips at the back and tie across the back, for you don't want any string marks over the breast of the bird. Refrigerate until roasting time.

ROASTING THE TURKEY

1. Preheat oven to 475° F.

2. Place the stuffed and trussed turkey, breast side up, in a shallow open roasting pan. Spread the skin with *butter*. Lots of butter! Use about half a pound for a 14-pound turkey, for this is what is going to keep the meat moist and flavorful. Add ½ *cup boiling water* to the roasting pan. Roast turkey in the hot oven for 30 minutes; then turn oven temperature down to 350° F. and continue to roast for about 4 hours, or until turkey is done, basting every half hour with the butter and juices in the roasting pan. When thighs and legs become a light mahogany color, cover them with a buttered cloth.

If your turkey is ready to serve but you're not ready to eat, cover the entire bird lightly with a sheet of foil and reduce oven temperature to 250° F.

3. When turkey is in the oven, put *the giblets, except the liver,* into a 3-quart saucepan and cover generously with water. Add ½ *teaspoon peppercorns, ¼ teaspoon thyme, 1 teaspoon salt, a few sprigs parsley, 1 stalk celery with leaves, 1 small onion,* coarsely cut. Bring water to a boil and then simmer for 2 hours, adding a little more water from time to time. Add *turkey liver* and simmer for 10 minutes longer. Strain broth into clean saucepan. You will need *1 quart turkey stock,* so add *water* if necessary. Chop liver and giblets, adding any little tender bits of meat pulled from the neck. Set aside.

TURKEY GIBLET GRAVY

1. When turkey is golden and tender, transfer it to a serving platter and put it back in the warm oven with the heat turned off.

2. Pour off all but *3 tablespoons of the fat* from roasting pan, taking care not to discard any of the *meat juices*. Place roasting pan over direct heat. Stir in ⅓ *cup flour*. Gradually stir in the *turkey stock*. Cook, stirring in all the wonderful crisp and brown bits of glaze from bottom and sides of pan to make a deep brown, shiny gravy. Add the *chopped giblets* and boil for 5 minutes, stirring occasionally. Correct seasoning with *salt and pepper*. Pour into gravy boat.

TURKEY ROYALE

Serves 6 to 8. Serve with rice or small boiled potatoes.

BUY

12 small onions
3 carrots
2 cans chicken broth, each 13¾ ounces
Scallions *or* green onions
Celery
12 medium mushrooms
8-ounce container heavy cream

HAVE ON HAND	*COOKWARE*
Bay leaves	Medium saucepan
Parsley	Large saucepan
White wine	
Garlic	
Butter	
Thyme	
Flour	
Lemon	
3 to 4 cups diced leftover turkey	
2 eggs	
Salt and pepper	

1. In medium saucepan put *12 small onions,* peeled, *3 large carrots,* scraped and sliced, *1 bay leaf, 1 sprig of parsley, 1 cup white wine,* and *2 cans chicken broth.* Bring to a boil and then simmer for 20 minutes.

2. Meanwhile chop *4 green onions, including the tender part of green stems;* peel and mince *1 clove garlic;* and slice the *heart of the celery with the leaves* and the *mushrooms.*

3. In large saucepan melt *6 tablespoons butter* and in it sauté the green onions for 2 or 3 minutes. Add the garlic, celery, and mushrooms, and *¼ teaspoon thyme;* cook over low heat for 10 minutes, stirring occasionally. Stir in *½ cup flour.* Gradually stir in *liquid from the simmering vegetables,* and season to taste with *salt, pepper,* and the *juice of 1 lemon.* Cook over low heat for 10 minutes, stirring occasionally.

4. Discard bay leaf and parsley from the vegetable mixture and add *vegetables* to the sauce. Add the *diced leftover turkey* and cook over low heat for 5 minutes longer. The liquid should not be allowed to boil after the turkey is added.

5. Just before serving, combine *1 cup of heavy cream* and *2 egg yolks* with a little of the hot sauce. Stir into the turkey mixture, and cook, stirring, for 3 minutes, or until hot but not boiling.

6. Empty into a warm serving dish and sprinkle with *minced parsley.*

ROAST HAMS ARE REALLY BAKED

You can bake a whole ham or half a ham, using the shank or butt end, whichever you prefer. It is really baked because a moderate oven heat is used.

Little or no advance preparation is needed for our modern hams. Commercial meat packers have taken over where individual farmhouses left off, and they pickle, cure, and smoke hams in an exacting manner, producing bland, uniformly-flavored hams that are partially or fully cooked.

The ideal weight of a smoked ham ranges from 10 to 12 pounds. Place the ham, or half a ham, fat side up, in a shallow roasting pan and bake at 325° F. for 2 hours, or according to directions on package. Since baking time varies with individual brands, it's a good idea to follow cooking directions on the outer wrapper, if there are any.

Meanwhile prepare a ham glaze, using a favorite recipe or one of the two recipes given below. Then remove ham from oven and discard all but about 1 tablespoon of the fat in roasting pan. Score the fat on the ham itself into 1-inch squares or diagonals. Return ham to roaster. Spread or brush with glaze, then stud the squares with cloves, or decorate in any way you want. Bake for 30 minutes longer, basting occasionally with juices in pan.

PORT WINE GLAZE
FOR A WHOLE HAM

Combine in small mixing bowl *2 cups light brown sugar, 1 teaspoon dry mustard, ½ teaspoon ground cinnamon or cloves, 1 tablespoon grated orange rind or orange marmalade, ¼ cup Port wine,* and *1 tablespoon reserved melted fat from roasting pan.*

APRICOT GLAZE
FOR A WHOLE HAM

Combine in a small saucepan *1½ cups light brown sugar, ½ teaspoon ground ginger, ¼ cup honey or maple syrup, ¼ cup apricot nectar,* and *1 tablespoon reserved melted ham fat.* Bring to a boil and simmer for 5 minutes, stirring constantly.

LEFTOVER HAM

Chances are there'll be a lot of it! Reserve one thick slice to bake in milk for a quick meal, and some thin slices for a salad platter or sandwiches. Finely chop or grind the rest. Package it in 2-cup quantities and freeze for future use, as in Ham Squares or a ham omelette or sandwich filling.

HAM SLICE BAKED IN MILK

Serves 4

HAVE ON HAND	*COOKWARE*
Ham slice cut from leftover roast *or* ham steak purchased separately	10 x 6 x 1½-inch baking dish
Potatoes	
Flour	
Dry mustard	
Onion	
Milk	
Butter	

1. Preheat oven to 375° F.

2. Place *thick slice ham* in oiled baking dish. Peel and slice *4 medium potatoes* and arrange slices on top of ham.

3. Combine *1 tablespoon flour, ½ teaspoon dry mustard, 2 table-spoons finely chopped onion,* and *2 cups milk.* Pour mixture over ham and potatoes. Dot with *1 tablespoon butter.*

4. Cover pan tightly with aluminum foil and bake in preheated oven for 1 hour. Remove foil and bake for 20 minutes longer.

HAM SQUARES

Serves 6

BUY

1 package corn-muffin mix
12-ounce can Mexican-style whole-kernel corn
Small can green jalapeño chili peppers
3-ounce can sliced mushrooms
Parsley

HAVE ON HAND	*COOKWARE*
Egg	8 x 8 x 2-inch cake pan *or*
Milk	baking dish
Onion	Medium saucepan
Butter	
Flour	
Salt	
Prepared mustard	
Ground cloves	
1½ cups ground cooked ham (about ¾ pound)	

1. Prepare *corn muffin mix with egg and milk,* following directions on box. Drain *can of corn;* seed and chop *2 jalapeño peppers or green chilies.* Fold corn and peppers into the muffin batter, and spoon batter into buttered pan.

2. Bake in a 350° F. oven for 30 minutes, or until the cornbread is golden and tests done.

3. While cornbread is baking, drain *liquid from can of mushrooms* into a 2-cup measure and add enough *milk* to make a total of *1½ cups liquid.* Chop *parsley* and set aside.

4. Peel and chop *1 small onion.* Melt *2 tablespoons butter* in saucepan, and in it sauté the onion and the drained mushrooms until onion is soft. Stir in *2 tablespoons flour* and *½ teaspoon salt* and cook, stirring, until mixture bubbles.

5. Stir in the *1½ cups milk mixture* and cook, stirring, until sauce thickens; then simmer for 1 minute longer. Stir in *2 tablespoons prepared mustard, a dash of ground cloves,* and the *ground ham.* Stir over low heat until serving temperature is reached.

6. Remove cornbread from oven and cut into 6 serving portions. Split each portion, and spoon ham mixture between and on top of the layers, shortcake fashion.

7. Sprinkle each serving with the chopped parsley.

A FEW APPETIZERS

A Few Appetizers

I'm not attempting here to go into the various nibble foods, dips, spreads, and canapés so frequently served with cocktails to stay hunger pains until dinner is on the table. You can find these in any general cookbook. And, if you have a blender, there is a good selection of quick appetizers (also hot and cold soups) in *The Blender Cookbook* which I wrote with Eileen Gaden.

Rather, I'm going to give you suggestions for first-course table appetizers that need no recipes, interspersed with a few of my favorite dishes for first courses.

CAVIAR

Caviar heads my list, for it is the perfect beginning to a festive meal. You have to adore caviar and feel in a very expansive mood to afford fresh Beluga—the best. But Coho salmon are now being caught commercially in limited quantities in the Great Lakes region. As a result, you can find golden fresh-water salmon caviar in delicacy shops. It is only slightly salted and its natural golden color is very attractive. Set the container of caviar into a bowl of cracked ice and take it to the table with a basket of hot buttered toast triangles. To serve, pile the caviar lightly and lavishly onto the toast and accompany with lemon wedges, sour cream, and chopped chives.

ANTIPASTO

A small plate of assorted cold foods, literally meaning "before the pasta," is a perfect prelude to almost any robust dish, especially spaghetti, Osso Buco, or Chicken Cacciatore. One great advantage of antipasto is that many of the items come straight from a can, bottle, or the delicatessen and require little preparation. Any or all of the following items belong in an antipasto selection whether arranged on individual serving plates at the table or presented on a buffet table laden with platters and dishes from which guests may help themselves. Provide a cruet of wine vinegar, another of pure olive oil, and a peppermill—and don't forget the garlic bread!

ANTIPASTO COMBINATIONS

Celery, fennel, and black and green olives
Anchovies and pimientos on shredded lettuce
Slices of mozzarella and provolone cheese
Small wedges of peeled, chilled honeydew or cantaloupe wrapped in paper-thin slices of prosciutto ham
Sardines, herring, tuna fish, or smoked salmon
Scallions, radishes, and carrot sticks
Pickled peppers
Pickled beets and/or pickled mushrooms and/or pickled artichoke hearts
Sliced tomatoes, or cucumbers or cooked cauliflower, vinaigrette
Cherry tomatoes stuffed with crabmeat
Sliced liverwurst and salami
Drained canned garbanzos (chick peas) moistened with mustard mayonnaise
Hard-cooked eggs, plain or deviled

ARTICHOKES

These make an excellent appetizer and can be served either hot or cold. When served cold they are generally accompanied by a room-temperature oil-and-vinegar sauce known as Sauce Vinaigrette, or with garlic mayonnaise. When served hot they are equally good with these same sauces, or with a hot butter-and-lemon-juice sauce seasoned with salt and pepper and, often, with finely minced garlic.

Buy fresh-looking green artichokes with tighty closed leaves.

ADVANCE PREPARATION:

Cut the stem of each artichoke off close to the bottom to give it a steady base on which to sit. Remove a row of the large outer leaves, for these are tough and fibrous. Then with a heavy sharp knife cut off about 1 inch from the top of the artichokes, or remove the point of each leaf with kitchen scissors.

TO COOK:

Arrange the artichokes on their bases in a large kettle, and barely cover with cold water. For 4 to 6 artichokes add 1 tablespoon salt, the juice of ½ lemon, and a clove of garlic if desired. Bring liquid to a boil, cover kettle, and simmer over low heat for 45 minutes. When a leaf is pulled easily from the base, or a fork easily penetrates the bottom, the artichoke is cooked. Turn off heat and let the artichokes rest in the hot water until ready to serve. They will keep hot for at least half an hour. If they are for later use, drain well and chill.

TO DRAIN BEFORE SERVING:

Remove artichokes from kettle with a slotted spoon and set upside down on a wire cake rack in the sink for a few minutes to let all excess water drain off.

Serve hot with Sauce Vinaigrette, lemon-butter-garlic sauce, Hollandaise, or Béarnaise.

Serve cold with Sauce Vinaigrette, Hollandaise, or lemon-flavored mayonnaise.

SAUCE VINAIGRETTE

Makes about 1 cup

½ teaspoon salt
½ teaspoon dry mustard *or* prepared Dijon mustard
Freshly ground black pepper
4 tablespoons wine vinegar
¾ cup olive oil *or* salad oil, *or* half of each

In a small bowl combine salt, mustard, and pepper. Stir in vinegar.
Gradually beat in oil with a fork. Keep at room temperature until ready
to serve, and beat lightly with a fork just before serving. Use for tossed
salads, artichokes, etc.

SAUCE VINAIGRETTE WITH GARLIC

If you like garlic as much as I do you will peel and mince a clove of
garlic and add it to the dressing just before serving. For a mild garlic
flavor, peel and halve a clove of garlic. Drop the halves into the sauce
and let them steep in it for half an hour or longer. Discard the garlic
before serving.

SAUCE VINAIGRETTE MAISON

Add to Sauce Vinaigrette *4 tablespoons finely chopped parsley, 2 tablespoons each chopped capers* and *sweet gherkins,* and *garlic* again if you
wish it—1 clove, peeled and minced. Beat lightly with a fork just before
serving. Makes about 1 cup, or enough for 4 to 6 artichokes.

DEVILED EGGS

Serves 12. And now hear this: There is a right way even to cook an egg.

TO HARD COOK EGGS:

Put fresh eggs into a saucepan with plenty of water to cover (at least one inch above the eggs). Bring to a rapid boil, reduce heat, and simmer for exactly 10 minutes. Drain immediately, and immediately cover with cold water to stop further cooking and prevent the unattractive thin layer of gray-green which often coats the gold of the yolks. As soon as the eggs are cool enough to handle, crack each shell all over in a myriad of little cracks, then hold the egg under cold running water while you easily peel the shell and thin inner membrane cleanly away.

12 hard-cooked eggs
½ cup mayonnaise
1 teaspoon dry mustard
¼ teaspoon salt *or* salt to taste
3 dashes Tabasco
1 tablespoon minced dill pickle
1 tablespoon minced pimiento-stuffed olives (2 large)
1 tablespoon chopped capers
1 tablespoon minced chives *or* green onions
1 pimiento and some parsley clusters for garnish

1. Halve eggs lengthwise and remove the yolks. Cut a thin slice from the underside of each egg-white half to help it stand upright on a plate.

2. Make a really smooth paste of the yolks, mashing well with a fork or pressing through a colander. Combine with remaining ingredients except pimiento and parsley.

3. Spoon yolk mixture into egg whites, piling high in center; better still, press mixture through a pastry bag fitted with a large fluted tube (it's easy and fun).

4. Cut pimiento into 12 long thin strips. Curl a strip on top of each egg to look like a tiny red rose and insert the stem of a sprig of parsley on one side.

5. Arrange on serving platter (or on a flat dish if the eggs are to be included on an antipasto plate) and cover with transparent plastic film. Keep refrigerated until ready to serve.

MUSHROOMS STUFFED WITH CRABMEAT

Serves 6

6 tablespoons butter
3 tablespoons flour
¾ cup chicken broth
¼ cup heavy cream
Salt, pepper, and cayenne to taste
1 tablespoon chopped green onions
1 teaspoon dry mustard
7½-ounce can king crab meat
3 tablespoons sherry
1 hard-cooked egg, chopped
1 tablespoon chopped parsley
1 dozen large mushrooms
½ cup fresh bread crumbs

1. In saucepan melt 3 tablespoons of the butter, Stir in flour and cook over moderate heat for 3 minutes, without letting mixture brown. Gradually stir in chicken broth and cream; cook, stirring, until sauce is smooth, thick, and bubbling hot. Season with salt, pepper, and cayenne. Set sauce aside.

2. In a skillet melt 1 tablespoon of the butter, and in it sauté the green onions until transparent. Add mustard and crabmeat; cook, stirring, until crabmeat is heated through. Stir in sherry and the sauce. Stir in egg and parsley. Set aside.

3. Wash mushrooms and dry them thoroughly on paper towels. Remove the stems, and save them in the refrigerator for some other dish.

4. In another skillet—one with a heat-proof handle, sauté the mushroom caps in the remaining 2 tablespoons of butter for 5 minutes, or

until lightly brown on both sides. Remove from heat and fill the under side of each cap with the crabmeat mixture. Sprinkle with bread crumbs and dot with butter. Set aside until needed.

5. Preheat oven to 450° F. Place skillet with stuffed mushrooms in the hot oven and bake for 10 minutes.

VEGETABLES À LA GRECQUE

This dish, as its name implies, is of Greek origin rather than Italian; even so, vegetable *à la grecque* are frequently included in an antipasto. The following recipe calls for artichoke hearts, but it is often made with tiny onions, mushrooms, and celery stalks. Actually, almost any vegetable can be substituted in this dish, which makes an excellent first course all by itself.

2 packages frozen artichoke hearts, each 10 ounces
1 cup water
½ cup olive oil
Juice of 1 lemon
1 tablespoon wine vinegar
1 stalk celery, chopped
1 clove garlic, minced
1 bay leaf
Coarsely ground black pepper
½ teaspoon salt
1 tablespoon coriander seeds, crushed

1. In saucepan combine all ingredients. Bring liquid to a boil; then cover and simmer for 8 minutes, or until vegetables are tender.

2. Empty into a serving bowl and chill for several hours or overnight before serving.

SHRIMP CECELIA

This is another excellent first-course appetizer served either alone or in combination with other savory cold foods.

1 pound cooked shrimp
1 cup mayonnaise
2 small sour pickles, minced
10 pimiento-stuffed olives, chopped
1 tablespoon chopped capers
1 tablespoon lemon juice *or* vinegar from capers
1 tablespoon chopped chives
Ground pepper
1 tablespoon chopped fresh dill *or* 1 teaspoon dried dill weed
A little salt, if needed

    1. If necessary, shell and devein the shrimp.

    2. Combine remaining ingredients. Pour the dressing over the shrimp; toss lightly; and refrigerate for several hours or overnight before serving.

CRABMEAT LOUIS

1 cup mayonnaise
⅓ cup French dressing
¼ cup chili sauce
2 tablespoons minced chives
2 tablespoons chopped green olives
¼ cup capers
1 teaspoon horseradish *or* dry mustard
Salt
Freshly ground black pepper
3 cups fresh lump crabmeat *or* Alaska king crab, broken into chunks

Lettuce
4 hard-cooked eggs
Quartered tomatoes

1. Combine mayonnaise, French dressing, chili sauce, chives, olives, capers, horseradish or dry mustard, salt, and pepper.

2. Arrange lettuce leaves in a chilled salad bowl and mound the crabmeat on top. Spoon dressing over crabmeat and garnish with hard-cooked eggs and tomato quarters.

REMEKI PO-PO

Makes 12. These are so good, you'd better count on 3 or 4 per guest.

½ pound chicken livers, fresh *or* defrosted
5-ounce can water chestnuts, drained
6 slices bacon, halved crosswise
1 teaspoon curry powder
½ cup soy sauce
½ teaspoon ground ginger
Quick Sweet-and-Sour Sauce

1. Rinse chicken livers and cut each in half, removing connecting tissue.

2. Cook livers in salted simmering water for 6 to 8 minutes, or until cooked through. Drain.

3. When livers are cool enough to handle, split each piece, then put it back together with a slice of water chestnut in between. Wrap each "sandwich" in a half slice of bacon and secure with a wooden pick.

4. Combine soy sauce, ginger, and curry powder. Marinate the prepared chicken livers in this sauce for at least 2 hours, turning occasionally.

5. Before serving, place the livers in shallow pan; broil for about 5 minutes, or until bacon is crisp.

6. Serve with Quick Sweet-and-Sour Sauce.

EGGS À LA RUSSE

Serves 4

8 hard-cooked eggs
1 cup mayonnaise
3 tablespoons chili sauce
1 tablespoon chopped green olives
2 tablespoons chopped chives
1 tablespoon chopped parsley
1 tablespoon minced green onion
Juice of ½ lemon *or* to taste
Pimiento for garnish

1. Peel eggs and cut in half lengthwise. Arrange them, cut side down, in serving dish.

2. Combine remaining ingredients and pour over eggs.

3. Garnish with strips of pimiento. Chill until ready to serve.

YOGURT CHEESE

Makes about 1 cup. In Lebanon, this soft, delicate, curd cheese is known as *labneh*. Serve with Real Hot Chicken Curry, or with thinly sliced, dark rye bread for cocktail canapés or cheese course.

1 pint unflavored yogurt
¼ teaspoon salt

1. Stir the salt into the yogurt.

2. Line a sieve with a double layer of cheesecloth and set into a bowl. Pour the yogurt mixture into the cloth-lined sieve, gather the ends of the cheesecloth together over the yogurt, and tie them closed with a string.

Tie the bag to the faucet of the kitchen sink, and allow the yogurt to drip overnight.

3. Next day, empty cheese into a bowl and refrigerate. It will stay fresh for several days.

QUICK SWEET-AND-SOUR SAUCE

This unusual sauce is really great—not only with Remeki Po-Po but also with batter-coated, deep-fried shrimp. It closely approximates the "plum sauce" served with egg rolls in Chinese restaurants.

2 tablespoons chili sauce
2 tablespoons black raspberry preserves
5 dashes Tabasco
½ teaspoon dry mustard

In a small bowl, combine all ingredients and mix well. Keep at room temperature until ready to serve.

A FEW SPECIAL
VEGETABLES

A Few Special Vegetables

PLEASE DON'T OVERCOOK
THE ASPARAGUS!

In advance of cooking, hold each asparagus stalk at about the center and break off the heavy white end at a point where the stalk snaps crisply. Asparagus grows in sandy soil, so often bits of sand lurk in the tips and beneath the scales. Soak stalks in cold water for a few minutes to loosen the sand. Then, using a vegetable peeler, strip off a very thin layer of the skin from each stalk below the tip, removing the scales at the same time. Hold the stalk at the tip end and strip away from tip to end, all the way around.

The tips cook more quickly than the stalks, and a special asparagus steamer, which is tall and narrow and holds the stalks upright, is well worth purchasing. Without this, a double boiler is best. Stand the stalks upright in the bottom of the double boiler, and fill it half way up the stalks with water. Bring water to a rapid boil, then cover with the upper part of the double boiler so that the tips steam while the stalks cook in the water. Check frequently until stalks are barely fork tender, for they will continue to cook from their own heat after they are drained. Cooking time is from 10 to 12 minutes, depending on the variety, age, and thickness of the stalks.

Drain, empty into a serving dish, sprinkle with salt and freshly ground pepper, and add a big chunk of butter.

BRAISED CAULIFLOWER

Serves 6. Serve with curries.

1 medium onion, sliced
2 teaspoons minced fresh ginger root, *or* ½ teaspoon powdered ginger
2 tablespoons vegetable oil
2 small *or* 1 large cauliflower, cut into flowerets
2 teaspoons turmeric
2 teaspoons cumin
1 teaspoon salt
½ teaspoon freshly ground pepper
1 tablespoon mustard seeds
½ cup water

1. In a skillet, sauté onion and ginger in the oil for 5 minutes, or until onion is transparent.

2. Add cauliflower and remaining ingredients.

3. Cover and cook for about 20 minutes, or until cauliflower is just tender; if necessary, add a little more water to keep the cauliflower moist.

CAULIFLOWER AU GRATIN

Serves· 6. Other vegetables, such as cabbage, carrots, or Brussels sprouts, may be substituted for the cauliflower.

1 large head cauliflower
½ teaspoon salt
2 cups milk
6 tablespoons butter
6 tablespoons flour
8-ounce container light cream
Dash white pepper
Salt to taste (about 1 teaspoon)
2 tablespoons Parmesan cheese

½ cup bread crumbs
2 tablespoons butter

IN ADVANCE:

1. Remove the green leaves from around the head of cauliflower and, with a heavy knife, cut out and discard the thick center core from the bottom. Cut the head into flowerets.

2. Put the flowerets into a saucepan with 2 cups of water and ½ teaspoon salt. Bring water to a boil, then cover and simmer for about 10 minutes, or until cauliflower is just fork tender. Drain well. Arrange cauliflower in a shallow baking dish.

3. In small saucepan heat the milk to simmering.

4. In medium saucepan melt 6 tablespoons butter. Stir in the flour, and cook, stirring, until mixture bubbles a moment. Remove saucepan from heat and let mixture cool for a moment. Then add the hot milk all at once, and stir vigorously with a wire whisk or wooden spoon until sauce is smooth. Return to heat and, stirring well the bottom and sides of pan, cook for about 3 minutes, or until sauce is thickened. Stir in light cream, a dash of white pepper, and about 1 teaspoon salt or to taste. Pour sauce over the cauliflower.

5. Mix cheese and crumbs and sprinkle over surface of the sauce. Dot with 2 tablespoons butter. Set aside until ready to cook.

TO BAKE:

6. Preheat oven to 375° F. Bake cauliflower for 20 minutes, or until top is crusty and golden and the sauce is bubbling.

RATATOUILLE

Serves 8. This is a delicious mélange of vegetables that are all at their peak in the fall months. It is good served either hot or cold with roasts, steaks, or chops.

1 cup olive oil
1 medium onion, sliced
3 cloves garlic, minced
2 small eggplants, peeled and sliced

Flour
4 small zucchini, sliced
4 green peppers, seeded and cut into strips
1 teaspoon freshly ground pepper
1½ teaspoons salt
2 tablespoons chopped fresh basil *or* 1 teaspoon dried basil
8 ripe tomatoes, peeled, seeded, and sliced

1. In casserole or heavy saucepan heat half the olive oil, and in it braise onion and garlic until onion slices are tender but not brown.

2. Dip eggplant slices in flour. Then, in a separate skillet, heat remaining oil and in it sauté eggplant for a few minutes on each side, or until lightly browned.

3. Arrange the eggplant and other vegetables in layers in the casserole. Add seasonings. Bring contents to a boil, cover and simmer for 30 minutes, or until flavors are well blended and mixture is thick.

TOMATOES PROVENÇALE

Serves 4. Goes well with steaks and chops.

4 large ripe tomatoes
Salt and pepper
½ cup fresh bread crumbs
1 tablespoon chopped parsley
1 clove garlic, minced
4 tablespoons soft *or* melted butter

1. Do not peel the tomatoes; wash them well and cut in half crosswise. Arrange the halves, cut side up, on a baking sheet. Sprinkle with salt and pepper.

2. Preheat oven to 450° F.

3. Combine bread crumbs, parsley, and garlic. Spread cut side of each tomato generously with the bread-crumb mixture, and sprinkle or dot with butter.

4. Bake in preheated oven for 10 to 15 minutes, or until tomatoes are barely tender and crumbs are a golden brown.

CURRIED FRESH CORN
AND GREEN PEPPERS

Serves 6

1 clove garlic
1 medium onion
2 green peppers
½ cup (1 stick) butter
1 tablespoon curry powder
½ teaspoon salt
8 to 12 ears fresh corn
8-ounce container heavy cream

1. Peel and mince the garlic. Peel and chop the onion. Seed and chop the green peppers.

2. Melt the butter in a skillet. Add garlic, onion, curry powder, and salt. Cook over low heat for 5 minutes, or until onion is transparent. Add the green peppers and sauté for an additional 5 minutes.

3. Shuck the corn and, with a sharp knife, cut the kernels from the ears, scraping cob with back of knife to remove all of the corn milk. Add the corn and juice to the skillet. Add the cream, and cook, stirring, until mixture begins to simmer. Cover skillet loosely and braise over low heat for 20 to 30 minutes, without allowing the cream to boil.

CRAIG'S CREAMED ONIONS

Serves 6 to 8

2 pounds small white onions
4 tablespoons (½ stick) butter
¼ cup flour
½ teaspoon salt
¼ teaspoon freshly ground pepper

1 cup milk
1 cup heavy cream
1 teaspoon thyme

1. Steam the unpeeled onions in a covered colander over boiling water for approximately 30 minutes, or until tender. Remove skins from onions.

2. In a saucepan, melt the butter. Remove saucepan from heat, and blend in flour, salt, and pepper.

3. Add milk and cream slowly, stirring constantly. Return to heat and bring to a boil, stirring constantly. Add onions and simmer for 2 minutes.

4. Stir in thyme. Serve immediately.

MUSHROOMS ESTRAGON

Serves 6

1 pound small mushrooms
4 tablespoons (½ stick) butter
Salt
Freshly ground black pepper
Juice of ½ lemon
1 teaspoon dried tarragon

1. Wash mushrooms and trim off stems close to caps. Reserve stems for another purpose. Dry mushrooms well on paper towels.

2. In skillet melt the butter until foaming. Place mushroom caps upside down in the hot butter; cook over moderately high heat for 2 minutes, or until mushrooms are lightly browned, shaking the pan frequently to move mushrooms around.

3. Sprinkle mushrooms lightly with salt, pepper, and the lemon juice. Sprinkle with the tarragon. Turn mushrooms over with a pancake turner and continue to cook for 2 minutes longer, again shaking pan frequently to keep the mushrooms from burning. Serve immediately. Otherwise, turn off heat and leave mushrooms in the skillet. Later reheat shaking the pan, for about 1 minute.

TURMERIC CUCUMBERS

Serves 4 to 6. Marvelous with any curried dish.

4 slim firm cucumbers
3 cloves garlic, minced
2 green onions, sliced
1½ teaspoons turmeric
1 teaspoon ground ginger
1 tablespoon salt
⅓ cup water
¼ cup vinegar
¼ cup sugar

1. Peel, quarter, and seed cucumbers; cut each quarter into thin strips. Put strips into a serving dish.

2. In saucepan combine the remaining ingredients. Bring to a boil and simmer for 15 minutes.

3. Pour the spicy liquid over cucumbers in serving dish. Chill for at least 2 hours, turning the cucumbers in the liquid occasionally.

SAVORY BAKED BEANS

Serves 6

1 pound navy *or* pea beans
½ pound salt pork
1 medium onion
2 cloves garlic
1 teaspoon salt
½ teaspoon coarsely cracked pepper
½ teaspoon crumbled sage
1 teaspoon dry mustard
¼ teaspoon allspice

1. Wash and pick over the beans. Then place them in a kettle, cover with plenty of cold water, and soak overnight. Next day, drain off water, cover with fresh water, and add the salt pork, onion, garlic, salt, pepper, and sage. Bring to a boil and simmer for 45 minutes to 1 hour, or until beans are just barely tender and their skins have burst, adding more water, if necessary, to keep the beans covered. Discard garlic.

2. Remove beans from heat. Take out the salt pork and slice. Place a few slices on bottom of a bean pot. Transfer the beans from the kettle to the pot, reserving the cooking liquid by removing the beans with a slotted spoon. Bury the onion in center of the beans and arrange the remaining slices of salt pork on top.

3. Combine the mustard and 1 cup of the bean liquid. Pour over the beans and sprinkle with the allspice. Cover the bean pot and bake in a 300° F. oven for 2 to 3 hours, adding a little more bean liquid if the beans become too dry. Remove cover from bean pot about ½ hour before serving.

SOPA DE ARROZ

Serves 6

3 tablespoons oil
1 cup raw rice
1 medium onion, peeled and chopped
1 clove garlic, peeled and chopped
½ green pepper, seeded and chopped
8-ounce can plum tomatoes
1½ cups chicken broth
1 cup drained garbanzos (chick peas)

1. In heavy 2-quart saucepan heat the oil. Add the rice and cook, stirring, until rice is coated with the oil. Add onion, garlic, and green pepper, and sauté over moderate heat until the onion is transparent, stirring occasionally.

2. Drain liquid from tomatoes. Mash tomatoes and add to rice along with the chicken broth and garbanzos. Bring liquid to a boil. Turn heat to very low, cover saucepan tightly, and cook for 45 minutes without dis-

turbing. Remove cover, toss mixture with a fork and let sit over low heat, partially covered, until ready to serve.

NOTE: If you buy a 1-pound can of garbanzos, you'll have a cup left over. Put them into a small bowl; stir in 1 teaspoon prepared mustard, ¼ cup mayonnaise, and 1 teaspoon lemon juice; mix well. Season with salt and pepper to taste. Let marinate overnight in the refrigerator, and serve next day on a bed of lettuce as either a salad or an appetizer.

RICE PILAF

Serves 3, but recipe may be doubled.

½ cup (1 stick) butter
1 medium onion, minced
1 clove garlic, minced
1 cup raw rice
13½-ounce can chicken broth

1. An hour or so before dinner, melt the butter in a heavy saucepan, and in it sauté the onion and garlic for 5 minutes, or until onion is transparent.

2. Stir in rice, and cook, stirring, until rice grains are well coated with the butter mixture.

3. Add chicken broth and bring to a rapid boil. Cover saucepan tightly, reduce heat to its lowest point, and cook, without raising the lid, for 20 to 30 minutes.

4. Remove lid, toss rice with a fork, then partially cover. Let saucepan and rice steam on very low heat until ready to serve. If you are lucky the rice will form a golden crust on the bottom, and no pilaf in the Near East would consider itself worthy of its garlic if it didn't have that golden crust.

5. When ready to serve, fluff the rice again with a fork and empty into a warm serving dish. With a spoon scrape the golden crust from the bottom of the pan and pile it on top of the pilaf.

SAFFRON RICE

Follow preceding recipe, but add ½ teaspoon of saffron threads along with the chicken broth.

RISOTTO

Serves 6

Butter
1 medium onion, peeled and chopped
2 cups converted rice
2 cans chicken broth (13¾ ounces each)
1 teaspoon saffron threads
½ cup water
Grated Parmesan cheese

1. In heavy saucepan melt 4 tablespoons butter. Add the onion and sauté for 5 minutes, or until onion is transparent.

2. Add the rice; cook, stirring, for 2 minutes, or until rice is well coated with butter.

3. Add the chicken broth, saffron, and ½ cup water. Bring liquid to a rapid boil. Cover tightly. Reduce heat to very low and cook without removing cover for 20 minutes.

4. Remove cover and fluff rice with a fork. Keep over low heat, partially covered, until ready to serve.

5. When ready to serve, toss rice again with 2 tablespoons butter. Empty into serving dish and sprinkle generously with the grated Parmesan cheese.

SWEET-POTATO CASSEROLE

Serves 6

3 pounds sweet potatoes
½ cup butter
½ cup sherry
¼ teaspoon nutmeg
½ teaspoon cinnamon
Salt and pepper to taste
Milk

1. Boil the potatoes in their jackets until soft. Drain, and as soon as they are cool enough to handle remove the skins. Then put the potatoes through a ricer, or mash until smooth.

2. Beat in butter, sherry, nutmeg, cinnamon, and salt and pepper. If potatoes are still dry, stir in enough milk to make a fluffy consistency. Pile into a buttered baking dish and sprinkle with additional cinnamon. Bake in a preheated 350° F. oven until very hot and nicely browned on top—about 30 minutes.

POMMES DAUPHINOISE

Serves 6. Perfect with any roast or pan-broiled meat, fish, or poultry. This is the best potato dish this side of heaven. It is simply sliced raw potatoes baked with a little garlic and cheese in heavy cream. So don't bother to count your calories. Just enjoy!

6 large baking potatoes
1 large clove garlic, minced
Salt
Freshly ground black pepper
1 pint heavy cream
Milk
½ cup shredded Gruyère *or* Switzerland Swiss cheese

1. Peel potatoes and drop into a bowl of cold water.

2. Preheat oven to 300° F.

3. Place a buttered shallow baking dish over direct low heat. Dry and thinly slice one potato at a time and spread the slices in the dish. When half the potatoes are in the dish, sprinkle with the garlic, salt to taste, and plenty of freshly ground pepper. Add enough of the cream to barely cover the potatoes and let cream come very slowly to a boil as the remaining potatoes are sliced and spread in the dish.

4. When all potatoes are in the dish, add remaining cream, and a little milk if necessary, to just cover potatoes. Sprinkle with salt and pepper. Bring cream to a gentle boil, then transfer baking dish to pre-heated oven.

5. Bake potatoes for 1½ hours. Sprinkle with cheese, and continue to bake for 30 minutes longer. If you are not ready to serve, turn oven to low and potatoes will remain hot and creamy for quite a long time.

HOMESTYLE POMMES ANNA

Serves 2

2 large baking potatoes
1 clove garlic
4 tablespoons butter
Salt
Coarsely cracked pepper

1. Peel the potatoes and, if you're not going to cook them right away, drop them into a bowl of cold water, but don't slice them until you are ready, because the slices curl and you want them to lie flat in the pan. Peel the garlic and drop it in too.

2. When you're ready to cook, place the potatoes on a chopping block and, with a very sharp heavy knife, or with a vegetable slicer, slice them as thinly as possible. Mince the garlic.

3. In a 10-inch heavy skillet melt half the butter. Arrange half the potato slices in the skillet, overlapping them in two or three layers to completely cover the bottom. Sprinkle with salt and pepper and the

minced garlic. Arrange remaining potato slices on top, again overlapping them in a regular spiral pattern. Sprinkle again with salt and pepper and dot with remaining butter.

4. Cover skillet and cook over moderate heat for about 8 minutes, or until potatoes are brown and a good crust has formed all over the bottom. You'll have to look occasionally to make sure they aren't burning, but usually your nose will tell you if you have your heat too high.

5. Now slip a pancake turner under the entire cake of potatoes and flip it over in one piece. Lower the heat, leave off the cover, and let the potatoes cook for another 8 minutes, or until again brown and crusty on the bottom.

6. Cut potatoes in half for easy serving and lift onto a serving dish, or invert skillet over a 12-inch serving dish and the potato pancake will slip out.

NOTE: You can double this recipe if you wish—in which case a 12-inch skillet would be used—but it becomes tricky to turn the potatoes. I have found that I can cut them in wedges (like pieces of pie) when they are brown on one side; I remove one wedge at a time, then I twist the pan around so it is in the opposite direction, and flip the wedge over into its original place. But better than this, use two small skillets when making enough to serve four.

SWISS FRIED POTATOES

Serves 4

4 baking potatoes
1 small onion, minced
¼ cup butter *or* bacon drippings
Salt and pepper

1. Place the potatoes in their jackets in water to cover, and boil until fork tender (about 40 minutes). Don't overcook. Drain and peel while hot. If you impale each potato on a two-tined kitchen fork you won't burn your fingers.

2. As soon as potatoes are cool enough to handle, cut them into thin strips or shred them coarsely on a cheese shredder.

3. In 10-inch skillet heat the butter or bacon drippings. Add potatoes and sprinkle with the onion and salt and pepper. Cook over moderate heat, turning and tossing potato strips frequently until lightly brown on all sides.

4. Lower heat, press potatoes firmly into a cake with a pancake turner or spatula, and cook for 8 to 10 minutes longer or until a golden crust forms on the bottom.

5. Turn potatoes, crust side up, onto a serving plate.

GNOCCHI ITALIENNE

Serves 4. Marvelous with roasts or veal dishes, or as a gourmet luncheon. For convenience, prepare this dish several hours in advance of serving, or even the day before.

4 baking potatoes
1 cup water
6 tablespoons butter
1 teaspoon salt
¼ teaspoon pepper
⅛ teaspoon ground nutmeg
1 cup flour
3 eggs
1 cup grated Parmesan cheese
2 tablespoons melted butter

IN ADVANCE:

1. Peel and quarter potatoes; then cook in boiling salted water until tender—about 30 minutes. Drain and dry well by shaking pan over direct heat for a few seconds. Put potatoes through a ricer and set aside. There should be about 2 cups.

2. In a saucepan combine ½ cup of water, the 6 tablespoons butter, the salt, pepper, and nutmeg. Bring to a boil, then simmer until butter is

melted. Dump in flour all at once; immediately raise saucepan above the heat and stir rapidly with a wooden spoon until the paste leaves sides of pan and forms a ball in the center.

3. Empty the paste into a mixing bowl and beat in the eggs one by one—a good time to use your electric beater. Continue to beat until mixture is thick, smooth, and glossy. Beat in ½ cup of the Parmesan cheese and all of the riced potatoes.

4. Spoon about 1 tablespoon of the mixture at a time onto a lightly floured board and, with the palm of your hand, roll paste into a plump cylinder about 1 inch long. When all the gnocchi have been formed, drop them into a shallow pan of simmering salted water and cook, uncovered, for about 15 minutes, or until the gnocchi puff and are firm. Be careful not to let the water boil or they will break apart.

5. As soon as the gnocchi are poached, remove them with a slotted spoon and place on paper towels to drain and cool.

6. Place the gnocchi in buttered shallow baking dish. Sprinkle with the melted butter and the remaining Parmesan cheese. Bake immediately, or cover with waxed paper and refrigerate.

TO BAKE:

7. Preheat oven to 400° F. and bake the gnocchi for 12 to 15 minutes, or until lightly browned. Reduce oven temperature to 200° F. until ready to serve.

POLENTA

Serves 6. A great starch accompaniment to chicken or veal—in fact, to practically any sauced or unsauced entrée.

2 teaspoons salt
6½ cups water
12-ounce package instant polenta *or* cream of wheat
    or 3 cups yellow corn meal
1 tablespoon olive oil
½ cup (1 stick) butter, melted
1 cup grated Parmesan cheese

IN ADVANCE:

1. Salt the water and bring it to a boil. Quickly empty the box of polenta into the boiling water and stir rapidly in one direction for about 1 minute, or until mixture pulls away from sides of pan. Lower heat if the polenta begins to cook too rapidly. (Cream of wheat take 3 to 5 minutes to cook; corn meal, 20 to 30 minutes.)

2. Measure the olive oil into an 8-INCH-SQUARE cake pan, and tip pan to coat bottom and sides with the oil. Spoon the polenta into the prepared pan and use a spatula to spread top evenly. Set aside to cool.

3. Empty polenta out onto a wooden board. With a string pulled taut between with both hands, cut the polenta into 32 long strips ¼ inch wide; then cut the strips in half. The rectangles will be ¼ inch wide, 4 inches long, and about 2 inches deep.

4. Butter a baking dish and fill with layers of the rectangles, placing the first layer lengthwise, the next one crosswise, and so on. Dribble a little of the melted butter over each layer and sprinkle with a little of the cheese. When dish is filled, pour remaining butter over the top and sprinkle with remaining cheese. Set aside until ready to bake.

TO BAKE:

5. Preheat oven to 400° F. Bake the polenta in the hot oven for 15 minutes. Reduce oven temperature to 200° F. until ready to serve.

FLUFFY BREAD-CRUMB DUMPLINGS

Makes about 12 large ones. Dumplings are one of my favorite accompaniments to stews and fricassees. They are usually made of drop-biscuit dough with the addition of a whole egg, but the lightest and best dumplings are a mixture of fresh bread crumbs and lots of eggs. And if you're going to make dumplings, you might as well make the best.

1-pound loaf sliced white bread
¼ cup water
½ cup finely chopped parsley

½ cup minced onion
Salt to taste
½ teaspoon nutmeg

1. Trim crusts from bread and reserve them for another dish or scatter them outside for the birds. Crumb the rest of the bread a few slices at a time in an electric blender, or rub it through a sieve.

2. Sprinkle the bread crumbs with the water and toss lightly with a fork.

3. Beat the eggs, add them to the crumbs, and toss again.

4. Add parsley, onion, salt to taste, and nutmeg. Mix well.

5. Drop by tablespoons on top of a bubbling stew or fricassee. Cover container tightly, and let the dumplings steam for 30 minutes. They will puff and be very light.

A FEW FAVORITE
EASY DESSERTS

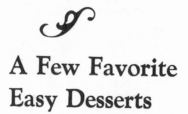

A Few Favorite
Easy Desserts

Some of the best desserts, in my opinion, are old-fashioned, homespun family favorites such as a Brown Betty, blueberry grunt, or a simple baked custard. I love to serve them as a contrast to an otherwise sophisticated meal. I do not have room here for all the desserts I like to make and serve, but I have made a selection of both American sweets and desserts that are more "French and fancy."

APPLE CRUNCH

Serves 6. Serve hot or warm with ice cream or whipped cream.

8 large baking apples (2½ pounds)
½ cup water
3 tablespoons quick-cooking tapioca
½ cup granulated sugar
¼ teaspoon cinnamon
½ cup seedless raisins
½ cup broken pecans
1 cup rolled oats
½ cup all-purpose flour
½ cup brown sugar
¾ cup (1½ sticks) butter

1. Peel, quarter, and core the apples. Butter a shallow 8-cup baking dish; fill it with the apples, and sprinkle them with the water.

2. Combine tapioca, granulated sugar, cinnamon, raisins, and pecans; sprinkle this over the apples.

3. Combine oats, flour, and brown sugar. Add the butter and crumble it into the flour mixture with your fingertips. Sprinkle this over tapioca mixture.

4. Bake in a preheated 375° F. oven for 45 minutes, or until golden.

PEACH BROWN BETTY

Serves 6. This is a wonderful old-fashioned dessert that is good any time of the year, but especially in the months when fresh peaches are at their best. If sliced canned peaches are substituted, they should be drained and the amount of sugar in the recipe should be reduced to ½ cup.

3 cups bread crumbs
½ cup (1 stick) butter, melted
8 large fresh peaches
1 cup sugar
¼ teaspoon nutmeg
Grated rind and juice of 1 lemon
8-ounce container heavy cream

1. Combine bread crumbs and butter in a small bowl and set aside.

2. Peel peaches, halve them, and remove pits. Slice peaches into a medium size bowl. Stir in sugar, nutmeg, lemon rind, and lemon juice.

3. Spread one-third of the crumb mixture into the bottom of a buttered casserole. Add half the fruit, one-third more of the crumb mixture, then the remaining fruit. Top with remaining crumbs.

4. Cover casserole and bake in a preheated 350° F. oven for 20 minutes. Remove cover and bake for 20 minutes longer.

5. Serve warm with whipped cream.

APPLE BROWN BETTY

Follow recipe above, substituting 4 cups peeled, cored, and sliced apples for the peaches.

MARSHMALLOW PEACH CRISP

Serves 6. Men and children always want seconds of this one. Serve warm with ice cream.

1-pound 13-ounce can peach halves
½ cup (1 stick) butter, melted
½ cup miniature marshmallows
½ cup chopped pecans
1 cup all-purpose flour
½ cup sugar
1½ teaspoons baking powder
½ teaspoon ground cinnamon *or* ginger
Dash of salt

1. Drain syrup from peaches into a 9 x 9 x 2-inch baking dish. Dice or slice the peaches and add to the syrup. Stir in butter and sprinkle with marshmallows and pecans.

2. In small mixing bowl combine flour, sugar, baking powder, cinnamon or ginger, and salt. Sprinkle on top of the peach mixture and stir in very lightly.

3. Bake in preheated 350° oven for 50 minutes, or until topping is browned.

PEACHES BAKED WITH COINTREAU

Serves 4

1-pound can peach halves in light syrup
½ cup sugar
4 tablespoons butter
2 tablespoons lemon juice
½ cup Cointreau
½ cup blanched slivered almonds

1. Drain peaches well. Arrange them, cut side up, in a shallow baking dish.

2. Cream together the sugar and butter. Put a heaping teaspoon of the butter mixture into center of each peach half. Sprinkle with lemon juice, Cointreau, and slivered almonds. Set aside until ready to bake.

3. Bake in a preheated 375° F. oven for 25 to 30 minutes. Serve hot right from the baking dish.

PRUNES IN PORT WINE

Serves 6

1 pound dried prunes
2 cups Port wine
¼ cup sugar
1 teaspoon vanilla
1 cup heavy cream, whipped
6 macaroons, crumbled

1. Soak prunes overnight in half the Port wine. Next day add sugar and remaining wine. Bring to a boil, then simmer for 3 minutes. Cool, stir in vanilla, and chill.

2. To serve: Empty prunes into a serving bowl or individual dishes and cover with whipped cream. Sprinkle with crumbled macaroons.

STRAWBERRIES ROMANOFF

Serves 6. A great dessert when fresh strawberries are in season—and that's most of the year nowadays. You can substitute fresh raspberries if you wish.

1 quart fresh strawberries
½ cup confectioners' sugar
¼ cup orange juice

¼ cup Curaçao
8-ounce container heavy cream

1. Rinse strawberries under cold running water. Remove hulls. Halve the berries lengthwise if large. Put berries into a serving dish and sprinkle with the confectioners' sugar, orange juice, and Curaçao. Marinate for several hours in refrigerator.

2. When ready to serve, whip the heavy cream until stiff, and pile it attractively over the berries.

NOTE: If you want to be really fancy, set the serving bowl into a larger bowl of crushed ice. And you can always garnish the top of the cream with several large berries.

FAST AND GOOD FRESH BLUEBERRY PIE

Serves 6

2 pints fresh blueberries
¾ cup sugar
3 tablespoons flour
Pinch of salt
Good pinch of nutmeg
1 tablespoon butter
1 tablespoon lemon juice
8-inch crumb crust, homemade or frozen

1. Empty berries into a colander and rinse well under cold running water. Pick over and discard any stems or tiny undeveloped green berries.

2. In a saucepan combine half the berries with the sugar, flour, salt, nutmeg, butter and lemon juice. Bring slowly to a simmer and cook, stirring, for 10 minutes, or until juice from berries is slightly thickened and berries are mushy.

3. Remove berry mixture from heat and fold in remaining raw berries. Empty into the crumb crust and chill until cold.

4. Serve with ice cream, whipped cream or sour cream, if desired.

CRUSTLESS DATE PECAN "PIE"

Serves 6

2 eggs
1 cup sugar
Dash of salt
1 teaspoon vanilla extract
½ cup soft bread crumbs
1 cup cut-up dates
1 cup coarsely broken pecans
Vanilla ice cream or whipped cream

1. Beat eggs lightly in mixing bowl. Stir in remaining ingredients.

2. Spoon into a buttered 8-inch pie plate and bake in a slow oven (200° F.) for 40 minutes. Raise oven temperature to 250° F. and continue to bake for 35 minutes longer, or until top is firm.

3. Cool and cut into wedges and serve, spooning sauce over each serving. Top with vanilla ice cream or whipped cream.

BAKED FRUIT COCKTAIL

Serves 6. Serve warm with whipped cream or ice cream.

1 cup granulated sugar
1 cup all-purpose flour
1 teaspoon baking soda
1 teaspoon salt
1 egg
1-pound can fruit cocktail
1 teaspoon vanilla
½ cup brown sugar
½ cup chopped walnuts

1. In a 6-cup baking dish combine sugar, flour, soda, and salt. Add egg, fruit with liquid, and vanilla, and beat well.

2. Combine brown sugar and walnuts and sprinkle over fruit batter.

3. Bake in a preheated 325° F. oven for 45 minutes, or until bubbling.

COLD LEMON SOUFFLÉ
WITH RASPBERRY SAUCE

Serves 6. This is the recipe that inspired this book (read the dedication)! Now, let me explain right away that cold soufflés are actually mousses set with gelatin in the refrigerator. They are not really soufflés, they are NOT baked in the oven, nor do they rise in any mysterious way. Traditionally, they are served in a soufflé dish which is collared to allow the mousse mixture to be piled up above the edge of the dish by a couple of inches. When the collar is removed before serving, the high and mighty cold mousse creates the illusion of a hot soufflé.

1 envelope plain gelatin
2 tablespoons water
6 lemons
¾ cup sugar
7 or 8 eggs (you'll only use the whites for this recipe)
8-ounce container heavy cream

1. From a roll of foil tear off a strip that's a little longer than the circumference of a 1-quart soufflé dish. Fold the strip in half lengthwise and tie it around the dish with a piece of string, letting the foil rise above the upper edge of the dish by about 1½ inches. Oil the inside surface of the foil collar. Set aside.

2. In a small saucepan soften the plain gelatin in 2 tablespoons water. Grate and add the rind of 4 lemons. Squeeze these lemons, and more if necessary, to make ½ cup lemon juice. Add the juice to the saucepan. Add the sugar, and stir over low heat until the gelatin and sugar are thoroughly dissolved and the liquid is clear. Chill for about 30 minutes, or to a syrupy consistency. It must be cold, but not cold enough to set.

3. Meanwhile separate 7 or 8 of the eggs, depending on size, to make 1 cup egg whites. The easiest way to do this is to crack one egg at a time

on the edge of a bowl or glass measuring cup. Separate the two halves and empty the egg into the cupped palm of the left hand. Let the white drain off into the measuring cup. Then tip the egg yolk remaining in the palm into a refrigerator container. Be careful not to break an egg yolk, for if even the slightest speck of yolk gets into your egg whites, they will not beat to a stiff smooth mass. If a drop of egg yolk does get into the whites, remove it gently with the sharp edge of an egg shell, taking up with it a small amount of the surrounding white. To preserve the egg yolks, add enough milk or cream to just cover them. Then cover the container and refrigerate until needed. They will keep for several days. If you wish to keep them longer, put the container in the freezer.

4. When the lemon mixture is cool and slightly thickened, beat the egg whites until very stiff and smooth, but not dry. Fold the egg whites into the lemon mixture thoroughly.

5. Beat the cream until stiff and fold this into the lemon-egg white mixture. You can beat the cream in the same bowl in which the egg whites were beaten, but you CANNOT REVERSE this procedure by beating the egg whites in the same bowl in which the cream was beaten, for any small amount of fat either in bowl or on beater will prevent the whites from mounding.

6. Spoon the dessert mixture into the collared soufflé dish, and chill for several hours, or overnight, until set. (It may be frozen if desired, but if so, remove from freezer several hours before serving).

7. Remove the aluminum foil collar before taking dish to the table. Serve with Raspberry Sauce.

NOTE: Save the leftover egg yolks for Hollandaise Sauce, French Chocolate Ice Cream, or Crème Brûlée.

RASPBERRY SAUCE AU KIRSCH

Makes 1½ cups

Partially defrost a *10-ounce package of frozen raspberries.* Empty it into the container of an electric blender, add *¼ cup sugar,* and blend on high speed for 20 seconds, or until smooth. Strain through a sieve to remove seeds, and stir in *2 tablespoons kirsch* if desired.

REFRIGERATOR CHEESECAKE

Serves 8

1 box zwieback
½ cup (1 stick) butter, melted
¼ cup sugar
1 teaspoon cinnamon
2 envelopes plain gelatin
½ cup cold water
3 egg yolks
½ cup sugar
½ cup milk
1 pound cream cheese at room temperature
Grated rind and juice of 1 lemon
1 cup heavy cream, lightly whipped
4 egg whites, stiffly whipped

1. Roll out zwieback with a rolling pin to make fine crumbs. Mix crumbs with the butter, the ¼ cup sugar, and cinnamon. Reserve one-fourth of the crumb mixture. Press remainder firmly against bottom and sides of a well-buttered 9-inch spring form pan. Bake the crumb crust in a preheated 400° F. oven for 10 minutes, or chill in refrigerator until firm.

2. Soak gelatin in the cold water for 5 minutes.

3. Blend egg yolks, the ½ cup sugar, and the milk. Cook over boiling water for 3 minutes, stirring constantly. Add soaked gelatin and stir until gelatin is thoroughly dissolved. Remove from heat.

4. Gradually beat the cooked mixture into the cream cheese, then strain through a fine sieve to remove any lumps. Add lemon rind and juice. Fold in the whipped cream and the stiff egg whites and blend lightly but thoroughly.

5. Pour into the prepared pan and sprinkle with the reserved crumb mixture. Chill in refrigerator for 3 hours, or until set.

CARAMEL FLAN

This is the Spanish version of a simple baked custard.
Serves 6

6 tablespoons granulated sugar
3 whole eggs
3 egg yolks
½ cup toasted blanched almonds
½ cup light brown sugar
2 cups (1 pint) light cream *or* half and half

1. Measure the granulated sugar into an 8-inch layer cake pan. Place pan over direct heat and stir the sugar constantly with a wooden spoon until it melts and turns a nice deep caramel color. Remove pan immediately from heat and place on a cool surface or the caramel will burn. Let the caramel harden.

2. Put the whole eggs and the egg yolks into the container of an electric blender. Add the almonds and sugar. Turn blender onto low speed and gradually pour in the cream.

3. Pour the egg mixture into the caramelized pan. Place the pan into a large shallow baking dish containing ½ inch hot water.

4. Bake in a preheated 325° F. oven for 45 minutes. Remove from oven, cool, then refrigerate for several hours or overnight.

5. When ready to serve, run a silver knife around the edge of the custard, invert the pan, and turn out custard onto a serving dish.

CRÈME BRÛLÉE

And this is the elegant and very French version of a rich custard.
Serves 6

4 tablespoons sugar
1 tablespoon cornstarch

6 egg yolks
3 cups heavy cream
2 tablespoons vanilla extract
1 cup light brown sugar

1. Gradually beat sugar and cornstarch into egg yolks, then continue to beat for 2 to 3 minutes, or until mixture is thick and pale in color.

2. Heat cream to simmering. Gradually pour the hot cream into egg yolk mixture, beating constantly.

3. Strain mixture into saucepan. Cook over moderate heat—stirring rapidly and continually with a wooden spoon and reaching all over bottom and sides of pan—until cream thickens just enough to coat the spoon. Be careful not to let the mixture boil. Remove from heat, and continue to stir rapidly for a minute or two in order to cool the cream.

4. Stir in the vanilla, then pour the cream into a serving bowl. Chill for several hours or overnight.

5. To caramelize the top, set the bowl into a shallow pan containing cracked ice. Sprinkle the brown sugar evenly over top of cream. Place bowl and pan in broiling section of stove; broil 3 inches from source of heat for 4 to 5 minutes while sugar melts and caramelizes. Be careful not to let it burn.

6. Serve immediately, or chill again for several hours and then serve.

LEMON SHERBET

Serves 6. A wonderfully refreshing dessert to serve in summertime or after a heavy meal in any season of the year.

6 lemons
2 cups sugar
2 cups water
2 egg whites
Fresh mint in season *or* a favorite liqueur

1. With a vegetable peeler strip the thin lemon-colored rind from 1 lemon; cut the strips into very fine shreds with a sharp knife. Put the shreds into a saucepan and add the sugar and water. Stir over low heat until sugar is dissolved, then bring to a boil over high heat and boil rapidly for 5 minutes.

2. Remove the syrup from the heat and set it aside. When syrup is cool, stir in ¾ cup lemon juice (the juice of 4 to 6 lemons). Pour mixture into refrigerator trays and freeze to the consistency of a solid mush.

3. Beat egg whites until stiff. Empty the frozen mush into a bowl and beat in the egg whites. Return mixture to freezer trays and freeze until firm.

4. Serve in sherbet glasses. Top with a sprig of fresh mint, or with a tablespoon of creme de menthe or other favorite liqueur.

FRENCH CHOCOLATE ICE CREAM

Makes about 1 quart

½ cup water
¼ cup sugar
6-ounce package semi-sweet chocolate pieces
3 egg yolks
2 cups heavy cream, whipped

1. In small saucepan combine sugar and water. Bring to a boil, and boil rapidly for 3 minutes.

2. Pour syrup into container of an electric blender; add chocolate pieces; cover and blend on high speed for 5 seconds. Add egg yolks; cover and blend on high speed for 10 seconds, or until mixture is very smooth, stopping to stir down if necessary.

3. Fold chocolate mixture into whipped cream. Spoon into refrigerator tray. Cover with waxed paper, and freeze for 2 to 3 hours before serving.

PEACH MELBA

10-ounce package frozen raspberries, defrosted
Vanilla ice cream
Fresh *or* canned peach halves

    1. Force defrosted berries through a sieve to remove the seeds. Chill the resulting purée, which makes about 1 cup.

    2. When ready to serve, put scoops of ice cream in individual dishes. Top each serving with a peach half, rounded side up. Cover peach with raspberry purée.

COUPE AUX FRUITS

Serves 4

10-ounce package frozen raspberries, defrosted
4 tablespoons kirsch
1 cup honeydew melon balls
½ cup diced pineapple
½ cup sliced strawberries
2 tablespoons granulated sugar
½ cup heavy cream, whipped
1 tablespoon confectioners' sugar
1 pint vanilla ice cream
Whole strawberries for garnish

    1. Empty defrosted raspberries into container of an electric blender and blend on high speed for 10 seconds. Strain through a sieve to remove seeds. Stir in half the kirsch, then set the sauce aside.

    2. In a small bowl combine melon balls, pineapple, sliced strawberries, and the 2 tablespoons granulated sugar. Add remaining kirsch and chill.

    3. Combine whipped cream and confectioners' sugar. Chill.

4. When ready to serve, put ½ cup fruit mixture into each coupe glass and top with a large scoop of the vanilla ice cream. Spoon about 3 tablespoons of the raspberry sauce over the ice cream, top with a glob of the whipped cream, and garnish with whole strawberries.

COUPE AUX MARRONS

Serves 6

¾ to 1 cup canned chestnut purée with sugar
1 quart vanilla ice cream
Chocolate Rum Sauce, heated
6 glacéed chestnuts

1. Put a large spoonful of chestnut purée in the bottom of each coupe glass. Top with a large scoop of ice cream, and spoon the hot chocolate sauce on top.

2. Garnish each serving with a glacéed chestnut.

CHOCOLATE RUM SAUCE

In a heavy saucepan, over low heat, stir 6 ounces semi-sweet chocolate pieces and ½ cup light cream until mixture is smooth and thick. Remove from heat and stir in ¼ cup Jamaica rum (or cognac). Keep sauce warm, or reheat it before serving.

ICE CREAM KONA

One serving

1 scoop vanilla ice cream
2 slices pineapple
½ banana

Shredded coconut
1 ounce Jamaica rum
1 tablespoon apricot preserves

1. Put ice cream into a large sherbet or coupe glass.

2. Halve the pineapple slices and arrange them around the ice cream. Split the banana half and place sections on either side of the ice cream. Sprinkle with coconut.

3. Combine rum and preserves, ignite with match, and spoon flaming over the ice cream.

CHOCOLATE DUMPLINGS

Serves 8

11-ounce can sweetened chocolate syrup
1 cup water
1 cup all-purpose flour
2 teaspoons baking powder
3 tablespoons butter
1 egg
1 envelope (1 ounce) liquid unsweetened chocolate
½ cup milk
1 teaspoon vanilla
½ cup semi-sweet chocolate bits
1 pint vanilla ice cream

1. In heavy skillet combine chocolate syrup and water; heat very slowly to simmering.

2. Meanwhile in mixing bowl combine flour and baking powder. Cut in butter with pastry cutter or 2 knives until butter is cut into crumbs.

3. Beat egg in a small bowl and stir in liquid chocolate, milk, and vanilla. Add all at once to flour mixture, and stir with a fork until flour is evenly moistened. Stir in chocolate bits.

4. Drop dough by rounded tablespoons into the hot chocolate sauce. Cover skillet and cook over low heat for 15 minutes. Spoon dumplings and sauce onto individual serving plates. Top with ice cream.

SHOO-FLY PIE FOR BREAKFAST— WHY NOT?

Rolling out the crust is considered by many to be the most difficult part of pie-making. Here you have a Pennsylvania Dutch pie that is better without a crust at all.

1½ cups all-purpose flour
1 cup brown sugar
½ cup butter
¼ teaspoon salt
½ teaspoon soda
⅔ cup hot water
⅔ cup molasses

1. Combine flour, sugar, butter, and salt; crumb the mixture by rubbing it between your hands.

2. Dissolve soda in hot water and combine with molasses. Pour into 8-inch pie plate, top with crumbs, and bake in a preheated 350° F. oven for 35 to 40 minutes, or until crumbs are lightly browned. Cool to lukewarm before serving.

BUTTERSCOTCH PIE

Serves 2 boys or 6 adults. Pie dough does not scares off the Dullinger boys to whom this book is dedicated! However, for timid (or busy) adults there are very good frozen pie crusts available.

1 frozen pie crust
2 tablespoons flour
2 tablespoons cornstarch
Dash of salt
¾ cup brown sugar
2 cups milk

3 egg yolks
1 teaspoon vanilla
1 tablespoon butter

1. Bake pie crust according to package directions. Cool.

2. In a saucepan combine flour, cornstarch, dash of salt, and brown sugar. Stir in milk. Bring to a boil over moderate heat and cook until thickened, stirring constantly. Remove from heat.

3. Separate 3 eggs. Reserve the whites in a cup or bowl. Beat the yolks into the hot sauce, one by one. Return sauce to low heat, and cook, stirring, for 2 minutes.

4. Remove from heat and stir in vanilla and butter. Cool a little, then pour into baked pastry shell. Top cooled pie either with meringue made from the egg whites, or with whipped cream.

MERINGUE TOPPING

In mixing bowl beat *3 egg whites* until frothy. Use an electric beater if you have one. Add *¼ teaspoon cream of tartar* (or *1 teaspoon lemon juice*) and continue to beat until whites are stiff enough to hold a peak. Gradually add *6 tablespoons sugar,* beating until meringue is stiff and shiny. Pile the meringue lightly on the cooled pie. To prevent meringue from shrinking, make sure it touches the edges of the pastry everywhere. With tablespoon or spatula, swirl topping into large curls. Bake in a preheated 425° F. oven for 5 to 6 minutes, or until peaks are attractively browned.

Index